Postmodernism and Public Policy

SUNY series in Constructive Postmodern Thought

David Ray Griffin, series editor

POSTMODERNISM
AND
PUBLIC POLICY

Reframing Religion, Culture, Education, Sexuality, Class, Race, Politics, and the Economy

John B. Cobb, Jr.

STATE UNIVERSITY OF NEW YORK PRESS, ALBANY

Published by
State University of New York Press, Albany

For information, address State University of New York Press,
State University Plaza, Albany, N.Y., 12246

Production by Kelli Williams
Marketing by Patrick Durocher

Library of Congress Cataloging-in-Publication Data

Cobb, John B.
    Postmodernism and public policy : reframing religion, culture, education,
sexuality, class, race, politics, and the economy / John B. Cobb, Jr.
        p.   cm. — (SUNY series in constructive postmodern thought)
    Includes index.
    ISBN 0–7914–5165–8 (alk. paper) — ISBN 0–7914–5166–6 (pbk. : alk. paper)
    1. Postmodern theology. 2. Christianity and politics. 3. Postmodernism–
Political aspects. I. Title. II. series.
    BT83.597 C63 2001
    146'.7—dc21   2001049331

10 9 8 7 6 5 4 3 2 1

Contents

Preface

In the twentieth century, in connection with changes in the sciences, in religion, and in the wider culture there emerged a movement that David Griffin has well labeled "constructive postmodernism." A number of philosophers have contributed. Of these, some of us believe that Alfred North Whitehead has provided the most systematic and profound conceptuality. Those who follow these philosophers remain on the fringe of the philosophical community, but some of their central ideas have emerged independently through the ecological and feminist movements, the encounter with primal and Eastern religious traditions, and the new physics. If these developments continue, the new century may see something like constructive postmodernism emerge as a strong, even dominant, force.

Like other comprehensive ways of thinking, this one has important implications for thought and action in all fields. Because constructive postmodernism is quite different from earlier philosophies such as Cartesian and Kantian forms of dualism, so are its implications. As one whose understanding has been captured by this kind of thinking, I have for many years been interested in exploring these implications.

David Griffin suggested that I write a book for this series that would summarize some of the proposals I have made in more detailed consideration of various topics in other books. A good deal of this book does just that on such topics as Christian theology, religious pluralism, ecology, and economics. Griffin has argued that theology in the constructive postmodern mode must be "public" in two senses: "it must make its case in terms of the criteria of self-consistency and adequacy to generally accessible facts of experience, and it must be directly relevant to matters of public policy."[1] This book intends to be that kind of theology.

Seeking to be public in the second sense led me to treat topics to which I have not given sustained attention in the past. These include education, gender, and race. On these topics I turned for help to Mary

Elizabeth Moore, Catherine Keller, and Thandeka. I am greatly indebted to all of them for careful reading of portions of the manuscript and for their criticisms and suggestions. Although the discussion of race still includes features with which Thandeka disagrees, her rigorous and insightful comments on several previous drafts have led me to fresh thinking and new formulations. My debt to her is particularly large, and I have yet much to learn from her.

I am also indebted to David Griffin. He read an early version of my manuscript and made many valuable criticisms and suggestions. He gave me special assistance in the chapter on governance. Because of his counsel, this is a very different book from what I first wrote. The staff of the Center for Process Studies, including a visitor from Hungary, Gabor Karsai, gone the second mile in helping me.

One of Griffin's reasons for inviting me to write this book was interest on the part of some Chinese constructive postmodernists. A translation into Chinese is in process. Being aware of this has also made me aware of how parochially American much of the book is. Several chapters deal only with the specifically American situation, and all reflect a perspective shaped by an American's experience. Perhaps, however, this is as it should be. The problems people face differ from culture to culture. To write chiefly about what is common to all cultures would lead to a level of high abstraction that might still remain distorting when applied to a different culture from one's own. The task is for all of us to approach the issues that face us in terms of the reality of our own communities. Often we can be stimulated and informed by what thinkers in other communities are doing. Perhaps, therefore, these examples of how an American works with a postmodern perspective can be of help in encouraging Chinese to find value in constructive postmodernisms in their quite different situation.

Although my suggestions on the various topics discussed in this book are heavily shaped by my appropriation of Whitehead's postmodern worldview, this does not mean that the implications I draw are dictated by that vision. Other thinkers who belong to the same general stream of thought will properly challenge the implications I have drawn for the topics discussed. The ensuing discussions should sharpen, clarify, and deepen our collective thinking.

Much is at stake. From my point of view as a constructive postmodernist, the major orientations that now dominate the university and the general culture—namely, early modernism with its doctrine of separate realms, late modernism with its materialism and atheism, and deconstructive postmodernism, which does not go far to provide a constructive alternative to these modernisms—are not helpful in treating some of the most critical issues of our time, especially human relations with the natural world. Unless a larger part of the cultural elite, as well as popular thinking and feeling, give much more attention to our internal relationships with one another and the wider world, the prospects for future life on this planet are bleak. To make clear that constructive postmodern thought makes a real difference in how we view our world, I have written this book. Perhaps some who are not interested in the philosophical debates as such may still join in supporting the practical and political implications of constructive postmodernism. Perhaps, also, some who appreciate the need to move beyond the modern world, but who have thought that move involved the rejection of every type of metaphysics, will see that there is an inclusive vision of reality that is supportive of many of their concerns and insights.

Introduction to SUNY Series in Constructive Postmodern Thought[1]

The rapid spread of the term *postmodern* in recent years witnesses to a growing dissatisfaction with modernity and to an increasing sense that the modern age not only had a beginning but can have an end as well. Whereas the word *modern* was almost always used until quite recently as a word of praise and as a synonym for *contemporary,* a growing sense is now evidenced that we can and should leave modernity behind—in fact, that we *must* if we are to avoid destroying ourselves and most of the life on our planet.

Modernity, rather than being regarded as the norm for human society toward which all history has been aiming and into which all societies should be ushered—forcibly if necessary—is instead increasingly seen as an aberration. A new respect for the wisdom of traditional societies is growing as we realize that they have endured for thousands of years and that, by contrast, the existence of modern civilization for even another century seems doubtful. Likewise, *modernism* as a worldview is less and less seen as The Final Truth, in comparison with which all divergent worldviews are automatically regarded as "superstitious." The modern worldview is increasingly relativized to the status of one among many, useful for some purposes, inadequate for others.

Although there have been antimodern movements before, beginning perhaps near the outset of the nineteenth century with the Romanticists and the Luddites, the rapidity with which the term *postmodern* has become widespread in our time suggests that the antimodern sentiment is more extensive and intense than before, and also that it includes the sense that modernity can be successfully overcome only by going beyond it, not by attempting to return to a premodern form of existence. Insofar as a common element is found in the various ways in which the

1. The present version of this introduction is slightly different from the first version, which was contained in the volumes that appeared prior to 1999.

term is used, *postmodernism* refers to a diffuse sentiment rather than to any common set of doctrines—the sentiment that humanity can and must go beyond the modern.

Beyond connoting this sentiment, the term *postmodern* is used in a confusing variety of ways, some of them contradictory to others. In artistic and literary circles, for example, postmodernism shares in this general sentiment but also involves a specific reaction against "modernism" in the narrow sense of a movement in artistic-literary circles in the late nineteenth and early twentieth centuries. Postmodern architecture is very different from postmodern literary criticism. In some circles, the term *postmodern* is used in reference to that potpourri of ideas and systems sometimes called *new age metaphysics,* although many of these ideas and systems are more premodern than postmodern. Even in philosophical and theological circles, the term *postmodern* refers to two quite different positions, one of which is reflected in this series. Each position seeks to transcend both *modernism*, in the sense of the worldview that has developed out of the seventeenth-century Galilean-Cartesian-Baconian-Newtonian science, and *modernity*, in the sense of the world order that both conditioned and was conditioned by this worldview. But the two positions seek to transcend the modern in different ways.

Closely related to literary-artistic postmodernism is a philosophical postmodernism inspired variously by physicalism, Ludwig Wittgenstein, Martin Heidegger, a cluster of French thinkers—including Jacques Derrida, Michel Foucault, Gilles Deleuze, and Julia Kristeva—and certain features of American pragmatism.[2] By the use of terms that arise out of particular segments of this movement, it can be called *deconstructive, relativistic,* or *eliminative* postmodernism. It overcomes the modern worldview through an antiworldview, deconstructing or even entirely eliminating various concepts that have generally been thought

2. The fact that the thinkers and movements named here are said to have inspired the deconstructive type of postmodernism should not be taken, of course, to imply that they have nothing in common with constructive postmodernists. For example, Wittgenstein, Heidegger, Derrida, and Deleuze share many points and concerns with Alfred North Whitehead, the chief inspiration behind the present series. Furthermore, the actual positions of the founders of pragmatism, especially William James and Charles Peirce, are much closer to Whitehead's philosophical position—see the volume in this series entitled *The Founders of Constructive Postmodern Philosophy: Peirce, James, Bergson, Whitehead, and Hartshorne*—than they are to Richard Rorty's so-called neopragmatism, which reflects many ideas from Rorty's explicitly physicalistic period.

necessary for a worldview, such as self, purpose, meaning, a real world, givenness, reason, truth as correspondence, universally valid norms, and divinity. While motivated by ethical and emancipatory concerns, this type of postmodern thought tends to issue in relativism. Indeed, it seems to many thinkers to imply nihilism.[3] It could, paradoxically, also be called *ultramodernism,* in that its eliminations result from carrying certain modern premises—such as the sensationist doctrine of perception, the mechanistic doctrine of nature, and the resulting denial of divine presence in the world—to their logical conclusions. Some critics see its deconstructions or eliminations as leading to self-referential inconsistencies, such as "performative self-contradictions" between what is said and what is presupposed in the saying.

The postmodernism of this series can, by contrast, be called *revisionary, constructive,* or—perhaps best—*reconstructive.* It seeks to overcome the modern worldview not by eliminating the possibility of worldviews (or "metanarratives") as such, but by constructing a postmodern worldview through a revision of modern premises and traditional concepts in the light of inescapable presuppositions of our various modes of practice. That is, it agrees with deconstructive postmodernists that a massive deconstruction of many received concepts is needed. But its deconstructive moment, carried out for the sake of the presuppositions of practice, does not result in self-referential inconsistency. It also is not so totalizing as to prevent reconstruction. The reconstruction carried out by this type of postmodernism involves a new unity of scientific, ethical, aesthetic, and religious intuitions (whereas poststructuralists tend to reject all such unitive projects as "totalizing modern metanarratives"). While critical of many ideas often associated with modern science, it rejects not science as such but only that *scientism* in which only the data of the modern natural sciences are allowed to contribute to the construction of our public worldview.

3. As Peter Dews points out, although Derrida's early work was "driven by profound ethical impulses," its insistence that no concepts were immune to deconstruction "drove its own ethical presuppositions into a penumbra of inarticulacy" (*The Limits of Disenchantment: Essays on Contemporary European Culture* [London: New York: Verso, 1995], 5). In his more recent thought, Derrida has declared an "emancipatory promise" and an "idea of justice" to be "irreducible to any deconstruction." Although this "ethical turn" in deconstruction implies its pulling back from a completely disenchanted universe, it also, Dews points out (6–7), implies the need to renounce "the unconditionality of its own earlier dismantling of the unconditional."

The reconstructive activity of this type of postmodern thought is not limited to a revised worldview. It is equally concerned with a postmodern world that will both support and be supported by the new worldview. A postmodern world will involve postmodern persons, with a postmodern spirituality, on the one hand, and a postmodern society, ultimately a postmodern global order, on the other. Going beyond the modern world will involve transcending its individualism, anthropocentrism, patriarchy, economism, consumerism, nationalism, and militarism. Reconstructive postmodern thought provides support for the ethnic, ecological, feminist, peace, and other emancipatory movements of our time, while stressing that the inclusive emancipation must be from the destructive features of modernity itself. However, the term *postmodern*, by contrast with *premodern*, is here meant to emphasize that the modern world has produced unparalleled advances, as Critical Theorists have emphasized, which must not be devalued in a general revulsion against modernity's negative features.

From the point of view of deconstructive postmodernists, this reconstructive postmodernism will seem hopelessly wedded to outdated concepts, because it wishes to salvage a positive meaning not only for the notions of selfhood, historical meaning, reason, and truth as correspondence, which were central to modernity, but also for notions of divinity, cosmic meaning, and an enchanted nature, which were central to premodern modes of thought. From the point of view of its advocates, however, this revisionary postmodernism is not only more adequate to our experience but also more genuinely postmodern. It does not simply carry the premises of modernity through to their logical conclusions, but criticizes and revises those premises. By virtue of its return to organicism and its acceptance of nonsensory perception, it opens itself to the recovery of truths and values from various forms of premodern thought and practice that had been dogmatically rejected, or at least restricted to "practice," by modern thought. This reconstructive postmodernism involves a creative synthesis of modern and premodern truths and values.

This series does not seek to create a movement so much as to help shape and support an already existing movement convinced that modernity can and must be transcended. But in light of the fact that those antimodern movements that arose in the past failed to deflect or even retard the onslaught of modernity, what reasons are there for expecting the current movement to be more successful? First, the previous antimodern movements were primarily calls to return to a premodern form of life and thought rather than calls to advance, and the human spirit does not rally to calls to turn back. Second, the previous antimodern movements either rejected modern science, reduced it to a description of mere appearances, or assumed its adequacy in principle. They could, therefore, base their calls only on the negative social and spiritual effects of modernity. The current movement draws on natural science itself as a witness against the adequacy of the modern worldview. In the third place, the present movement has even more evidence than did previous movements of the ways in which modernity and its worldview *are* socially and spiritually destructive. The fourth and probably most decisive difference is that the present movement is based on the awareness that *the continuation of modernity threatens the very survival of life on our planet.* This awareness, combined with the growing knowledge of the interdependence of the modern worldview with the militarism, nuclearism, patriarchy, global apartheid, and ecological devastation of the modern world, is providing an unprecedented impetus for people to see the evidence for a postmodern worldview and to envisage postmodern ways of relating to each other, the rest of nature, and the cosmos as a whole. For these reasons, the failure of the previous antimodern movements says little about the possible success of the current movement.

Advocates of this movement do not hold the naively utopian belief that the success of this movement would bring about a global society of universal and lasting peace, harmony and happiness, in which all spiritual problems, social conflicts, ecological destruction, and hard choices would vanish. There is, after all, surely a deep truth in the testimony of the world's religions to the presence of a transcultural proclivity to evil deep within the human heart, which no new paradigm, combined with a new economic order, new child-rearing practices, or any other social arrangements, will suddenly eliminate. Furthermore, it has correctly been said that "life is robbery": A strong element of competition is inherent within finite existence, which no social-political-economic-ecological order can overcome. These two truths, especially when contemplated together, should caution us against unrealistic hopes.

No such appeal to "universal constants," however, should reconcile us to the present order, as if it were thereby uniquely legitimated. The human proclivity to evil in general, and to conflictual competition and ecological destruction in particular, can be greatly exacerbated or greatly mitigated by a world order and its worldview. Modernity exacerbates it about as much as imaginable. We can therefore envision, without being naively utopian, a far better world order, with a far less dangerous trajectory, than the one we now have.

This series, making no pretense of neutrality, is dedicated to the success of this movement toward a postmodern world.

David Ray Griffin
Series Editor

Introduction

We live in an era of "posts." We speak of post-liberal, post-industrial, post-Western, post-Constantinian, post-Christian, post-colonial, post-nationalist, post-humanist, post-patriarchal, and, most paradoxically and importantly, postmodern. Although there are faddish elements involved in this rhetoric, it should be taken seriously. The sense of a radical break with the past, partly observed and partly hoped for, comes to expression in this language, and the language sharpens the observation and fuels the hope. The choice of terminology also suggests that there is greater clarity about what is being superseded than about the new affirmations that are to replace it.

Most of the terms are reasonably clear, at least in specific contexts, in the sense that that which is being superseded is fairly definite. We know that much of Africa and Asia was ruled in the first half of this century by European powers and that, politically speaking, this is no longer true. Most former colonies in Africa and Asia are now independent countries. Yet the marks of colonialism still shape them. To say that their situation is post-colonial can be given quite exact meaning.

In a broader sense the value of the rhetoric in each case, and in this case in particular, may be disputed. One may argue that the former colonies are not really free from colonial rule, that that rule has simply changed form. Whereas once their governments were directly controlled by European nations, now their elected officials must do the will of transnational corporations and transgovernmental financial agencies such as the World Trade Organization, the International Monetary

Fund, and the World Bank. One may argue that the situation is not so much post-colonial as neo-colonial, and that "post-colonial" obscures this important historical fact.

"Post-patriarchal" is also fairly clear. Feminists have made us keenly aware of the extent to which society for thousands of years has been based on the control of women by men. Our recorded histories are of the thoughts and acts of men. The few women who figure in this history have played roles largely shaped by the male culture.

The difficulty in understanding what is meant by post-patriarchal, then, is not with the meaning of "patriarchal." The difficulty is with the sense in which that world is being superseded. Is a post-patriarchal world an object of hope? Or is it claimed that in some measure it is being realized here and now? In the realm of thought, much literature in many fields has changed. At the very least many have been conscientized with respect to the patriarchal character of inherited habits and customs and modes of thought so that these are now topics of critical discussion rather than simply taken for granted. Perhaps that situation itself can be called post-patriarchal even if, through vast stretches of culture, patriarchy still reigns.

The ambiguities of the term "postmodern" are far greater. Given the dominant usage of the term "modern" until recently, "postmodern" is paradoxical. In common speech "modern" often still means whatever is most advanced, most up-to-date, most current. This changes as culture changes, so that it is never superseded. Given that usage, "modernists" may be opposed by conservatives or traditionalists; they may be opposed by those who emphasize the importance of recovering some features of the past by calling themselves "neo" this or that; but they cannot be opposed by "postmodernists."

The serious use of "postmodern" depends on freezing the "modern" in terms of some of the dominant features of the recent past. This has happened in various fields. Alfred North Whitehead contributed to this development in his book *Science and the Modern World*.[1] Here he objectifies "modern" thought as an historical phenomenon, noting its strengths, but also discussing developments that break its boundaries. For him the modern world is most clearly that of the sixteenth through the nineteenth centuries. Of course, when he published the book in the 1920s he knew that the habits of mind he described as modern were still widely prevalent.

Whitehead undertook to present a convincing alternative to modern ways of understanding the world. In place of the material substances posited by early modern thought, he proposed that events are primary. The unit events of which the world is composed are like organisms in that they are internally related to their environments, which are made up of societies of other unitary events. Each such event is a subject in the moment of its occurrence, receiving the past into itself and actively constituting itself so that it will, in turn, affect its future. As soon as it has fully become, it is an object of which subsequent events take account. Thus Whitehead overcomes the dualism of subjects and objects.

Similarly, human experiences are examples of the events that make up the world. They do not stand aside from the others. There is no dualism of humanity and nature. And finally, every event has both physicality and mentality in some incipient degree. The world is not made up of minds and bodies but of events that have both mental and physical characteristics in varying degrees.

Whitehead did not use the term "postmodern," but by the 1960s some of his followers were doing so.[2] By that term, we meant the full implications of twentieth-century developments in science, philosophy, and other fields. The new beginning to which Whitehead pointed in philosophy was William James, who rejected the starting point of modern philosophy in sense experience and the reification of consciousness. In science the new beginning was relativity and quantum theory. Whiteheadians continue to use "postmodern" in this sense. This book follows this pattern. Above all it investigates the implications for a variety of current issues of Whitehead's vision of a world of internally related events.

Histories of "modern" philosophy typically begin with Descartes in the seventeenth century. Whitehead locates Descartes in an ongoing movement of scientific-philosophical thought originating a century earlier. But he recognizes the important role of Descartes in restructuring philosophy on the basis of the thinking human subject. For Whitehead, as for philosophers generally, Descartes is the father of modern philosophy.

"Modern" as a philosophical label goes back to the fourteenth century. William of Ockham's nominalism was called the *via moderna,* and a continuity can be traced between that and the dominant styles of modern philosophy. But it is probably better to call this a foreshadowing of modern philosophy than its full appearance.

Although the "modern" period in philosophy has been understood to have a beginning, until very recently it had no end. Standard texts brought the story of modern philosophy as close to the time of the writer as they could. The implication was that whatever is happening now and will happen in the future will be a part of the continuing story of modern philosophy. To identify a fresh beginning in the twentieth century that would have to be considered a break with modernity was not part of the usual picture.

What historians call "modern" history is likely to begin somewhat earlier. Some date it as early as the fall of Constantinople in 1453, with the resultant spread of classical learning to the West. The Renaissance is viewed as the cultural break with Medievalism. Although most historians recognize the importance of science, they do not make as much of the philosophy and science of the period as did Whitehead. For them, the basic characteristics of the modern period, in distinction from its predecessor, may be secularization, or nationalism, or colonialism, or humanism, or individualism, or belief in progress, or Eurocentrism. Once the term "modern" is clearly identified, historians can join in speaking of the postmodern, meaning either that the public historical situation has changed or that the elite culture has turned in another direction.

In other fields, the use of the term has differed. In my own field of theology, it has been more common to speak of theology's response to modernity than to speak of modern theology. We do speak of Friedrich Schleiermacher, who wrote early in the nineteenth century, as the father of "liberal" theology, and we mean by "liberal" what could easily be called "modern." Schleiermacher recast the whole of theology intentionally in terms of the cultural situation of his time.[3] Religious experience replaced scripture and tradition as the fundamental norm for reflection about Christian faith. Because Schleiermacher has been called "liberal," recent movements replacing his turn to religious experience by a turn to language have called themselves "post-liberal"[4] rather than "postmodern," despite their affinities to important forms of the latter. On the other hand, many scholars in the field of religious studies have adopted postmodern styles and methods, and a few theologians have done so also.[5]

Near the end of the nineteenth century the term "modern" was used by some Roman Catholics in France[6] and the United Kingdom,[7] by some Anglicans,[8] and by some Protestants in the United States. They all called for an end to compromise with the best knowledge of the day and for its wholehearted acceptance. They understood that this required radical reformulation of Christian doctrine, but they were convinced that there was truth and value in Christian teaching that survived any cultural and intellectual change. This could be appreciated and genuinely realized only through thoroughgoing abandonment of efforts to hold on to received doctrine for its own sake.

Pope Pius X suppressed modernism in the Catholic context, but a clear echo of the modernists' concerns could be heard in Vatican II. In Protestant circles modernism lost much of its influence because of the rise to dominance of Neo-Orthodoxy. But with the decline of Neo-Orthodoxy it has, under various names, regained importance. American modernism provides much of the background for the acceptance of the Whiteheadian form of postmodernism.

Toward the end of the nineteenth century a group of American Protestants centered at the University of Chicago adopted the label "modernists." They meant that Christian thinking should be completely recast in terms of current historical, philosophical, and scientific thought. Shailer Matthews's *The Faith of Modernism*[9] was a clarion call for such a shift in the churches.

Matthews used "modern" to mean contemporary, not as affirming the distinctive emphases of the previous three centuries. He was particularly interested in the new science that was emerging when he wrote, believing that it offered fresh opportunities for relating religious and scientific thought. He denied that there is any unchanging essence to Christianity, holding instead that it is a sociohistorical movement.

Matthews emphasized the dependence of doctrine on changing cultural situations in ways that are quite congenial to more recent cultural criticism. For example, he was critical of the continued use of monarchical language in the church because of the support it gave to authoritarian ways of thinking of God and human relations. Given the terminology that came into vogue later in the century, he would no doubt have preferred to call himself a "postmodernist." Whiteheadian theological postmodernism is more a development from Matthews's modernism than a repudiation and reversal.

In painting, also, "modernism" named movements of the nineteenth and twentieth centuries.[10] In a museum of "modern art" we expect to see the paintings of expressionists and more recent schools that became far more abstract. In short, modern art was a movement away from the realism that had dominated Western painting since the time of the Greeks. It placed primary emphasis on form rather than on any kind of representation. In many respects it has more affinities with some forms of postmodernism in philosophy than with what postmodernists generally call modernism, although philosophical postmodernism can also reject this formalist preoccupation.

Clearly, what is meant by "postmodernism" has less significance when the "modern" that is superseded is a short-term school in a particular field rather than a long-lasting historical epoch. This book will use the term "modern" to refer primarily to the creative developments in the four hundred years from 1500 to 1900. It is obvious that through the earlier centuries of this period, habits of mind shaped in the Middle Ages continued to dominate in much of society and education. It is only the creative new ideas emerging during the period that are "modern."

In a similar way, most of our institutions and education are still thoroughly modern. The postmodern period began early in the twentieth century, but modern habits of mind still dominate. Most of us who call ourselves postmodernists agree that much of modernity is now destructive and threatens the future of the Earth. Accordingly this book undertakes to employ the new basic assumptions that have become available chiefly in this century to propose changing directions in a variety of fields.

Diverse topics bring different meanings of "postmodern" to the fore. It is not important to define the term narrowly. Sometimes the focus may be on going beyond humanism; sometimes, patriarchy; sometimes, nationalism; sometimes, the mechanistic worldview of modern science; sometimes, the subjectivism and dualism of modern philosophy. Sometimes features of modernity will be affirmed as well as criticized; sometimes there will be only polemic against them. Sometimes premodern ways of understanding will be treated with great appreciation; sometimes the postmodern that is proposed will be quite different from anything that has preceded it.

Most postmodernists have moved beyond modernism in a quite different direction from Whitehead's. They rightly note his continuities with features of modernism they have rejected. Ironically, Whiteheadians see in these critics continuities with late modernity that we believe should be rejected. But the issue of who has broken most fully with modernity is not important. Indeed, it may be desirable to maintain continuities. The real question is who can propose directions and policies that hold promise for the future. If premodern or modern policies show themselves best, they should be adopted. But in field after field, fresh approaches are required that are free from some of the habits of mind that have been inherited uncritically from the modern period.

A major problem, perhaps *the* major problem, confronting humanity today is the threatened collapse of the natural system on which all humanity depends. Modernity's dualistic and anthropocentric habits of mind long delayed attention to this problem and continue to impede an appropriate response. The abandonment of comprehensive philosophical thinking in favor of analysis and phenomenology and existentialism has contributed to the inability of most philosophers to assist society in redirecting its activities. The prevalence of philosophical doctrines that imply that the natural world exists only in and for human experience and language has had catastrophic effects in this respect. This move away both from the affirmation of the independent reality of nonhuman things and from the quest for a comprehensive vision is characteristic of late modernity. The renewal of naturalistic realism and of cosmology in a new key is what we now need.

Those familiar with the dominant schools of postmodernism know that these judgments are quite antithetical to those of most of their members. For them the quest for a "master narrative" can be nothing other than an effort to impose one's will on others. It is inherently "hegemonic." The effort to speak realistically about the natural world is the continuation of "correspondence thinking" and "logocentrism" that are at the heart of the modern project. Obviously, postmodernists who hold these views are highly suspicious of the efforts of persons like myself to address public issues. They will be alert for expressions of my privileged position as a white, middle-class, Euro-American male, whose social location has been in the church and the university.

Readers of this book should, indeed, discern the distortions that this social location inevitably introduces. This recognition is important from my perspective as well as that of the critics of this kind of project. Our difference is that I do not consider the effort to engage in comprehensive thinking as in itself a distortion. I believe it can be carried out with sensitivity to its dangers.

The dominant forms of postmodernism have continued the secularizing process of modernity. They have no place for a holy or divine reality. This neglect is reinforced by their rejection of realism in general and their avoidance of the cosmological project. Whitehead, on the other hand, reopened the discussion of God. He rejected the dominant understanding of God in both the classical and the modern worlds.[11] In particular he opposed the idea of an omnipotent deity controlling everything and unaffected by what happens in the world. But he found a place for a pervasive divine indwelling in all things, calling them into a process of becoming, giving them freedom to transcend their past, and receiving them as they perish, moment by moment, into the divine life.

By definition, working on policy proposals for our society is a constructive task. Hence this is a work in constructive postmodern thought. However, fruitful construction cannot take place without extensive deconstruction of our heritage. For example, of central importance to Whitehead and to deconstructive postmodernists alike is the deconstruction of the modern self and the patriarchal deity. Nor are those who devote themselves to the deconstructive task without constructive goals and proposals. There are certainly differences between us, but there are also many opportunities for working together.

Although this book aims to suggest policies, most of the content of the following chapters will not be directly on new policies as such. Helpful proposals can come only as issues are reframed. To reframe the issues means to view them in an unaccustomed way. Most of what the book offers are ways of reframing the issues. When that is done, fresh solutions suggest themselves.

The proposals that emerge from these discussions are not entirely new. In some cases the book only offers partly original reasons for supporting already widely considered policies. Our human ability to transcend our histories is limited. Also, there is extensive fresh discussion taking place that is already proposing creative new responses to our problems. Each of us may give a different twist to the formulation of these problems, but I am, no doubt, even more dependent than I realize on the work of others. Also, there is a great deal I have not read in which the ideas presented here may be much more adequately articulated and defended. I hope this is the case.

I am a Christian theologian. Postmodernists have learned the importance of publicly clarifying the point of view from which we speak; so I begin here by acknowledging the shaping force of Christian faith in my life and thought. My having been formed and informed by the Christian tradition and community deeply affects my perception of all the questions with which this book deals. This does not mean that I argue at any point from the authority of Christian teaching. Even in inner Christian discussion, appeals to authority are problematic. In discussion with others, they are irrelevant and unacceptable. Christian insights belong in the public discussion if they commend themselves by their intrinsic value. The same is true of the insights of physicists, neoliberal economists, ecofeminists, sociologists, Buddhists, humanists, and everyone else. All of us should examine the sources of our ideas as well as the cultural forces that have shaped us and share this information with our dialogue partners as fully as we can. On the other hand, our ideas should not be prejudged because of prejudices against the traditions that have shaped us.

I regret having to make this request for tolerance. It would be good to be able to take tolerance of Christianity for granted. Unfortunately, in recent decades the public image of "Christian" has been captured by persons whose views are an unattractive mixture of premodern and modern modes of thought, often lacking in compassion. They have left the impression with many in our culture that to bring a Christian voice into the public discussion is to argue from the authority of a particular tradition and to try to impose the policies one supports on the basis of that authority on the wider, pluralistic society. Many, I think most, Christians reject that approach, but we who do so have now become the "silent majority."

I devote the first chapter to my understanding of Christianity. In one sense, it is a quite traditional view, centering in Jesus Christ. In another sense, it may qualify as "postmodern." In the early 1970s I worked out a view of Jesus Christ that I called postmodern.[12] This Christology offers a way of understanding who we Christians are that allows us to get beyond some of the dilemmas that confronted us in late modernity as we adjusted to a radically pluralistic context. It also explains the Christian reasons for engaging in the discussion that occupies the remainder of the book. Since how Christians understand themselves is important for everyone, the chapter should be of interest to all, not just to those who identify themselves in this way.

Chapter Two presents a postmodern way of thinking about religious pluralism. Its main thesis is that at the deepest level differences among beliefs of the great religious traditions are more often complementary than contradictory. It points out the possibilities for future relationship among traditions in light of this complementarity; it then offers its own recommendations. It recognizes that what it offers is a *Christian* postmodern approach. That is, it does not undertake to say how other communities of faith should deal with plurality. It is my hope, however, that this understanding of how to relate to an "other" can have wider relevance to issues of religious pluralism and of how diverse groups, whether religious or cultural, can learn from one another.

Religious diversity is intimately related to cultural diversity, although they are not identical. Chapter Three takes up the challenge of cultural diversity within a single society—the United States. It points to the difficulty of shared action for the common good when there is no agreement on basic values. It points out that when normative values are removed from the public world, only the supposedly neutral values of the market remain. It applies the discussion to education, considering the alternative of separate schools for each culture. Given the risks in that response to pluralism, it also suggests an experiment in identifying common values arising out of the multicultural situation itself.

The discussion then moves in the fourth chapter to questions of gender and sexuality. The ideas in this discussion are borrowed from feminist literature, which has unquestionably led the way in reframing questions about gender. The chapter examines a few points where puzzles and paradoxes arise in that feminist literature, and proposes that a postmodern ontological analysis of the relation of body, soul, and self can cast light on these questions. With that same analysis it approaches the issue of homosexuality. It argues that society should support responsible expressions of homosexuality as it does of heterosexuality. The ideal context for both is committed, loving relations of equals. Society should sanction and celebrate homosexual unions that embody such relations.

Chapter Five extends the topic of the natural, introduced in the discussion of gender and sexuality, to the whole of the world. It undertakes, through a continuing discussion of body and soul, to identify the point at which human behavior transcends nature and can even become anti-natural. This entails an alienation from nature that began long ago and came to a climax in the modern period. The cultural alienation expresses itself in actions that are threatening the well-being of the natural world. These actions occur especially in the economic order, which acts out the basic implications of modern thought with regard to relations among people and with nature. The chapter concludes by suggesting an alternative, postmodern approach.

Acting out the assumptions of modernity, the economy has become global. It can no longer be controlled by any national government. This raises in acute form the problem of governance. Assuming that representative government should control economic actors, Chapter Six notes the possibility that world government could respond to this need and argues that it should do so if the economy remains global. It also sketches out a more decentralized pattern of government by local communities and communities of communities that would embody the traditional Catholic teaching of subsidiarity and better express the postmodern understanding of the importance of community. This pattern could also give more play for multiculturalism in political life. It would require a parallel decentralization of the economy.

Chapter Seven takes up critically the notion of community, which is presented only positively in Chapter Six. It shows how communities, while necessary and desirable, are also sources of evil. It illustrates this in the area of race, noting that whites created the white race to be a community over and against black slaves. It describes how to this day the identification of Americans of European descent as "whites" blocks possibilities for a healthy society in which blacks could participate fully. The chapter also considers class, which has played a much smaller role in American history than has race. It notes that the current trend is toward much sharper separation between the elite and the masses who are being dispossessed. It considers the possibility that an alliance of African Americans and dispossessed Euro-Americans can generate a countervailing force to the total control of political life by the upper class.

Chapter Eight reflects about the nature and role of ethics in public life in a multicultural society. Is ethics any less culturally conditioned than are values generally? Can society work as a unit without shared ethics? Alternately, should each group, following its own value system, simply throw its weight into the public realm seeking to impose its values by its political power? The abortion debate is taken as a test case. The conclusion is that postmodernists, while respecting the views of others and their right to act on them, will also express and act on their own convictions. This leads them to seek to make space for variety, but there are also instances in which definite positions must be taken and argued for as convincingly as possible.

Chapter One

Can Christians Contribute to the Postmodern World?

I. Christianity as Obstacle and Resource

Christianity has lost its dominant role in the Western world. In many countries it is no longer politically established as the official and state-supported religion, and even where such support exists it has declining significance. More important, Christianity no longer occupies the primary place in the commitment system of most citizens. Even most of those who attend church have their basic attitudes and convictions shaped by sources other than the Christian community and its traditions. In the eyes of many intellectuals and opinion-makers, the church is an anachronistic institution.

In view of this situation, beginning a book on postmodern social policy with a chapter on Christianity seems odd indeed! As explained in the Introduction, one reason for doing so is to put my cards on the table. As a Christian theologian, my own reflections on the social issues with which this book deals are formed and informed by the Christian tradition.

But there are other reasons for attending to religious communities and convictions in general and to Christianity in particular. Despite centuries of secularization, religious beliefs continue to play a large role at deep levels in shaping cultural and social life. As we encounter people formed in diverse religious traditions, we become more aware that even what we have known as secularization has roots in our particular religious tradition, that often what we have defended as simply rational appears so to us because of our religious heritage.

Even the most secular Americans acknowledge the importance of Islam and Judaism on the world scene. That the Catholic Church is a power to be reckoned with on a variety of social issues has long been apparent to those interested in social change. More recently, conservative Protestants have made their voices heard in influential ways. There is widespread concern about the rise of what is sometimes called religious "fundamentalism" all over the world, sometimes as a protest against the forces of Western secularism. Within the United States the diversity of religions is recognized as in tension with unified social and educational practices.

Those who view Western culture from without have no difficulty in seeing that even in its present, highly secularized form, it is, for good and ill, an outgrowth of Christianity. When secular Westerners treat their own values as religiously neutral, others may experience this as a new form of cultural arrogance and imperialism. In an increasingly pluralistic context, to ignore the historical fact of our shared Christian tradition inhibits effective response to social and cultural problems.

Furthermore, avowed Christian commitment is far from dead. Globally, Christianity claims the largest number of adherents of any religious tradition. Although many of these adherents are only nominally Christian, many others are serious. This is true even in the Western countries where secularization has gone the farthest.

Most secular thinking identifies Christianity as an obstacle to postmodern change (and even to modernity). Christianity is seen as informing one among the multiple religious and cultural traditions out of which a postmodern, secular, or pluralistic culture must be formed. Since Christianity has been dominant in the past, much of the deconstruction that is needed is of this particular tradition. The presence of large numbers of committed defenders of this tradition makes the needed deconstruction difficult. It may be important to understand this tradition, but it seems to many moderns and postmoderns unlikely that one can look to it for help.

The reality, however, is more complex. Some Christians understand their tradition in ways that turn it into a positive resource for moving into the postmodern world. Furthermore, these ways of understanding are not imposed on the community from without but arise from its own internal reflection.

This chapter takes up four topics. First, how is Christianity to be understood? Several possible answers are considered, including understanding Christianity as a cultural-linguistic system. Section II proposes that we understand it, instead, as a particular sociohistorical movement with great capacity for change and development. It is Christian because Jesus is its central and pivotal figure, and in every period the movement looks back to the events centering in Jesus for inspiration.

For this reason the subsequent sections focus on this centeredness in the Jesus-event. Section III asks who Jesus was. Is it reasonable for Christians today to continue to attribute special authority to him? Section IV turns to his teaching as a guide to how we can now understand ·salvation, or that toward which our efforts are properly directed. The discussion focuses on the *basileia theou,* often translated as the Kingdom of God. Section V discusses "Christ" as the living power that Christians find in their lives and world as they are informed by Jesus. It explains this to be the power of creative transformation.

Section VI completes the chapter with a discussion of what this means for the Christian way of being in the world today. What constitutes faithfulness? The question is brought to bear on the currently controversial topic of physician-assisted suicide.

II. What Is Christianity?

Whether Christianity is an obstacle to moving forward into a postmodern world, or a resource for doing so, depends on how its adherents understand the significance of their faith. What does it mean to be a Christian? Most of the major answers lead to making Christianity an obstacle. But there is another way of understanding faith that makes it a resource.

We can consider a few of the answers to our question in a highly schematic way. (1) The dominant premodern answer was otherworldly. The other world was divided into realms of rewards and of punishments. Since these were everlasting, their overwhelming importance could not be denied. To be a Christian was to be recipient of the grace of Jesus Christ through the church. This grace mediated God's forgiveness for sins and the gift of a destiny of blessedness.

(2) In modernity, attention shifted to this world. Belief in life after death was long retained because of the assumption that hope for rewards and fear of punishment after death encouraged socially desired behavior in this life. By the nineteenth century, however, the appeal to rewards and punishments in another world largely disappeared among leading Christian thinkers. The focus was on the Christian formation of life here and now. To be a Christian was to be a member of

that community that participated in the highest form of religious experience and life.

(3) As modernity advanced, the claim that Christianity is superior to other religious traditions and communities lost its persuasiveness. That claim has been superseded by the view that all the great religious traditions are paths to the same goal. As paths they are quite different, but their success in reaching the goal is relatively equal. The goal may be understood as loving communion with neighbors, as proper response to the holy, as union with ultimate reality, or, more recently, as transformation from ego-centeredness to centeredness in the Real.[1] Since Christianity offers a successful and effective path to the ultimate goal, those who have been formed by the Christian tradition have every reason to continue to pursue that path.

From a postmodern perspective, this effort to find or impose unity on diverse communities is objectionable. However generous the intention, the effect is hegemonic. Inevitably, the goal that is affirmed as common to all expresses the values of the writer and silences the voices of those who have other priorities and commitments. This is true even if some members of the diverse traditions can recognize their ends in what is asserted to be the universal goal.

(4) The influence of postmodernism on Christian theology is most visible among those who have renounced any universal claims. They recognize Christianity as one community among others, with its own distinctive traditions and practices. To be a Christian is not to compare Christianity with others and make claims either to superiority or to equality. It is not to try to impose Christian teachings on society as a whole. It is to immerse oneself in one's own community, appropriating its values and meanings more deeply, and living from its stories and rituals.

The argument for this understanding of Christianity is familiar to many postmodernists. It begins with the rejection of the notion that language mirrors an objective and independent reality. According to this view, there is no access apart from language to a "real" world, and hence there can be no correspondence of language to that world. Instead, the world we inhabit is a linguistic one.

This means that Christian doctrines are not to be viewed as assertions about how things are in and of themselves. They are not to be believed in this sense. Instead, they constitute a system of symbols and meanings that can order understanding and life. Christianity thus understands itself as a cultural-linguistic system.[2]

This kind of theological postmodernism has the advantage of abandoning all Christian claims to hegemony, of leaving to others the equal right to shape their lives according to their preferred system of meanings. This is certainly a gain. Furthermore, Christians formed in this way can be counted on to serve not only one another but other neighbors as well, without imposing their own meanings and values on them. They will make a positive contribution to meeting some of the needs of society.

It is not clear, however, that Christians who accept this understanding of what faith means can contribute, as Christians, to the shaping of policy in the wider society. If they do so, it seems, they do not act as Christians but in some other capacity. Yet the inherited symbol-system encourages concern for society as a whole. And the good of society cannot be attained simply by the virtue of individual actors.

There is another way for Christians to understand themselves that grows more naturally out of their tradition and yet breaks, as fully as does the cultural-linguistic proposal, with both pre-modern and modern views. This is the understanding of Christianity as a sociohistorical movement. This interpretation goes back to the American Protestant "modernism" discussed in the Introduction, which has many affinities to postmodernism.

According to this understanding, which is mine, to be a Christian is to locate oneself in the Christian community. This community is a changing one, growing out of a long history and moving into an uncertain future. Being a sociohistorical movement does not, of course, differentiate Christianity from other major traditions. What differentiates the Christian movement is its particular origin and history. It originated in events in Israel centering on Jesus and the community that grew up around him. Crucial for the development of this community was its interpretation of the nature and mission of Jesus after his death and his appearances to his followers. For simplicity, this complex of historical occurrences can be called "the Jesus-event."

But origination in that event does not by itself define the movement as Christian. That Western secularism also has roots in that event does not imply that all Western secularists are now Christians. Even those who recognize their roots are not necessarily Christian. The Christian movement regards the originating events as normatively significant. Some Marxists, secular humanists, existentialists, and post-Christian feminists recognize that their origins lie in the Jesus-event, but no longer find it a source of norms. They do not consider themselves Christians, and their preference should be respected.

Normally, the Christian community understands the Jesus-event as located in the history of Israel and finds much of normative importance in that earlier history. Normally, it gathers for regular occasions of renewal of its memory both of that earlier history and of the Jesus-event itself. Normally, it places great weight on the written records of Israel's life and of the Jesus-event, that is, on the Bible. Much else can be said of its usual practice. But a definition should include only enough to establish boundaries within which there may still be great diversity. No matter how carefully those boundaries are drawn, furthermore, there will be many borderline instances. This does not disqualify a definition.

Beliefs are important to this sociohistorical movement. Subgroups within the community may not be able to work together if they disagree too much on the meaning of the founding events. Today it is hard to understand the intensity of feeling aroused by disagreements on Christology and Trinity in the early church because these differences are not the ones that divide us today. But at that time they were bound up with the way salvation was understood, and a great deal depended on that.

More understandable to us today are the theological quarrels that gave rise to the Reformation. But they, too, are fading in importance. Lutherans and Catholics can now agree on common formulations without overcoming their practical differences, brought about by a long history of separate development.

In the nineteenth century, denominations split over slavery, an issue we can still understand. Today the most divisive issues among Christians in the United States are abortion, women's ordination, and homosexuality. To what extent these will cause institutional divisions within the church remains to be seen, but they are already dividing the Christian movement.

Obviously, being a part of the Christian movement does not determine how one thinks on all issues. This is partly because Christian identity does not exclude the influence of other social forces. Much thinking in the church becomes subservient to these other forces. Many passionately affirm as essential to faith beliefs and attitudes whose sources are quite external to the tradition. But disagreements also occur because equally faithful people disagree as to the meaning of the Jesus-event for our time and as to the most faithful responses for the church to make to new challenges.

The theological task is both to clarify disagreements and to take a stand in relation to them. To be theological, the stand must intend to be Christian. The more fully this intention is clarified, the better the theologian fulfills the task. But theologies that excel in this way still disagree, and there are profound changes over time.

This understanding of Christianity has some of the advantages of the cultural-linguistic form of postmodernism. It leaves entirely open the self-definition of other religious communities, imposing nothing on them. It makes no attempt to reduce their otherness to sameness, or to prejudge them in any way as inferior, equal, or superior to Christianity. In short, it is not hegemonic.

This way of understanding Christianity recognizes that beliefs are culturally shaped and have their role and meaning within the community. They are not ultimate statements about absolute truth. Believers are not to be required to accept them if they do not commend themselves by their own persuasiveness and illuminating power.

But the sociohistorical school is not committed, as is the cultural-linguistic school, to a way of thinking that prevents speaking of God, the world, and the human past as having a reality independent of our thought and language. In responding intellectually to changing situations, the church attempts to reformulate its teachings as well as possible. Good teachings are not only those that conform to past teachings or shape the lives of members well. They are also those teachings that conform as fully as possible to the best knowledge of the time. That knowledge has some, always fragmentary and imperfect, correspondence to the way the world is. The church should strive to formulate its teaching more accurately.

For example, the scholarship of the past two hundred years has given us a much more accurate account of how the Bible was formed and who Jesus really was. Of course, there are still legitimate debates about these matters. Among those who take the historical evidence seriously, however, the parameters of the debates have changed. Some of the assumptions underlying past doctrines are now exposed as highly implausible. The church should reformulate its teaching in light of this increased knowledge of history so that it will correspond more closely to what probably took place.

Similarly, there have been enormous advances in our knowledge of the natural world. We are quite sure now that the world is far more than six thousand years old. Our teaching about creation has changed to take this into account. This is as it should be. As the Big Bang becomes more and more the likely story about the origins of our cosmos, our teachings should reflect this new understanding. In this way they are more likely to correspond to what actually occurred.

Even though church teaching obviously has changed over the centuries, many Christians are disturbed by this relativization of doctrine. Some Christians attempt to establish one set of doctrines as eternally fixed regardless of changing culture, historical study, and natural science. These doctrines, they declare, are of the essence of Christianity. Others recognize that no linguistic formulations can have this absoluteness, and they appeal to prethematic convictions, orientations, or styles of life. This move greatly eases the problem.

Nevertheless, the effort to establish some unchanging pattern that must characterize all Christians moves in a direction different from that of the sociohistorical school. It may well be that there are some teachings and practices that have characterized all serious Christians for two millennia. But it is a mistake to identify them as the unchanging essence of Christianity. In this new century we may discover problems with what has characterized all of us until now. If our fresh reflection about the meaning of our history for our new situation leads us to abandon those teachings or characteristics, we will not be less Christian for that. On the contrary, to refuse to change for the sake of a supposed unchanging essence would be a lapse of faithfulness.

III. Jesus

The central teaching of the Christian movement is about Jesus and "Christ." The question is how we are to understand the originating events of our movement and what they call on us to do today. Jesus is at the center of those events.

For two centuries reflection about Jesus has been in part an investigation of history. What really happened back then? Modern historiography can help to answer that question.

The question for Christians, however, goes beyond the capacities of modern historians because modern historiography cannot deal with God's agency. While learning as much as possible from historians, theologians ask: How was God involved in the Jesus-event? The importance of that question shows that Christology cannot be separated from the doctrine of God.

The complexity of the church's task is already clear. We cannot answer our question without the help of historians, but the assumptions that modern historians have written into their craft prevent them from even asking the question that has been most important to the Christian movement. One solution is for the movement today to accept the assumptions built into modern historiography that God does not act in the world. It would then be possible simply to adopt the consensus of historians, when there is a consensus, and move on from there.

Another solution has been to minimize the role of historians by grounding our affirmations as to what happened on the testimony of the earliest witnesses. We may regard that testimony itself as the decisive initiation of our movement.

The Whiteheadian form of postmodernism offers another option. Christians can bring their understanding of God's presence in the world into relation with what we learn from historians who omit this. We can thereby come to fresh judgments as to how God was present in Jesus and in the early church. This enables us to take seriously the efforts of the church fathers to understand God's incarnation in Jesus even while realizing that some of the issues they raised and the conceptual categories available to them were different from ours.

Whitehead makes this possible by providing a postmodern philosophical grounding for the widespread Christian belief that God is present and active everywhere. In a quite technical sense, God is immanent in all things. If so, God was immanent in Jesus and in the community that surrounded him and subsequently developed into the church.

Given this starting point, the problem in formulating a Christology is quite opposite to that which confronted the church fathers. For them, thinking of creatures and God as externally related substances, the problem was how to affirm that, nevertheless, in this one unique case, God was internal to a human being. Since for them supernaturalism was no problem, they could do so easily by thinking of some portion of the human Jesus as replaced by the divine. But they resisted this option, because the assertion of the full humanness of Jesus was important to them. Accordingly, they developed the idea that one being could be commingled with another without loss of distinctness. In doing so they moved toward a doctrine of internal relations. They employed this doctrine also in understanding how the members of the Trinity mutually constituted one another. Whitehead believed that in their reflections on the Trinity and the incarnation, the Alexandrian and Antiochene theologians made a fundamental metaphysical advance over Plato by developing a doctrine of internal relations.[3]

Christians can now begin where the church fathers ended. Not only was God present in Jesus without reducing his humanity in any way, but also God is present in all of us. Hence the literal affirmation of incarnation is unproblematic. But the doctrine of incarnation was not simply about God's presence in the world. It was also about the unique authority and nature of Jesus. It is this that now challenges us.

That Jesus played a unique role in the Christian movement is not in question. What *is* in question is what kind of authority we should give him today. The founder of a movement may not be regarded as particularly insightful or wise. One can acknowledge the contribution without returning to her or him for guidance in future situations. Yet to this day the church continues to look to Jesus and to those most closely involved in the Jesus-event as authoritative. Is that warranted? Or is it simply a habit that was developed when people supposed that one in whom God was incarnate would be all-wise and inerrant?

These questions are fundamental for present practice. The church is a community that not only originated in the Jesus-event but also seeks to be informed by the memory of that event. When it ceases to find the event normative, it will cease to keep the memory alive through scripture reading, sacrament, and sermon. The Christian movement will end.

Although the question of the authority of the event is not identical with that of how God was present in Jesus, the relation has always been close. If there was nothing unusual about the way God was present in Jesus, then are there other grounds for attributing special authority to him? If so, what are they? If there was something unusual about the relationship, then this should be affirmed and clarified so that both the nature of the authority that follows from it for believers and its limitations can be understood.

Given the fact that God is present in all people and that Christians have looked to Jesus with particular admiration, the simplest answer would be that Jesus conformed more fully to God's aim than have most others. Few Christians doubt that this is the case. The truth of this judgment warrants attributing authority to Jesus as an example of goodness and spiritual greatness. Further, an unusually good person is also more likely to have accurate insights than others are. Hence, it is appropriate to attend to his teaching. Nevertheless, this judgment would not justify singling Jesus out to the extent that the church continues to do in its liturgical life.

A second point that is not particularly controversial is that the mission Jesus performed is unique. Just how we identify that mission is controversial, but some elements are historically undisputed. Whether intentionally or not, Jesus initiated the movement within which Christians now find themselves. That movement was far more open to Gentiles than was the dominant Judaism of the day. Because it has in fact been remarkably successful among Gentiles, the movement has had world-historical importance.

Does this give us reason to accord any particular authority to Jesus' words and deeds? Apparently not. Since Jesus himself did not envision the sort of events that followed, it is hard to see why, on the grounds of his unique work, we should pay particular attention to his teaching. That teaching was not directed at us. And further, as practical advice, most of it is questionable.

Nevertheless, Jesus' contemporaries were impressed by the implicit claim to authority of Jesus' teaching, and it still carries its own weight today. Even when people know that they will not act directly on what he taught, many feel grasped by it as having a truth that they can neither incorporate nor neglect. Is there any explanation of the unusual nature of Jesus' teaching and actions?

The Whiteheadian form of postmodernism suggests a possibility that is worth exploring. It does so by deconstructing the modern self and putting in its place a self that can be constructed in a variety of ways. It does this through its doctrine of "prehension."

A prehension is the way one actual entity includes another. The Introduction briefly explained that actual entities as conceived by Whitehead are not little substances but events that are "occasions of experience." Each such event is constituted by the way other events flow into it. This inflowing is the causal efficacy of past occasions for the one that is now becoming. From the side of the occasion that is becoming, the act of including a past event is a prehension.

The most important prehensions in ordinary occasions are of the immediate environment. This environment always includes God. In the case of a human experience, it also includes not only the neuronal experiences in the brain, but one's own immediate past experience. The deconstruction of the continuous self prepares for reconstructing the self out of a succession of human experiences.

In ordinary adult human experience, at least in the modern West, the single most determinative prehension with regard to one's self-determination is that of one's own personal past. It is the prominence of this prehension that has given rise to notions of a substantial self. Whiteheadian postmodernists affirm that this connection is what establishes one's sense of personal identity through time.

As one examines one's own experience, one can distinguish this continuation of the personal past into the present from the roles of other elements that participate in constituting the experience. One easily thinks of "I" and "they." Although the decision that culminates the self-forming occasion of experience grows out of all of these, if it is not primarily determined by the prehension of the personal past, one is likely to feel some loss of autonomy and control.

There is something else operative in each moment—the prehension of God, drawing one into responsible freedom. Normally one feels this, like the other influences, as coming from without. One may be grateful for it as a gift; or one may be resistant, because it calls for taking risks one does not want to take. One may feel guilt because one experiences a rightful demand that one refuses. But in all these instances there is a clear difference between oneself as the continuation into the present of the personal past and the divine presence experienced as grace or judgment.

As long as this difference exists, part of one's experience in each moment will be the feeling of tension between what one has become and what one might have become. One will be in some measure guilty and defensive. One's perception of the world will be colored by this tension and the resultant defensiveness. In traditional theological language, one will be concerned to justify oneself. One will view others as supporters or threats, not simply as what they are in themselves. In short, one will be self-centered.

But there are other possibilities. The prehension of the personal past may lose any significant role in the present. Buddhist meditation moves in that direction but without highlighting God's presence in the occasion. Some forms of Western mysticism, in contrast, may lead to so setting the personal self aside that the organizing principle of the occasion is the prehension of God. Mystics who have attained that experience should be recognized as having a certain authority.

Jesus does not seem to have been that kind of mystic. He impresses us as having had a strong self. According to the gospel accounts, the tension between his personal self and the call of God was occasionally intense. This tension is depicted especially in the story of the temptations in the wilderness and the struggle in the Garden of Gethsemane. Although the evidence for their historicity is very indirect, the inclusion of these stories shows that the first Christians did not suppose that Jesus' relation to God precluded such struggle.

On the other hand, what comes through in many of Jesus' sayings is a lack of tension, an absence of defensiveness. Jesus seems to speak out of immediate perception of the situation, a perception that is not distorted by self-concern. Is such perception intelligible?

If Jesus' prehension of his personal past and his prehension of God were sometimes so related as to function as a unity in determining what each of his occasions of experience became, then the apparent absence of tension, doubt, and defensiveness would follow. Jesus would speak with authority, knowing that what he perceived was what was there to be perceived—that, in a sense, he saw as God saw. There would be then, at times, the union of the divine and the human persons that the church fathers struggled to articulate.

To accent the distinctiveness of the way in which God was present in Jesus, we could restrict the term "incarnation" to this type of immanence, using the term "immanence" elsewhere. Alternately, we could speak of incarnation everywhere and describe the different forms that it takes.

The teachings resulting from such a structure of existence have the authority of direct insight but do not provide practical guidance for the behavior of those who are still caught in the midst of tension and defensiveness and social expectations. They provide norms by which we can judge the direction that our lives, our church, and our society are taking. We can work for circumstances in which actual behavior could more easily conform to these norms. Because these insights stand in tension with all human achievements they are an inexhaustible source of challenge.[4] This is their peculiar authority for Christians.

IV. Salvation

A religious community offers its members some vision of the goal of life, some ideal toward which to strive, or some end for which to hope. Buddhism points toward enlightenment as the supreme end. It is the Buddhas, the enlightened ones, whom it reveres and who speak to it with authority. Christianity names its goal salvation, and identifies Jesus as the Savior. When the Christian movement is clear both about the salvation for which it hopes and its role in relation to that salvation, it is vital and vigorous. When that is not the case, its energies are difficult to mobilize.

Unfortunately, the understanding of salvation in the old-line Protestant churches has become vague and diverse. There are still some who take the term to apply to what happens to individuals after they die or to vindication at the last judgment. But there are many who focus on salvation in this life instead. Of these, some identify salvation in psychological terms, others, in existential terms. Still others have stopped using the term altogether.

In such a situation, identifying Jesus as Savior has little meaning. From what does he save us and to what? For some Christians, the answer is that he saves us from sin and guilt. This answer has strong traditional support especially among Protestants. For many Christians, however, it now has little power. They are not sure whether they are "sinners." The clear-cut legalistic statements of an earlier generation are largely gone from the old-line churches. In any case, it is not clear how Jesus saves us from sin. The doctrines of atonement that were long central to Christian teaching have lost persuasive power. If one is having a problem with guilt feelings, one is more likely to get help from a therapist than from one's church.

For some, Jesus has saved us by showing how deeply God loves us. This frees us from fear and assures us that, when we seek forgiveness, God is ready and willing to extend it. We do not have to appease an angry God. This is plausible and meaningful for many, but the threat of punishment from an angry God seems quite remote to most. Perhaps this kind of salvation, effected by Jesus, has been all too successful in wide sections of contemporary Christendom. One has to remind oneself that people once feared God's wrath in order to appreciate one's current lack of fear. If this exhausts the meaning of salvation, salvation seems somewhat peripheral to more burning concerns.

One reason for the difficulty of defining salvation is that the word has many uses in the Bible. Often salvation has quite practical historical meanings. A city is saved from a siege. A child is saved from disease. A people are saved from bondage in Egypt. We continue to use the term in these ways today, but most Christians distinguish this use from the theological one.

In my judgment, we would benefit from taking Jesus' authority seriously on this topic. He provides a way of moving past the diversity without excluding many of its elements. At the heart of his teaching was the proclamation of the *basileia theou*, the "realm of God."

Jesus' parables give little concrete idea as to what happens in the *basileia*. They speak instead of its supreme value and of how it comes. But the parallel line in the Lord's Prayer speaks volumes. The *basileia* is where God's will is done on earth. Jesus called people to prepare for this changed order.

It is fortunate for us that we have no record of Jesus spelling out the political, social, and economic arrangements of the *basileia*. We are left free to read into it our own understanding of God's aims in the world. Of course, if we are Christians, what we read in will be deeply influenced by the Jesus-event.

Jesus' expectation was of a transformed earth where God's purposes are realized. Those who thought it would come soon were disappointed. But understanding salvation in terms of the healing of the planet with all its human inhabitants remains a worthy definition. It directs our attention to the suffering of the present day and indicates the importance of working for the transformation of society and the renewal of the Earth.

As a sociohistorical movement, Christianity can clarify its sociohistoric goal by aiming at the *basileia*. Indeed, in the early part of this century, when this way of understanding Christianity was most widespread, the goal was identified as the coming of the Kingdom of God. But this formulation of Christian hope came under severe critique. During the era of the "social gospel," to which I have been referring, many people saw the activities in which they were then involved as ushering in the Kingdom quite unambiguously. Some spoke of "building" it.

The expectation that it was already coming and would soon be present in a fuller way was proven hopelessly wrong by two world wars. History showed that this understanding of salvation had relied far too much on human effort and had greatly underestimated the corruption of human actions by sin. It had also conceived the Kingdom of God in modernist terms.

But the reaction went much too far. Instead of continuously correcting the interpretation of the *basileia*, placing stress on the divine initiative and emphasizing the deep ambiguities that beset all action in history, leading theologians directed the church away from Jesus' message altogether. When the idea of the *basileia* was retained it was given an apocalyptic meaning that disconnected what was expected of God from any human efforts. Some defined salvation in a radically individualistic, existentialist way. Popular piety in the United States adopted psychological categories.

Partly as a result of these moves the church has become ineffective in the public world at a time when that world desperately needs salvation. A bold recovery of Jesus' proclamation of the realm of God, which fills it with concrete and realistic accounts of the solutions that

Christians can propose for the existential, moral, psychological, social, political, economic, and ecological problems of our day, could galvanize and unify the energies of the church and enable it to serve the world.

V. Christ

Section III dealt with Jesus and his specific authority for the church, Section IV, with the realm of God that he proclaimed. We have proposed that in Jesus the church discerns an unusual relation to God, one that undergirds or explains the authority many find in him. As a result we call Jesus the Christ.

But the term "Christ" has not been limited to Jesus. We find Christ in the church and in other believers as well. We even encounter Christ outside the boundaries of the church. When we say "Jesus," we attend to a past historical figure, but when we say "Christ," we are often speaking of the ongoing working of God in the world.

We do not, however, speak of Christ in complete disconnection with Jesus. It is in and through Jesus that we discern Christ's presence elsewhere. And that presence elsewhere is enhanced by Jesus' special efficacy in the church.

What marks the presence of Christ, that is, of God's efficacious presence in the world as known in and through Jesus? In Jesus himself the presence was marked by a unity of his personal past and God's indwelling. Because of this he is for Christians uniquely "the Christ." In us, formation "in Christ" rarely takes that form.

Among believers, much more commonly, Christian formation takes the form of repentance. Repentance is the English translation for the Greek word *metanoia,* a word frequently on the lips of Jesus in the gospels. Unfortunately, the English word has lost much of the meaning of the Greek. It tends to name only regret and, perhaps, desisting from some sin. *Metanoia,* in contrast, refers to a change of direction more than to regret for the past. Jesus' call for *metanoia* is not for a return to the past but for an orientation toward the future, toward that new way of ordering matters that he calls the *basileia.*

It is thus the encounter with a new possibility that calls forth *metanoia* in Jesus' message. In the first generation of believers, it was the encounter with the message of Jesus' resurrection and the new possibility that God has brought about through that. Throughout the history of the movement, encountering the message of Jesus has often evoked *meta-noia*. But it also occurs through the words of the preacher who is calling for *metanoia* in new circumstances. The Christian life is entered through *metanoia* and continues as one of repeated *metanoia*.

Metanoia is understood to be the work of God. It comes about because God addresses the soul and calls for change. God also empowers the soul to change accordingly. To the extent that God is heard and a positive response is evoked, there is *metanoia*.

To avoid the accent on regret for the past and to emphasize that it is divine working, this *metanoia* can also be called "creative transformation." God's effective presence known in Jesus is Christ, and Christ transforms. Most of the time, this transformation is very slight and hardly noticed either by the person involved or by others. But there are also dramatic instances.[5]

Whitehead shows us philosophically what is happening in creative transformation. In each moment, the prehension of God introduces a range of possibilities that go beyond, and are thus in some tension with, the mere outcome of the causal forces of the past. These new possibilities enable the occasion to bring unity out of the multiplicity of forces operative within it. God lures toward the realization of the best way of doing this. The rudiments of creative transformation are present in every occasion, at least wherever there is life.

But there are times when the many that are becoming one include elements that are in marked tension with what has constituted the personal self up until then. Newly encountered ideas may be incompatible with the old at the level at which they are presented. Either they must be silenced, or one must give up what has been valuable in the past. Otherwise there will be an unsatisfactory mixture of the two. There is, however, an alternative. One may move forward to a new level at which the two apparently exclusive alternatives are brought into a larger unity.

For this advance to take place, novel possibilities must play a large role. God's presence in the occasion must be peculiarly efficacious. When the novel possibility is actualized, the older value is retained, but in a larger whole that includes the other as well. One's personal identity, with its rootedness in tradition, is not diminished, but one's identity and tradition are expanded and transformed. This is growth, but growth of a specific kind. It is a full-fledged instance of creative transformation. Here Christ is peculiarly manifest.

Christ works most immediately and directly in individuals. By working through many individuals, however, creative transformation can occur also in historical movements, including the Christian one. We discern Christ in the early church's assimilation of the best of the classical world, its later incorporation of scientific thinking and modern historical scholarship, its new appreciation of sexuality as it learned from the sexual revolution, the profound transformation of the Catholic church that occurred in the Second Vatican Council, and the transformation of American society through the leadership of the black church in the civil rights movement. We discern Christ also in political events such as the nearly bloodless transformation of the Union of South Africa into a democracy inclusive of all its people.

Christ's work is enhanced by the encounter with new ideas that prove convincing to Christians. The church did not accept all pagan thinking, only that which commended itself to Christian sensibilities. Its openness to science was not a concession to secular knowledge but an expression of its understanding of God as creator. Its repentance for its millennia-long teaching against sexuality was grounded in a recovery of biblical understanding. The Second Vatican Council was rooted in decades of study of tradition and the way it developed.

VI. The Nature of Faithfulness

Christians vary greatly in their judgments of what relation to the past constitutes faithfulness. One extreme view is that the Bible contains all truth and wisdom, that it presents one coherent position, and that our task is simply to believe what it teaches and to obey its injunctions. At the opposite extreme are Christians who quote Augustine to the effect that we should love God and do as we please, drawing the conclusion that acting as love calls us to do exhausts the meaning of faithfulness for us.

The major response to this situation within the contemporary American Protestant old-line churches is to call for "renewal." Renewal can take many forms. Those who reject repetition of outdated teaching and legalistic morality, but want to be faithful to the larger tradition, argue that we must recover important elements of our tradition that we have lost, but they differ as to which elements should be reemphasized.

This call is usually set against the background of a church that tends to conform to the world around it, a church whose inner divisions simply mirror those of the surrounding society. In Germany this kind of church was described as "culture Protestantism." Easily co-opted by Nazism, it stands as a warning to all future churches not to surrender their distinctive identity by uncritical acceptance of the surrounding culture. When belonging to the Protestant church is simply one of the things the culture prescribes, and when the church is not expected to challenge the culture or make significant demands on its members that put them in tension with the culture, then we have culture Protestantism. There is a great deal of culture Protestantism in our American churches today.

In its most general form, the argument is not that the church should replicate any particular earlier form. It is that it should truly be the church, having its own integrity in contrast to whatever social norms emerge in the society. Its thinking and practice should grow out of its own sources and traditions, not simply reflect the cultural environment. Instead of doing market research to determine what people want and then adapting itself to fill those needs, a renewed church would make its own judgments as to what people need. To this point there is broad agreement among serious Christians.

There are, however, two major ways, other than simple repristination, in which the church can move to realize this end.

One is *renewal* as such, emphasizing the deepening of the distinctive character of Christianity in some separation from the culture. The other is *transformation,* including renewal, but only as a step toward the development of new forms.

The most interesting form of renewal is that discussed in Section II as cultural-linguistic theology. The type of transformation that I call creative transformation has been described in Section V. These have been presented as two forms of postmodern thinking about the nature of the church. This section will explore them somewhat further with special reference to their implications for policy.

The cultural-linguistic school issues a richly informed call for renewal. Instead of adopting the language of the wider community, a renewed church would recover its own symbols and live deeply into them. These symbols would not have to be translated into some other language, because people would come to find that they provide their own meaning, that they interpret the world in their own way. Where the distinctive teaching of the church calls for action or protest beyond its borders, Christians will act. But their chief responsibility is for the faithfulness of the church in its own life, not for the solution of the world's problems. Until they know who they are and how this is rightly expressed in action, they do well to work on their own renewal.

A renewed church would make no effort to dominate society. It would support the full freedom and equality of other groups and organizations, religious and nonreligious. It would not seek to proselytize or convert or to gain advantages for itself through government action. On the other hand, it would have little interest in cooperating with other groups or in engaging in dialogue with them. Its focus would be on its interior revitalization and faithfulness.

Understanding the church as a cultural-linguistic system can allow changes on the surface, but such a system has an unchanging deep structure. Whatever changes occur must conform to that structure. Accordingly, although Christians will not attempt to impose their views on the larger culture, traditional patterns of moral behavior are likely to be supported in the inner life of the church.

A renewed church would not concern itself with whether its actions were liberal or conservative according to the politics of the outside world. It would act as its traditions and teachings require. On issues of race its position would be unequivocally for full equality and participation of all in the life of the church. The Bible and the tradition provide no justification for racism.

But with regard to the issues now dividing the church, renewal is likely to be traditional. An example is physician-assisted suicide. Suicide is not an issue on which the Bible speaks directly, but the tradition has opposed it strongly. One can discern here part of what renewalists see as the deep structure of Christianity. It is committed to the affirmation of each individual's life. It is firmly against any practice that, for temporary gain or advantage, cheapens life. It calls for the community to surround any who are suffering with its love and support and to encourage them to face the ordeal with courage. To do otherwise would be to abandon the fullness of Christian life and to compromise with the wider culture.

The alternative to renewal is transformation. It cannot occur apart from deepening the church's rootedness in the tradition. Without that, efforts to transform would be likely to lead to a culture Protestantism that is clearly faithless to Christ. The ideal of transformation follows from the understanding of the church as a sociohistorical movement. Such a movement maintains identical elements over long periods, but it is also always changing. For transformationists there is no essence or deep structure to block such change. One cannot specify in advance what changes will occur and what will remain the same.

Change is of many types. Some of it is bad. The loss of distinctive moorings and the assimilation to the culture that renewalists rightly bemoan are examples of destructive changes. Against them Christians should stand fast. But there are other changes that are called for by the gospel itself. As noted previously, *metanoia* is a key biblical name for the needed change.

Metanoia means taking a new direction. It is evoked by the contrast between what is and what might be—what may become. It is, thus, oriented to a new future, what Jesus named the realm of God. To engage in *metanoia* by orienting ourselves to that new future is in some measure already to participate in it.

Section V proposed that this *metanoia* be called "creative transformation" and that Christians identify this transformation with what God does in them. The paradigm instances are those in which Christians encounter challenging differences and need to incorporate new insights without weakening their commitment to their own truth and wisdom. Creative transformation occurs through God's gift of a novelty that enables people to encompass the newly encountered wisdom by moving to a larger vision. Where creative transformation occurs, there is Christ.

Viewing the church and Christ in this way leads to judgments about norms for the Christian movement that differ from those of the renewalists. There is agreement that Christians need to recover our rootage, but how we do so depends on a more comprehensive picture of both our origins and our goals. Part of the goal proposed here is to recover sufficient vitality as a Christian movement that we can encounter the vast wisdom generated outside the Christian tradition and be enriched by it.

The Christian movement that results from serious learning from others will be quite different from the more isolated and exclusivist one of which we are heirs, but it will not have lost its continuity. What has been truly learned in its own history will not be forgotten. It will not be less Christocentric than it has been, but it will find in Christ not so much a reason to defend past ideas and practices as the power and motivation to open ourselves to new challenges. As we grow in this way, our faith in Christ will deepen. We will no longer divide our allegiance between Christ and other sources of wisdom.

This transformationist understanding of faithfulness leads to different results with respect to currently troubling issues. Physician-assisted suicide was used previously as the test case for renewal. It will serve here as well.

When the church, as a sociohistorical movement stemming from the Jesus-event, encounters new ways of thinking in the culture around it, it must decide whether it is called to change. If the new ways of thinking do not strike it as having merit, as in the case of new movements of white supremacy, the church responds with principled opposition. But if the new ways of thinking contain ideas with which it has not previously dealt, ideas that on the surface have merit, then it is called to study with an open mind.

Physician-assisted suicide has this latter character. It responds to a problem, now common, that was rare in the past, that of people continuing to live when they prefer to die. Whereas death was once almost always an "enemy," coming before it was wanted, today it is often a longed-for friend. Whereas when death came too soon, physicians rightly prolonged life as long as possible, now that it often comes too late, physicians should help patients who responsibly seek their assistance to die.

To take this position is to deny that human life as such is of absolute worth. It is to say that helping people to fulfill their purposes is sometimes of greater importance than keeping them alive. Love and respect for others is expressed better by taking their wishes seriously than by imposing on them one's own sense of the worth of prolonging their lives. For the transformationist, love of the neighbor calls us to take her or his desires as a claim upon us, setting aside rules or supposed absolutes that prevent us from doing so.

For a transformationist, the fact that there is no explicit support for suicide in the tradition does not count against it in a changed situation. Reaffirming old views, just because they have been strongly established for a long time, is not faithfulness to Christ.

Chapter Two

Religious Pluralism and Truth

I. Introduction

A major reason for rethinking the nature of Christianity and Christian teaching has been the Christian awareness of the presence and value of other religious communities and their teaching. Chapter One offered a reformulation responsive to this problem. It did not go far to show how this new approach works out for Christians in their concrete understanding of the varied religious traditions or in shaping their actual relations to other traditions.

This issue is important not only because of the practical and theoretical problems posed to Christians by the insights of other traditions, but because the encounter with them has eroded Christian confidence in its own claims to truth. One of the reasons for modern religious doubt, both outside and within the churches, has been the diversity of religious truth claims.

This doubt has been justified in many respects. Religious communities, especially those of the Abrahamic family, have tended to formulate their beliefs in opposition to one another. When these are treated as claims to absolute truth, they contradict and exclude one another, so that all but one tradition must be false. As moderns came to take a more comprehensive view, they concluded that there was little basis to favor one tradition over the others. They found the most probable conclusion to be that all were false.

A second response, emerging into prominence in late modernity, is to reject the association of religious faith with truth claims. Clearly there are ways of ordering life and society, of transmitting values, of telling stories, and of relating to one another that have proved durable and meaningful to millions of people over millennia. These are the great religious traditions. They deserve respectful study, but their beliefs can be understood in relation to their practices without regard to their objective truth or falsehood. Even their claims of absolute truth for these beliefs can be understood and respected with detachment. Truth claims are an interesting phenomenon to be understood, like others, in anthropological, psychological, and sociological ways.

Viewed in this light, the fact that there are highly diverse religious traditions is not a problem. The fact that some people order life in one way does not invalidate the different ordering by others. The world is richer for these differences.

This way of looking at religion is often thought of as postmodern. It is so in its appreciation of religious diversity and its respect for the integrity of each tradition. But it is postmodern only when modernity is understood in terms of its pre-Kantian form. It is clearly a continuous development of the post-Kantian abandonment of efforts to describe an objective reality and of its emphasis on the constructive work of the human subject. To Whiteheadian postmodernists, this treatment of religion is, therefore, a new expression of late modernity.

This approach appears, at least at first glance, to be far friendlier to religious communities than the skepticism it supersedes. But this friendliness may, in fact, prove to be more erosive of the traditions than the previous animosity. It may be that the religious traditions cannot survive apart from some of the beliefs that are, in this post-Kantian approach, no longer taken seriously as truth claims.

This chapter is an exploration of this double challenge, with a postmodern response. It proposes that the diversity of religious truth claims can be accepted without arousing skepticism about all if they can be shown to be mutually complementary rather than in conflict. The following section asks whether the differing truth claims of the Abrahamic faiths can be so formulated as to avoid contradicting one another. It notes that even when this is done, they all depend on a doctrine of God that has become radically problematic, partly because it is absent from some other religious traditions such as Theravada Buddhism.

Section III examines Buddhism to see whether, as is sometimes supposed, it actually provides a form of religious understanding that is independent of all questionable truth claims. The conclusion is that it does not—that it, instead, offers some very persuasive and important claims of its own.

These Buddhist claims differ from those of the best-known forms of Hindu Vedanta. Both traditions believe that their understanding of reality is confirmed in their meditative experience. This apparent conflict offers a special challenge to reflection about the mutual complementarity or contradictoriness of religious traditions. Section IV offers a response to this challenge.

Buddhism was introduced partly because its apparent lack of need for a doctrine of God adds to doubts about the justification of believing in God as required by the Abrahamic faiths. Do the denials of God in many Buddhist writings and the affirmations in most Abrahamic ones entail a contradiction? Or can we understand experience in such a way as to see a valid place for both Buddhist and Abrahamic affirmations? This is the topic of Section V.

Section V answers that once again a complementary relationship can be established. But it does so by identifying God as an immanent element in experience, whereas in the Abrahamic traditions God's transcendence has been of great importance. Section VI considers the kind of transcendence that can be affirmed without coming into contradiction with Buddhism.

II. The Abrahamic Faiths

The Abrahamic faiths confront the challenge of both modernity and postmodernity with special intensity. They have presented themselves as systems of belief, and they have formulated these beliefs in part in explicit opposition to one another. It seems that one must choose among them—that if one set of beliefs is correct, then the others must be wrong.

It is supposed, for example, that God is either Trinitarian or not. If God is Trinitarian, then Christianity is the true religion and Judaism and Islam are false. Similarly, either Mohammed is God's prophet or he is not. If he is, then Islam is the true religion and Judaism and Christianity are false. Either God's one covenant is with the Jews or it is not. If it is, then Judaism is the true religion and Christianity and Islam are false.

In fairness to Judaism and Islam, Christians must acknowledge that these two traditions are not as dogmatically oriented as Christianity. Accordingly, their exclusion of each other and of Christianity has not been as unqualified as the traditional Christian exclusion of all who did not accept Jesus Christ as God incarnate and unite with the church. Even in Christianity, moreover, the actual teaching has generally been somewhat more nuanced. Nevertheless, there has been so much mutual exclusion on the basis of absolutist truth claims that the skeptical response was warranted. Since all claims could not be true, given the exclusivist understanding of such claims, most religious truth claims must be false. What reason is there not to suppose that all such claims are false?

This threat of general skepticism opens the way to appreciating the widespread postmodern depreciation of doctrinal assertions as claims to truth. But to abandon truth claims in this way would undercut their basic message and meaning for believers. For example, all the Abrahamic faiths have always believed that God is an active agent independent of their opinions about "Him." Their style of life and social organization, their ideals and practices, have all developed around this truth claim. It is not clear that they can survive if they shift to an understanding of "God" as simply an aspect of the symbol system and liturgical life of their particular culture.

Does this need for beliefs mean that the healthy survival of each tradition depends on its continuing to make exclusivist truth claims that reject the truth claims of the others? If so, it might be better if the religious traditions would simply fade away. A world like ours cannot afford mutually rejecting communities of believers. But there is an alternative. Each tradition has the resources within it to rethink the meaning and value of other traditions without surrendering its own most precious affirmations. This rethinking, however, requires hard work, not casual generalizations.

Because the most disastrous feature of exclusivistic Christian teaching has been its ancient and continuing polemic against Judaism, the greatest amount of theological rethinking has been in regard to Judaism. Historically, Christians have often taught that the new covenant in Jesus Christ *superseded* the old covenant with the Jews. But this is not the only possible interpretation of the new covenant. It can also be understood as *supplementing* the old one. In that case, Christians can affirm that it is through this new covenant that they, as Gentiles, are brought into saving relation with God without supposing that the old covenant with the Jews was in any way abrogated. The two covenants are complementary rather than contradictory.

Trinitarian thought, also, need not involve truth claims that contradict the faithful Jewish and Muslim affirmations of God's unity. That the divinity known in Jesus Christ and in the ongoing life of the church and the world is the same God who is creator of all things does not deny the unity affirmed by Jews and Muslims. It is even possible to find analogies to this kind of Trinitarianism in their teachings. Only if Trinitarianism entails that there are three metaphysical beings within the divine realm does it contradict the divine unity, and many Christians do not understand this to be orthodox teaching.

Work of this kind takes advantage of the postmodern view that beliefs are closely related to the lives of the communities that hold them. It understands that Christology grows out of the community that has found its relation to God through Jesus Christ. Many of its affirmations, therefore, would not be appropriate for Jews or Muslims. But Jews and Muslims need not deny that these beliefs are genuinely true for Christians. Christians may correctly affirm Jesus to be Lord and Savior without implying that the failure of Jews to relate to him in this way invalidates their relation to God through the Abrahamic and Mosaic covenants. Jews can even affirm the reality of the resurrection of Jesus without ceasing to be Jews.[1]

Consider also the question as to whether Mohammed is The Prophet. This claim is central to Islam, and it places Mohammed at the center of history for Muslims. Must Christians deny it because of their belief in the centrality of Jesus?

No. The fact that Jesus constitutes the center of history for Christians does not preclude the fact that Mohammed constitutes the center for Muslims. That Jesus is the center of history is a confessional statement for Christians, not a claim that objectively speaking this is the only possible way of reading and being informed by history. Christians and Muslims may discuss with each other the respective advantage of their different readings of history. In the process there may be conflicts of truth claims, but that is not inevitable.

Muslims assign a high place in their history to Jesus. Some of the statements in the Koran are highly problematic for Christians, but basic Christian claims about Jesus are not denied. In the past, Christians have not reciprocated by providing Mohammed with a theologically important role in their understanding of history. This has limited the possibility of complementarity between the two traditions.

Hans Küng has done more than any other Christian theologian to remedy this weakness.[2] He sees no reason that Christians should deny to Mohammed the title of "The Prophet." No doubt there are particular Muslim teachings about the dictation of the Koran by God through

Mohammed that Christians cannot accept. But that Mohammed brought God's message, continuous with that of the Bible, to millions and even billions of people is historical fact. As we emphasize that it is indeed a biblical vision that pervades Islam, there is no reason not to celebrate this accomplishment and to honor the one through whom it occurred.

Relativizing doctrines in this way, that is, by understanding them as relational doctrines, does not, like the dominant postmodern way, deny their truth claims. It asserts that Jesus truly is the Lord and Savior of Christians and potentially of others as well. Lord and Savior are relational terms and apply only as the relation does or can occur. But they do not depend entirely on the contemporary Christian for their validity. They depend also on who Jesus was, what he did, the community around him, how it responded to his death, and what resulted historically from all of that.

How these past events, objective to us, are now understood affects the meaning of the affirmations of Jesus' Lordship and Saviorhood for Christians today. Their validity depends on objective facts about Jesus and his relation to us. There are truth claims involved. The outcome of the continuing debates about the historical Jesus is relevant to the contemporary faith of Christians. Of course, the positions taken by the scholars are influenced by their own social locations and religious values, but their positions are also influenced by more objective considerations. Their truth claims about history must be taken seriously. Learning about the past is not mere projection on the past.

Whereas in the eighteenth century, skepticism was directed chiefly to those beliefs that divided the Abrahamic faiths from one another, today it is more likely to be directed also to what unites them—their affirmation of God. It is argued that great religious communities, especially Buddhist communities, have no need for that affirmation. Clearly, then, it is not warranted by the general nature of religious experience. If it is not affirmed on the basis of a supernatural revelation—and thus placed beyond open discussion—it must be argued for in the courts of reason. Although the debate continues, the preponderance of opinion is that the philosophical arguments for theism are unconvincing. Hence many believe that it would be better for religious communities to reorder their thinking without this questionable teaching.

This argument is plausible. Religious experience globally does not demonstrate any necessary connection to the God of Abraham. If religious experience is held, nevertheless, to be a reason for belief, then it must be a particular type of religious experience. The clearly theistic type occurs in communities where belief in God is prevalent. It can hardly be doubted that this belief informs the experience. Hence, this fact seems to weaken any evidential value of the experience with regard to the objective truth of the belief.

The problem for the Abrahamic faiths is severe, especially for those branches of these faiths that are most open to intellectual and cultural developments. To abandon realistic belief in God is to break radically with tradition, to lose the deepest principle of motivation, to give up the religious basis for self-understanding, to surrender the grounds of hope. Although these are drastic changes, there are thousands of Christians who have personally passed through this crisis and remained faithful participants in the life of the church. A few congregations have organized around such changes. They appeal to those seekers who want to be part of a religious community but are turned off by traditional affirmations.

All of this is to be respected. But most of those who lose faith in God leave the church altogether. If this is the only option for open-minded people, then the future is likely to consist of a conservative, exclusivistic, closed-minded Christianity, on the one side, and unbelievers on the other. Nontheistic Christianity is unlikely to serve as a third force. There is more promise in the continuing growth of Buddhism among those former Christians who are no longer believers in God.

III. Buddhism

The problem raised for Buddhism by the postmodern critique of truth claims is far less obvious. Indeed, many Buddhists see no problem at all. They view postmodern developments as supportive of the ancient Buddhist critique of conceptual thought.

Whereas Christianity understands itself as an historical movement that orders life in response to beliefs about God and Jesus Christ, Buddhism can understand itself as a practice. In many forms of Buddhism, this practice is meditation, although a whole way of life can be associated with that meditation. Part of the meditative practice entails the surrendering of attachment to beliefs and concepts.

Underlying the whole approach, nevertheless, are beliefs that involve truth claims. Some of them are negations, and these get support from most forms of postmodern thought. For example, if there are in fact unchanging substances underlying all things, then Buddhists are wrong. Buddhists may give up attachment to any particular metaphysical view, but this fact does not mean that Buddhist practice is entirely neutral among metaphysical systems.

There are other respects in which the dominant forms of postmodern thought are quite different from Buddhism. It seems, at least superficially, that if they are right, then Buddhist practice is misguided. The most important difference lies in the relation of language and experience.

Typical postmodern thinking stresses the primacy of language. If experience is discussed, it is asserted that it is not only informed, but even formed, by language. There is no such thing as a nonlinguistic experience.

Buddhist practice, on the other hand, seeks just such an experience. Language and conceptuality do indeed inform ordinary experience. But this fact is viewed as reason to see ordinary experience as distorted. The task of meditation, at least in some Buddhist traditions, is to get past this distortion and to realize what is as it really is, not as it is presented to us through language.

Some Buddhists might well reply that it is not necessary to formulate truth claims about pure experience. One may, probably must, let all such things go. Nevertheless, the practice does not make sense unless something of this sort—something like pure experience—can be at least approximated.

Some postmodernists might assert that although no experience can be freed entirely from the effects of language, these effects can be reduced. In that case, the issue would be only whether Buddhists have exaggerated the degree of success that some have achieved. Such a qualification, however, would run counter to the general tone of deconstructive postmodernism. For this school, the effort to attain relative freedom from language and to arrive at a culture-neutral experience is fundamentally misdirected.

Buddhism can hardly be separated from some further beliefs. The practice would make little sense if the experience attained through it were not regarded as valuable. Of course, those who do not wish to make objective claims about value could say merely that some people find it attractive. The Buddhist tradition has, however, claimed much more. If Buddhists in general were persuaded that enlightenment is only one of many possible conditions prized by persons of diverse temperaments and cultures, this conclusion would be a break from the tradition hardly less than the Christian abandonment of belief in God.

At one level, it is obvious that not everyone pursues enlightenment. In that sense, there is strong evidence in favor of the relativizing of this goal. To be a Buddhist, however, is to recognize that, whether one pursues it or not, enlightenment is the highest goal. On what grounds can this truth claim be asserted?

It is asserted chiefly on the grounds that what is experienced in enlightenment is reality as it is. That is, enlightenment is the attainment of truth. Apart from it, everyone lives in some measure of delusion. Most people may settle for this, but Buddhists do not suppose delusion to be of equal value with truth.

The attainment of truth could be regarded as one goal among others. But for Buddhists, as for most religious believers, it involves and contains the other values. The attainment of truth, and only that, brings true happiness. Buddhists understand happiness as serenity, a state of being in which no outward event can trouble one. One is free from guilt and from anxiety. One lives fully in each moment.

The effort to achieve this perfect happiness might be viewed as selfish, and this issue has been debated within Buddhism. But the state of happiness is also a state of perfect compassion for others. Compassion is a complete empathy with the other and results in acting for the other. In this way enlightenment is the goal that encompasses all those goals that can lay any claim on ultimacy.

If there is no nonlinguistic experience, if no experience puts one into relation with reality as it truly is, if the attainment of wisdom does not bring serenity and compassion, then Buddhist teaching is mistaken and the huge investment made in Buddhist practice makes little sense. Truth claims, accordingly, play a role for Buddhists not unlike the role they play for Christians. The rejection of all truth claims would be devastating for both.

Buddhists can argue, of course, that their truth claims are vindicated by actual experience. One is not required to accept them on faith or to try to demonstrate them by rational argument. In a sense this is true, but it is also an exaggeration. The full experience of enlightenment is rare. Most Buddhists do not suppose that they know any fully enlightened person; certainly they do not claim to hold to this ideal through personal experience, and they have no expectation of doing so. Large branches of Buddhism have arisen out of the conviction that the attainment of enlightenment in this world is no longer even possible. Their hope lies in their faith in the attainment and vow for them of a figure of bygone ages, Dharmakara, who became Amida Buddha.

In terms of modern historiography, however, Dharmakara must be judged mythical.

If Buddhists grant that experiential evidence for their claims is modest and disputable, then their appeal, quite properly, is to the approximation of enlightenment to which meditation more commonly leads. If meditation brings a measure of freedom from the distorting effects of ordinary conceptuality, if it brings a measure of serenity, if it makes people more compassionate, then it provides evidence that, as one moves further along these lines, true enlightenment is possible and remains the full ideal. Belief in the truth claim, however, still goes beyond what actual experience warrants.

The truth claim about the supreme value of enlightenment is codependent with other truth claims about the nature of reality. That means that Buddhist truth claims include ontological or metaphysical assertions. Buddhists emphasize that all verbal formulations about the nature of reality are surrendered on the way to enlightenment, but that does not mean that there is no correspondence between these formulations and the reality finally realized. It may be asserted that these beliefs belong only to the sphere of *upaya* or "skillful means," but usually that doctrine itself depends on a contrast between the way things really are and the way they are ordinarily experienced. The ontological element, although more equivocal than in Western traditions, cannot be avoided.

What, then, is the Buddhist view of ultimate reality? It is formulated in many ways. One widespread name is "Buddha-nature," which is understood to be the true nature of all things. This is not, however, simply a statement that whatever that nature turns out to be, this label will be attached. On the contrary, there is a rich discussion of Buddha-nature.

The Buddha-nature is understood as *pratitya samutpada* or "dependent origination." To affirm this doctrine is to deny any kind of substance. A substance has its being in itself, independently of other things. It acts and is acted on without being affected in its interior state. It underlies the flux of things rather than participating in it.

Substance thinking was important for some schools of Hinduism. *Atman* or self was understood to be a substance. According to this Hindu vision, the true self is the subject of action and is acted on, but it is unchanged in the process. Change belongs to the level of the phenomena, the content of experience, not to the entity that experiences. One's true self is found beneath the flow of experience.

Buddhist thinkers consistently rejected this notion of an underlying substantial self, teaching instead the doctrine of *Anatman* or "no self."

Buddha-nature is nonsubstantial. This means that I do not exist and then act. I come into being only in the acting. I do not exist before being affected by others. I come into being only as they affect me. Thus I originate in dependence on them. What I am at any moment is a reflection of what others are. It is a mistake to try to discover my true self in separation from the self that emerges out of the others in dependent origination. Once I have abandoned the idea of a substantial self, I can affirm the true self as what becomes moment by moment through dependent origination. The same is true of all other entities.

This view of the way reality really is, it is recognized, runs counter to the way it is depicted in ordinary language and conceptuality. For this reason, freeing our experience from the ordering effects of language is extremely important. Mere belief that this is an accurate account of Buddha-nature by no means ensures that one actually experiences things in this way. The *realization* of Buddha-nature requires radical retraining of the mind. This is what meditation is about.

The point here is only to note the importance of the belief that reality is different in this way from the ordinary ways of experiencing it and thinking about it. This belief supports the conviction that enlightenment is the supreme goal and that its effects are as claimed.

IV. Buddhism and Hinduism

History shows that it is not enough to see beliefs as simply arising from practice. Beliefs of this sort shape practice, and both sets of beliefs claim vindication through practice. Much Hindu practice, because of Hindu beliefs, aims to shut out the phenomenal world in order to realize the true self. Much Buddhist practice, because of Buddhist beliefs, opens itself to that world without the barrier of language or conceptuality.

Furthermore, there is good evidence that both forms of practice are successful. An experiment involving Hindu yogis and Zen meditators was conducted at St. Sophia University in Tokyo some years ago. The subjects were hooked up with equipment that measured their brain waves. There was also a control group of people who did not have a particular meditative technique.

After the subjects had time to enter their meditative state, a raucous buzzer was sounded, and this was repeated at irregular intervals thereafter. The results with the control group were as expected. They responded quite strongly at first, then decreasingly as they became accustomed to the interruption. The yogis did not respond at all. The Zen meditators reacted moderately, repeating the same response each time.

What is striking in these results is that the meditation is shown to accomplish what it sets out to do. The Hindu cuts off relation to the external and attains a consciousness that is free from it. The Buddhist is open to what is, as it is, and responds to what happens, as it happens. There is no added reaction due to irritation or to the violation of expectations.

This illustrates again the importance of beliefs about the way reality is. If a Buddhist were persuaded that the self is substantial and can only be realized through disconnecting from the phenomenal world, this belief would affect the nature of meditational practice. As long as one believes that Buddha-nature is dependent origination, the practice that leads to the experiential realization of this truth will be favored.

The two practices as such do not contradict each other. Both occur, and both are effective. Reality must be such as to allow for both. But the theories as usually expounded were understood, at least by Buddhists, to be antithetical. *Anatman* contradicts *Atman*. We are back to a situation in which the skeptic is led to think that both cannot be true. In this view, if there is equal evidence for both, then neither is to be believed.

We have here a classic case of apparent contradiction between religious truth claims, both of which are equally supported by experience. Is there any escape from this conclusion? Can they both be true, or must the notion of truth and falsity simply be dismissed, as by so many postmodernists, as irrelevant?

The task would be to develop an understanding of reality that accounts for the fact that both Hindu and Buddhist meditation achieve what they seek. This account could not include the contrasting doctrines in just the form in which they have been presented. The *Anatman* doctrine was formulated as a rejection of *Atman*. The doctrine of *Atman* that was there rejected cannot be affirmed without declaring the Buddhist wrong.

Still a doctrine of *Atman* that fits the Yogic evidence might be formulated in such as way as not to contradict the doctrine of dependent origination. The substantialist metaphysics is far less central to Hindu thought and experience than is the nonsubstantialist teaching to Buddhism. Many Hindus in fact deny that they think of the self as a substance.

A reformulated Hindu account of yogic experience is beyond the scope of this book, but it is present already in Hindu literature. A fascinating example can be found in the writings of Sri Aurobindo, who had a series of quite varied mystical experiences, one of which he described as Buddhist.[3] His account is largely free from substantialist assumptions. Although it leads to a vision of reality that includes much that is typically absent from Buddhist thinking, it is not flatly contradictory. Perhaps the totality of things is such that both Buddha-nature and much of what Aurobindo finds in the cosmos are there to be found.

In this case, one main reason for skepticism is removed. Perhaps diverse meditational disciplines lead to the realization of diverse features of an extremely complex reality. One is properly skeptical of the claim that the features highlighted in one tradition are the only important features. But one need not be skeptical of truth claims about them that leave room for other truth claims about other features of the totality. There is no reason to reduce all such claims to the horizon of particular languages.

V. Buddha-Nature and God as Complementary

The preceding sections have argued that truth claims are important to both the Abrahamic faiths and to Buddhism, but that these claims need not be formulated in exclusivist ways. Differences that have been presented as oppositions can be reformulated as complementary. That is, both claims may be true in their central affirmations, and they may be shown to cohere in a larger framework. This type of postmodern approach is possible, however, only on the basis of a new realism.

Although the deconstructive form of postmodernism removes the contradictions among religious traditions, it does so by defining them in terms of incommensurable symbolic systems. One can say nothing about a common world to which they belong. The quest for an overview that would allow them to complement one another is regarded as a forbidden, hegemonic move. The avoidance of contradiction is achieved by the translation of each tradition's truth claims into elements within its own private symbol system. It is stipulated that these elements cannot refer to anything outside the system; they refer only to one another.

The preceding sections pursued another avenue. They showed that many very different truth claims, when carefully formulated, do not contradict one another. Often there is sufficient evidence to lend them credence when the supposed counterevidence for other truth claims is seen as complementary.

The value of this approach can be illustrated from the field of medicine. In the modern West, allopathic medicine, with its emphases on chemistry and physiology, triumphed. A well-worked-out theory of the body underlay this medicine and was reinforced by its brilliant success. One can hardly doubt that what allopathic medicine teaches about the nature of the human body is true.

Meanwhile, however, Chinese medicine had developed around a quite different theory of the nature of the body. Chinese science had studied a pattern of energy flows through the body and learned how to stimulate these flows. Chinese doctors had found that this stimulation could be healing. It could also anaesthetize parts of the body.

Western doctors who observed the resulting acupuncture were impressed. They could not deny the evidence of its effectiveness, even though it was not based on the Western understanding of the body. To their great credit, they led the American Medical Association to approve the practice of acupuncture.

It seems that the human body is far more complex than Western science had recognized. There are important patterns of activity within it that differ from those the West had studied. This did not mean that what the West had learned about the body was erroneous. As long as neither science claims exhaustiveness for the patterns it has discerned, there is no contradiction between them. They can be regarded as complementary.

If one believes that the totality of reality is far more complex than can yet be thought or even imagined, then one will seek to view the insights of different communities and traditions as hypotheses about some feature of the way things are that should be seriously considered and tested. Where the insights in question seem credible in themselves, even if they do not fit well with what one has previously thought, one will try to expand one's understanding of the totality so as to include the new insight.

Such expansion requires adjustments elsewhere as well. Sometimes these adjustments are illuminating in themselves and add confidence with respect to the new insight. The whole of one's understanding and every part thereof should remain open for further expansion, correction, questioning, and testing. The process is open-ended.

It is in this spirit that we approach the question of Buddha-nature and God. Historically, most Buddhists have drawn from their understanding of Buddha-nature the conclusion that there is no God, at least, in the traditional Christian sense. This denial was originally directed against the Hindu doctrine of Brahman, understood as the divine substance underlying all things. It was directed also against worship of the many gods of the Hindu pantheon. In this role, it was a judgment not so much of nonexistence as of unimportance. These gods cannot help move one to enlightenment, and, indeed, attachment to them blocks the road.

As Buddhists confronted the God of the Abrahamic traditions, they found similar problems. This God was typically conceived as substantial and so contradicted what was believed about Buddha-nature. This God was also depicted as a being to whom people were called to cling. In Buddhist perspective, even if this being existed, one should ignore it so as to move forward to enlightenment.

There seems to be here a direct contradiction. The Abrahamic faiths affirm both the reality and the supreme importance of God. Buddhism has typically denied both.

The question is, then, whether the truth claims of the two communities can be turned from contradiction into complementarity. This goal, obviously, could be attained only by changing the usual formulations of the Abrahamic doctrine of God, because these formulations do contradict the Buddhist understanding of Buddha-nature. To simplify this discussion, further comments will be limited to Christian formulations.

The alternative would be to argue that it is the Buddhist doctrine that must be changed, but that would be a mistake. To adopt a substantialist view of Buddha-nature would be the end of Buddhism. On the other hand, as with the Hindu case, the role of substance thinking in Christianity is far from necessary for the preservation of faith. It is far less present in the Bible than in the Hellenized Christian tradition. Many theologians, quite apart from concern with Buddhism, have worked to free Christian thought from its influence.

Similarly, although the note of clinging to God has been prominent in Christian literature, it is not the only way in which the believer's relation to God is depicted. Faith or trust is primary. The assurance that is involved in such faith allows the believer to attend to other matters, not to be preoccupied with the relation to God. Faith is at least as much a letting go as a holding fast. In encounter with Buddhism, the value of the emphasis on letting go can be more clearly learned.

Most Christian thinkers who have sought to bring reconciliation between Christianity and Buddhism have not only desubstantialized God, but also largely identified God with Buddha-nature. This move makes sense for those who have previously identified God with Being Itself. Being Itself seems to be answering the same question for the West that Buddha-nature answers for Buddhists. Just as for Buddhists, everything that is is an instance of Buddha-nature, for Westerners, everything that is may be seen as an instance of Being. We may ask what Being, of which each being is an instance, is in itself.

The problem has been that Being Itself, at least in the influential formulation of Paul Tillich, has the taint of substance. Being Itself is sometimes described as the "ground of being." It seems to underlie the beings and express itself in them.

Recognizing this, some Christians have worked to remove that taint. When they do so, the similarity with Buddha-nature becomes apparent. Starting with such identity, it is possible to see Buddhism and the Abrahamic faiths as complementary expressions of the human apprehension of, and relation to, one and the same feature of the totality, now called either Buddha-nature or God.

Some Christians, especially those in the tradition of apophatic mysticism, find this solution satisfactory. They have long since left behind as primitive the more personal characteristics, so prominent in the Abrahamic God. They do not find the absence of these characteristics in Buddha-nature troubling.

For many Christians, however, especially those bound more closely to biblical categories, this reinterpretation of God undercuts their deepest convictions. The problem is not so much the desubstantialization of Being involved, but the initial identification of God with Being Itself.

Tillich himself made explicit the problematic character of the identification he espoused. He spoke of Being Itself as the God *beyond* the God of the Bible, clearly recognizing that there is a marked difference between the biblical understanding of God and the notion of Being Itself.[4] Being Itself is not *a* being, not even the Supreme Being. It is, instead, the being of every being. It does not act in the way in which a being such as a person acts. It cannot be acted upon. Only with great difficulty can it be connected with moral concerns. It supports mystical tendencies in Christianity rather than historical ones. In short, Being Itself is *very* different from the God of the Bible and of most Christian piety. Accordingly, it cannot play the same religious roles.

Tillich, thinking that we must choose between the God of the Bible and Being Itself, opted for the latter. By contrast, Heidegger, his mentor in thinking about being, insisted that Being-Itself is *not* God. Although Heidegger strongly opposed the classical doctrine of God as *causa sui* and rejected any idea that God is the source of the being of things, he emphasized that he was not an atheist. He considered it important that his analysis of being and beings leaves open the question of God for appropriate inquiry. He lists God as one of the beings that may be, and in his conversation with theologians emphasizes that the door is open for theological reflection about God. He supported Heinrich Ott in his effort to think about God in a compatible way.[5]

The drive to find commonality in that with which all religious traditions deal is modern. Postmodernists allow difference to stand. This postmodern sensitivity to difference suggests that it is worthwhile to pursue an alternative possibility. Perhaps, as the theory of Heidegger and Ott implies, we can affirm the reality both of Buddha-nature and of God, while recognizing that they do not name the same feature of reality. In this task, the philosophy of Whitehead is particularly helpful.

The reader may have noticed that the exposition of dependent origination was similar to Whitehead's account of how in each event the many become one. As in Nagarjuna and many other Buddhists, whatever is is an instance of dependent origination, so in Whitehead every actual entity is an instance of the many becoming one. The language is different, but the idea is remarkably similar.

There are, of course, differences. For Whitehead all the actual entities that participate in the constitution of the new entity are in its past. For some Buddhists this is not the case. But this is a discussable difference that does not affect what is of most importance to Buddhists. Some Buddhists find Whitehead's account helpful in giving a more rigorous explanation of their understanding. It is clear that what Buddhists mean by Buddha-nature plays a central role in Whitehead's philosophy under the name of creativity. Indeed, creativity belongs to the category of the ultimate. Some important conclusions that Whitehead draws from his analysis are repetitions of those drawn long ago by Buddhists.

Whitehead's overall vision, nevertheless, is not Buddhist. It contains emphases that move in a distinctively Christian direction. For Buddhists, what is most important is to realize that we are instances of Buddha-nature. For Whitehead, the past entities that compose our experience in each moment differ, and attention to those specific entities is crucial for the understanding of that momentary experience. For most Buddhists, the distinction between past and future is minimized. For Whitehead, it is accented. For most Buddhists, accordingly, historical understanding is secondary. For Whitehead, it is central. Buddhists do not thematize human freedom. Whitehead does. Ethical issues do not pervade Buddhist meditation. For Whitehead they are part of the structure of human existence.

These contrasts suggest that Whitehead finds an element in the coming together of the many to form the new one that is not discussed in Buddhist literature. It is a force that makes for health and growth. It provides alternatives to the sheer determination by the past. It also urges the adoption of that alternative that provides the greatest immediate satisfaction combined with the greatest contribution to the relevant future. It pushes for the expansion of the recognition of relevance. Its presence makes both possible and necessary a decision, a final self-determination as to just how and what that occasion of experience will become.

Whitehead describes this element as an aim that participates in constituting every occasion. Accordingly, there is a purposive element pervading the world. What happens is not wholly determined by the causal efficacy of the past. It is also shaped by present purpose.

As it finally expresses itself in the determinative decision of the new entity, the aim has been modified. But it is present in the occasion from the beginning. As one of the many that become one, it is called the "initial aim." Apart from its presence, the future would be simply the outgrowth of the past, moral judgments would be illusory, and the course of events would be without meaning.

It is important to understand that this purposive element in all things is directed not to some one grand attainment of the whole, but to the outcome of that one momentary occasion—both for what it can be in itself and for its effects in the relevant future. The aim in one occasion can compete with that in others. The aim of the predator to get food conflicts with that of the prey to escape. Yet there is some overarching coordination of aims so that, where conditions allow, life appears and takes more diverse and complex forms. The fact that conditions in this universe do allow for this development is suggestive of a more general aim operative in things.

This purposive element pervasively present in the world is clearly of great significance for Christians. It is not denied in Buddhist teaching, but neither is it highlighted. In the Abrahamic traditions, it is associated with God. Whitehead also makes this connection.

That it need not be denied by Buddhism in order to affirm the dependent origination of all things is important. It is similarly important that it is asserted and emphasized by Whitehead in the context of his doctrine of the many becoming one. Clearly there is no contradiction between the two doctrines. In Whitehead's own work they play complementary roles. "The many become one and are increased by one."[6]

This increase is a function of the decision that brings new actuality to the many. This decision occurs because one of the many in every instance is the God who calls each occasion to be something more than the sheer outcome of its past and draws it toward realizing what value it can.

Whitehead, as a child of Christianity, assumed that religious meaning is associated with temporal passage, history, morality, freedom, responsibility, ordered novelty, novel order, and the future. This assumption led him to use the religious word "God" in association with that element in things that introduces all that. It evidently did not occur to him that there was religious meaning also in the realization that in every moment each thing is nothing other than the many becoming one. But clearly there has been, and is, great religious meaning in that realization.

The postmodernist can, then, allow the deep difference between Buddhism and Christianity to stand without rejecting the basic truth claims of either. God and Buddha-nature are by no means identical. Yet they are both features of what is. Both have the utmost existential importance, but attending to one leads to a very different sense of reality and of one's place in it than attending to the other. These differences are not contradictions, although they can easily lead to contradictions when not carefully formulated.

Although God is emphasized chiefly by the Abrahamic faiths and Buddha-nature chiefly by Buddhists, neither tradition is wholly lacking the complementary element. As noted previously, mystics in the Abrahamic traditions have often moved in the direction of seeking their own deepest nature. This move has sometimes been related to the idea of Being Itself; and the realization of the identity of oneself with Being Itself, as in Meister Eckhart, has not necessarily involved substantialist categories.

On the other side, some Buddhists, especially in the Pure Land tradition, have thought of a power in things that works for their salvation. Also, followers of the Lotus Sutra, such as Nichiren Buddhists in Japan, affirm the reality of something very much like the God here discussed. Thus, both traditions have had some experience with the complementarity, as well as the tensions, involved.

More recently, a good many individuals have undertaken to embody both traditions within themselves. The most famous example is Thomas Merton who, without ceasing to be a Christian, undertook to become "as good a Buddhist" as he could.[7] But there are hundreds, perhaps thousands, of others. It is true that most of them have brought God and Buddha-nature closer together than has this proposal, but they have still deeply appreciated the differences between the two ways of being. The experience of complementarity is playing a growing and promising role in the emerging postmodern religious world.

VI. God's Transcendence

In the previous section, "God" was associated with the "aim" in all things apart from which they would not be at all. More exactly, the initial phase of this aim is the prehension of God in each occasion. The presence of a purposive element in human life is subject to ready verification, and this analysis of its relation to freedom and morality is open to phenomenological testing. It is as well grounded as the Buddha-nature and, at least to Westerners, somewhat more obvious.

For many people in the Abrahamic tradition, however, this account of God in purely immanent terms implies that the "God" described is not the God of Abraham. The meaning of the word "God" in the Abrahamic traditions may not be bound to substance metaphysics, but it is bound to transcendence. If this transcendence is abandoned in order to establish complementarity with Buddhism, that price is too high. On the other hand, the introduction of transcendence may destroy the complementarity for which the preceding section argued.

The likelihood that any doctrine will satisfy all is remote. That cannot be the goal. But the concern for divine transcendence is inherent in almost all forms of Christian faith. Indeed, it is not absent in Whitehead. The question whether honoring this concern destroys the complementarity established at the level of immanence is an important one.

The word "transcendence" means many things. For some it means that God's nature and being are of a different metaphysical order than that of creatures. To assert transcendence in that sense would be to contradict central Buddhist thinking directly. Furthermore, binding Christian doctrine to particular metaphysical judgments of this sort is not generally regarded as necessary or even desirable. Hence, that demand need not be met.

In the present context, the idea of transcendence that is required to establish connection to biblical thinking is, at a minimum, that God is not simply an aspect of creatures. God must also be an actuality whose being is by no means exhausted in its presence in creatures. Further, this actuality must be radically different from any other, in that it has a necessary role in all things, its present and continuing existence is independent of all other things, and awareness of it uniquely inspires awe and adoration. Our two questions are: (1) can transcendence in this sense be affirmed coherently with the immanentist account above and, if so (2) must it destroy the potential complementarity with Buddhism?

With regard to the first question, Whitehead himself moved far in the direction indicated. This move resulted, in part, from the coherent development of his system of thought, in part, from his desire to do justice to religious experience, including his own spiritual sensibility. I will explain.

Whitehead believed that nothing could participate as part of the many becoming one that did not first have its own actuality. For example, the previous occasion of one's experience could not affect the present one if it had not first occurred in its own right. All the ingredients of the present occasion are aspects of other actual entities. The initial phase of the aim can be no exception. If it plays a divine role, then we can call the actual entity that is present in the new occasion in this way "God." That God is actual is a systematic requisite for God to function as described previously.

For anything to be actual is for it to be something for itself. It must have a subjective aspect. Accordingly, God must be conceived as a subject. Because God is present directly in every entity whatsoever, God is cosmic in scope and everlasting through time. In these respects, God is profoundly different from the creatures. That this God evokes awe and devotion is natural.

There is another side of God that is less directly attested. Positing it fits and completes Whitehead's systematic vision. It expresses also his own religious concerns. Actually, this completion ties the doctrine of God back into the Buddhist doctrine of dependent origination.

Every actual entity is di-polar. It has both physical and mental aspects. The physical aspect is its inclusion of other actual entities. Its mental aspect is its inclusion of possibilities. The role of God discussed thus far is that of the mental pole. But God should not be conceived as a metaphysical exception. God also has a physical pole, constituted by the reception of the creatures into the divine life. God is also an instance of the many becoming one. All creation becomes one in God.

The second question asked above was whether in the process of affirming transcendence the complementarity achieved with Buddhist thought is destroyed. Is it possible in principle for a Buddhist to acknowledge that God, understood in this way, can be a part of what is? This is different from asking Buddhists to believe in God's reality. There may be good Buddhist reasons for indifference and skepticism, just as many Christians will have no religious interest in dependent origination. The issue is whether essential Buddhist insights are violated by these theistic affirmations.

If God's nature were asserted to be other than Buddha-nature, such a contradiction would occur. In this vision, however, God, too, is an instance, the one perfect instance, of the many becoming one. But can one instance of the many becoming one play a role in the whole of things radically different from any other? Although that idea is offensive to some Buddhists, it is not entirely absent in the Buddhist tradition. To Gautama Buddha himself is attributed much that renders him profoundly distinctive. In the cosmic roles sometimes assigned him, he differs from God chiefly in that his divine role begins in time with his enlightenment.

A closer approximation to the view of God suggested here is found in Pure Land Buddhism. Central to this form of Buddhism is faith in the Primal Vow by which all sentient creatures can be saved. Today the stories of the origin of the Primal Vow in the legendary past are often demythologized. When this happens, the vow is understood to characterize reality at all times. It is embodied in Amida who can be equated with a cosmic and everlasting form of the Buddha-body.

A still clearer teaching about what Christians can call God is to be found in the Lotus Sutra, one of the most influential of Buddhist scriptures. Here, in addition to the many Buddhas inhabiting the many worlds, there is one universal and everlasting Buddha. This Buddha is represented through or manifested in all the more particular Buddhas, such as Sakyamuni. Thus Sakyamuni is, at the deepest level, this universal Buddha.

This universal Buddha is far removed from the impassibility and the omnipotence of the God of classical Christian theism. Buddha is above all compassionate, seeking the salvation of all, and often frustrated by human resistance. But the Sutra's analogy of the universal Buddha with a loving father certainly shows its resonance with the God of the Bible. It is fully compatible with the ideas proposed from the Christian side previously stated.[8]

The details are not important here. The argument is simply that an everlasting cosmic embodiment of Buddha-nature is not excluded by fundamental Buddhist insights. Such a being has the transcendence required for Christian faith. For Christians to name such a cosmic embodiment "God" does not destroy the complementarity of God and Buddha-nature.

Chapter Three

Culture and Education

I. Introduction

Chapter Two discussed religious diversity and how it could be respected without rejecting the claims of the different traditions. This issue is important for those who are serious about their convictions. If, in this postmodern age, adherents of the several religious traditions understand themselves and one another in the light of this possibility, the new vision will help to ease the conflicts that are now often described in terms of religious differences.

Nevertheless, although a postmodern vision of religious pluralism will help, it will certainly not solve the problems. What are called religious conflicts today are usually more accurately described as ethnic or cultural. Theological differences between Catholics and Protestants play a minor role in the struggles in Northern Ireland. The struggle in Palestine/Israel is not over differences in belief and practice of Muslims and Jews, although the Jews' belief that God gave them the land of Canaan does play a significant role.

The line between religion and culture is often difficult to draw. Christians complain that Christmas has been so commercialized and secularized that it is no longer a religious festival but a cultural one. Certainly, many who have their children hang their stockings for Santa Claus have disconnected this practice from any religious meaning. But Jews experience Christmas even in its more secularized expressions as still a Christian festival. For many of them, it is important that their gift-giving take place at a different time.

As a nation we long ago separated church from state, and for many this has meant that religious beliefs should play no direct role in politics. But it is impossible to separate politics from culture, and cultures are religiously saturated. Belief in God, for example, is part of the dominant culture; so politicians invoke God regularly. Atheists are very much aware that belief in God, by informing the culture, continues to play a large role in the national life.

We try to deal with religious diversity by distancing public policy from specific religious convictions, but we cannot distance public policy from culture without separating it from values altogether. Cultures are the effective bearers of value for most people. A multicultural society poses particular problems for public life.

These problems come to sharpest focus in public education. Schools are intended to serve all children, and in a multicultural society that means that they serve children from many cultures. But education is historically the major means by which children are acculturated. Must this function now be abandoned by schools and left entirely in other hands? Must public schools be value-free? Is that possible?

Section II provides a general discussion of the relation of religion and culture. Section III considers the phenomenon of multiculturalism and the problems it poses for social unity. Because these problems are particularly acute for a society that promotes public education for its children, Section IV sketches the history of schooling and its present problems, and Section V considers the implications of multiculturalism for schooling. Section VI proposes an understanding of teaching that may help. Section VII then draws some conclusions from these reflections about the role of the university.

II. Religion and Culture

Because primal cultures are not compartmentalized, they have no distinct religious institutions. In them the idea of "religion" does not occur. Nevertheless, from a modern Western perspective, these cultures are pervasively religious. The reason they do not have "religions" is that they have no secular sphere. Every aspect of life is influenced by the stories that inform their cultures. These stories, which are replete with features and figures that we now call religious, provide guidance about the roles to be played in the tribe and how life is to be lived. There are special ways in which these stories are transmitted.

There are special ceremonies that organize time and the successive stages of life.

What Western scholars have recognized as "religions" came into being in the first millennium B.C.E. As society became more fragmented, individuals ceased to find adequate meaning in traditional values and communal life. Awareness of cultural diversity, no doubt, also raised questions about the adequacy of the beliefs involved in particular cultures. People wanted to know what is truly real and what that reality implies for how they should live.

In China some sought to understand nature and adapt personal life to its deepest patterns. Others focused on the social and political order, showing how true virtue is formed in human relationships. These, in turn, lead to the excellent performance of duties that serve the whole of society.

Science, philosophy, and religion share a common ancestry in the quest to order life as reality requires. In Greece the former two predominated, but we misunderstand Greek science and philosophy if we do not see that their deepest purpose was normative, and hence religious. This purpose is clear in the later stages with Stoics, Epicureans, and Neoplatonists, but it is true already with the Pythagoreans and Socrates.

In India, the religious purpose of scientific-philosophical inquiries is even clearer. Debates about the nature of physical reality and the human soul were closely related to meditational practices designed to attain spiritual liberation. To this day, Buddhists who engage in refined discussion of the nature of human and natural reality repeatedly remind their Western colleagues that the purpose is not to satisfy human curiosity but to pave the way to enlightenment.

In Israel, the preoccupation was with the religious question of what God is doing and what God requires of humanity. There was much less of what moderns recognize as science or philosophy. Instead, the primary concerns were with history and morality. These concerns focused on the people of Israel; nevertheless, they moved to a level of universality that had great appeal beyond Israel's borders.

Religion as the conscious quest for personal and communal meaning was disruptive of society. The Athenians condemned Socrates as a corrupter of youth. Several Jewish prophets were killed. Jesus died on a cross.

This quest for universal truth was deeply shaped by the cultures in which it occurred, but it transcended cultural boundaries. The quest brought with it the critique of cultures, and it changed the cultures in which it arose. It also transcended them. The communities it produced developed ideas and practices that could be found attractive in other cultures.

These religious movements claimed universal validity for the beliefs and practices they advocated. As these claims were found convincing by more and more people, the relation or religion to culture changed. Over large parts of the Earth, the new universalistic religious loyalties transformed the primal, tribal, and local patterns. They became, in Paul Tillich's language, the "substance" of new cultures. Tillich taught that religious beliefs and practices provide the basic meanings and values for a culture.[1]

China became Confucian, and Confucian influence extended far beyond China's borders. India developed innumerable religious forms, whose adherents lived together in relative peace. These forms have come, collectively, to be called Hinduism. Buddhism challenged this loose consensus and contested it in India for some years. Though it failed to displace Hinduism there, it spread through much of eastern Asia, supplementing Confucianism and living in uneasy tension with it. When the Roman world was Hellenized, it was the influence of Socrates that triumphed. Eventually this influence was trumped by that of Israel mediated through the Jesus-event. Islam transformed part of the resultant Christendom again.

All these religious traditions have teachings about the nature of reality in general, and they aspire to prescribe the way of salvation for all. They became established and transformed the cultures that accepted them. This transformation was particular to each culture. Vietnamese Buddhist culture is not identical with Tibetan Buddhist culture, and both differ from Japanese Buddhist culture. Nevertheless, they are all recognizably Buddhist.

When religious teachings have reshaped a culture, the religious tradition can still be distinguished from its cultural embodiment. Most participants in the culture are unlikely to study the religious teachings that have shaped them or to practice the full disciplines prescribed by the religion. Even those who undertake to do so are still deeply affected by aspects of the culture that have not been transformed by the religious tradition. At the same time, many serious religious believers are troubled by the gap between the true meaning of the tradition and the way in which its influence has been appropriated in the culture.

Sometimes the difference is quite dramatic. In Japan the main income of Buddhist temples comes from ceremonies for the dead held at specified intervals after their death. These ceremonies assume that the spirits of the dead live in some other sphere but have an uneasy relation to their descendants. They require appeasement. Beliefs of this kind have no source in Buddhism; in fact, they derive from an understanding of death and existence beyond death that is in conflict with standard Buddhist teaching.

This is an extreme case. In general, the relation between the universalistic teachings proclaimed in a religious tradition and the cultures it informs is much closer. For example, although few participants in any Buddhist culture claim to have reached enlightenment, the doctrine of no-self cuts against the emergence of separated individuals. Persons from Buddhist cultures are likely to be both fascinated and appalled by the individualistic assertiveness that those who have been acculturated in Christendom take for granted.

Although the religious traditions play a large role in shaping basic attitudes and values, it is through the whole complex pattern of beliefs, values, and practices that make up a culture that these are chiefly transmitted. For this reason, the universalistic and often radical religious teachings are in fact transmitted mainly in diluted and modified form. Sometimes the dilution and modification are necessary to adapt teachings oriented to individual salvation to the needs of an ongoing community. For example, primitive Christian teaching provides little practical guidance for the family and civic community so crucial to a continuing culture. The culture also typically reduces the radical demands of the religious teaching so as to allow for more relaxed enjoyment of life.

In the public world, therefore, interreligious contacts and conflicts are usually not between the fullest meanings of the several traditions along the lines discussed in Chapter Two, but between cultures. Christians quarrel rather little with the teachings of the Koran, but they are often very critical of Muslim restrictions on the activities of women. The licentiousness to which Muslims object in contemporary Christian cultures is only indirectly related to Christian theology, and much of it is deplored equally by serious Christians.

A more adequate account of the relation of religious teachings and cultural reality requires the extension of the term "religion" in less accustomed ways. In recent centuries new efforts arose to understand reality universally and to comprehend the meaning of that understanding for the way individual and collective life should be organized. These efforts arose in Christendom and testify, largely unintentionally, to their origins. Their careers have been sufficiently independent of Christendom and important in themselves to warrant separate mention. I refer to "secular humanism," and Marxism, which can be regarded as quasi-religions.

Secular humanism is the product of the Enlightenment. It honors individual human beings and emphasizes their autonomy and responsibility. It also calls for their rights to be respected. It typically understands social relations as contractual. It looks to science to tell us about the nature of reality and to technology and education to solve our problems. Its ethics are typically utilitarian. It sees nature primarily as that which is investigated. It tolerates traditional religious beliefs as long as there is no effort to impose them on others. It affirms participatory democracy as the best way to settle our disagreements and move to action.

Marxism shares with secular humanism the sense that traditional religions have outlived any usefulness they may once have had. It shares the conviction that science has now superseded philosophy and religion as the proper source of knowledge about the world. But it regards secular humanism as reflecting the point of view of persons who are satisfied with the status quo and are insensitive to the profound injustices inherent in it. It believes that participatory democracy is in fact an instrument of maintaining the economic status quo. The real problems are created by an economic system that exploits workers for the sake of enriching the bourgeoisie. The solution is to organize the workers to take over the means of production so that all may share the fruits.

Secular humanism and Marxism, like the great religious traditions before them, reflect the cultures out of which they come. But they also transcend these cultures and offer insights into universal truth that have commanded assent far beyond them. Where Marxism superseded traditional religion as the ideology of a people, it undertook consciously to transform culture, often quite ruthlessly. In the process, it took on diverse forms in different cultures. In short, it has played a role in the twentieth century much like the roles played in the past by the first wave of universalistic religions.

At present it seems that Marxism is in retreat as a quasi-religion. China remains officially Marxist, but even there Marxism evokes diminishing loyalty among thoughtful people and has diminishing influence in practice. Nevertheless, the basic Marxist analysis of the global historical situation still has convincing power, and the Marxist dream of a classless society continues to draw sensitive people, appalled by the widening gap between rich and poor. Cuba's Marxist culture remains attractive to many, despite the suffering caused by the U.S.-imposed economic embargo.

Secular humanism has never had the separate organization of either the traditional religions or Marxism. It has not displaced other reigning ideologies in the dramatic way of past religious conversions or Marxist revolutions. Postmodernists are attacking it as outdated modernism.

Nevertheless, secular humanism remains a quasi-religious ideology of great power and a major contender for leadership in a multicultural world. It has greatly changed the culture of Western Christianity, making much of it post-Christian. Its doctrine of human rights has emerged as a global consensus enshrined in the United Nations declaration. Its celebration of science and technology shapes cultures around the world. Most formal education is currently directed to its ends. When we discuss multiculturalism, we should take the legacy of the Enlightenment seriously as one of the cultures involved, perhaps the dominant one.

III. Multiculturalism

Until quite recently, it has been assumed that a society required a dominant culture. Certainly most societies had one. In countries such as Japan and Korea, for example, citizenship in the state and ethnic identity are intimately connected.

Some of these dominant cultures were quite tolerant of minorities and allowed them to maintain subcultures as long as they accepted their subordinate roles. A few states were composed of more than one cultural group, usually somewhat separated geographically. Switzerland had French-, German-, and Italian-dominated cantons. Canada was predominantly British but included the predominantly French province of Quebec. Belgium had both French and Flemish sections.

In Latin America nations are typically composed of a mixture of indigenous people and European conquerors. Fashioning a common society out of this diversity is a still incomplete task. In post-colonial Africa, nations emerged with boundaries drawn by the colonizing powers that had little relation to traditional tribal areas. This has exacerbated the problem of nation-building.

The United States is composed of immigrants from many countries living side-by-side with the surviving native population. The task was understood to be that of assimilating all into a single culture based on English as a language and Protestantism and the British Enlightenment as a system of values. Native Americans resisted this process most consistently. Most of the immigrants, in contrast, wanted their children to be assimilated in this way.

There were exceptions among the immigrants as well. Roman Catholic leaders recognized the Protestant character of the dominant culture and resisted integration into it. Today, however, although they maintain many parochial schools, their assimilation has come a long way. Blacks were long excluded from the dominant culture in the South, although they greatly influenced it. Recent efforts at assimilation throughout the country still encounter difficulties, and many blacks now prize their distinctive culture and linguistic forms.

This shift among blacks has led to a major cultural change in the past two or three decades. The culturally specific character of our public life has been named and recognized as unjust to those whose cultures are different. Instead of assuming that a nation needs a homogeneous culture, a postmodern appreciation of diversity has emerged. A chorus of voices, which had long been unheard, is now singing loudly of the richness of their cultures as well as the pain they have experienced in being devalued by the dominant culture.

American society is feeling its way toward a new kind of multiculturalism. It is seeking to avoid public actions that support one culture over others or that are offensive to the members of any of the cultures that make it up. Progress is halting, with traditional practices such as Christmas celebrations continuing to receive public support despite considerable opposition.

Despite the progress, the goal is difficult to envision. Do we want our public life to be uninfluenced by any culture? Would that mean that public life cannot support any moral or aesthetic values? Or do we consider the quasi-religion of the Enlightenment to provide the neutral culture into which all should be assimilated?

There seem to be several possibilities for a multicultural society. One is to decentralize to smaller and smaller units within which enough agreement may be possible for value-laden corporate acts to occur. A second is to leave the question of the values to be followed to the electoral process, allowing the majority to impose its values on minorities. A third is to discover what values are shared by all the major cultures that are represented and to act on those. A fourth is to work toward new formulations of values, including multiculturalism itself, that can be affirmed by members of most of the cultures involved. This effort would require each of the cultures to recognize the need to grow and change in order to adapt itself to the new multicultural situation, while leaving as much room as possible for diversity. For a constructive postmodernist, this fourth possibility seems the most promising approach.

The practical issues of multiculturalism come to focus most urgently and poignantly around education in general, and public schooling in particular. A value-neutral educational system seems to be a contradiction in terms. But what values can the system act upon? The remainder of this chapter responds to this question.

IV. Schooling

Education is a large part of what goes on in any society. Infants come into the world with neither information nor habits. They must be informed and acculturated. Every society provides for this education in a variety of ways. Primal societies include education as an integral part of the life of the community. The whole community participates in sharing its stories and rituals and teaching the practical skills needed for successful living.

Socrates taught us to think of another role of education. He argued that people have implicit knowledge that a skillful teacher can draw out. The word "educate" expresses this understanding. This is one way in which education can lead beyond acculturation to universal truth. Subsequent educators have shown that human beings can be helped to articulate their historical and empirical perceptions as well as universal ones.

As society became more complex, education was needed for specialists in various fields. Such education was typically a matter of a master craftsman sharing knowledge and skills with an apprentice, but it could include something more like classroom instruction. With increasing specialization and the need for literacy, this schooling became more important. It became a separate institution with its own professionals.

In China ideally, at least, these schools were for the brightest boys without regard to their social status. In them the classics were studied intensively as a means of character formation and learning the traditions in terms of which the graduates could serve and guide society.

The Jews were also deeply convinced of the importance of schooling. Their goal was to enable all of their males to study the Torah, so that their lives might conform to Jewish teachings. For centuries the literacy that they maintained gave them important roles in a largely illiterate Europe.

Although the reason for schools as separate institutions was the need to impart information and skills, schools continued, as part of the educational system, to play the role of acculturation. The acculturation might be into the special culture of a profession, but, intentionally or not, it was also acculturation into the larger society.

Medieval Europe created great universities whose function was to prepare students for the professions of law and medicine and above all the clergy. These, too, immersed students in the classics. But they also cultivated a lively intellectual life, encouraging students to think critically and constructively.

In the North Atlantic countries, the advent of print and the rise of Protestantism worked together to encourage the extension of schooling to a wider public. Previously, the priest was thought of as mediator between the laity and God. It had sufficed, therefore, that the priest could read and instruct the laity in what they should know. The Reformers, in contrast, introduced a view more like that of the Jews. They insisted that *all* Christians should be priests, meaning that they should be in direct relation to God. All people, or at least the male heads of households, needed to be able to read the Bible for themselves.

The Enlightenment increased emphasis on education, and schooling grew more and more important. In the United States, the early nineteenth century brought a movement for public schools for all. The ideal of universal schooling provided by the government is now entrenched in most of the world. This development constitutes the context for the present discussion.

In the century preceding World War I, the system of schooling in the United States was two-tiered. The public schools were for everyone. Their function was acculturation of a particular sort. The United States was a nation of immigrants. Most of those coming in during this period were from Europe, but chiefly from parts of Europe that had not been strongly represented in earlier immigration. They spoke different languages and brought diverse cultural traditions. The task of the school was to turn their children into effective and productive citizens of the United States. Because the United States was a democracy, its citizens needed to be able to participate in democratic processes.

This goal required their acculturation into "American" culture. This was the culture established in the colonies primarily by British settlers. The Catholic immigrants were assigned a peripheral role. "American" culture was a British Protestant culture, already influenced by the Enlightenment and by the colonial and revolutionary experience.

Acculturation included the learning of skills and the communication of information. The question was: What skills and what information? The most important skill was the mastery of the English language. The most important information was the history of the United States and the European sources of its culture. Acculturation also included values and behavior patterns that could be modeled and required within the school.

Although most youth ended their formal schooling with the completion of the public school program (or less), some went on to higher education. The dominant form of higher education at that time was the liberal arts college. Whereas the purpose of the public schools was to produce good American citizens, the purpose of the colleges was to produce leaders for American society. Such leadership required a deeper and more critical understanding of the Western tradition and its values. It required the ability and motivation to continue a process of self-education throughout life.

Leadership also required an inner cultivation. Leaders needed to internalize the values of Western civilization, specifically in their Protestant form, and to act in terms of them. They should be able to give direction to society's response to ever-new problems in terms of these values. Their task was not merely to internalize and transmit the culture of the past but also to participate in its further development.

Elements of this understanding of both public schools and higher education continue to the present time. But they are no longer dominant. Today the dominant purpose of schooling is understood to be economic rather than social and political. In terms of the values of contemporary American society, it is more important to enable students to function well in the market than to prepare them to be good citizens.

The shift with respect to higher education occurred quickly after World War II. Whereas prior to the war the dominant image of higher education was the private or church-sponsored liberal arts college, after the war it quickly became the state university. Of course, the states had played an important role in higher education earlier, and liberal arts colleges have not disappeared. But during this period, while private colleges grew slowly, the states poured huge resources into the expansion of their university systems.

Before World War II, state universities often modeled themselves on liberal arts colleges. They included professional schools and graduate schools, but these were usually peripheral to the colleges. There were also state teachers colleges and agricultural and mining schools, but the prestige was with the liberal arts colleges.

Research-oriented universities, in distinction from liberal arts colleges with associated professional and graduate schools, also existed before World War II. They had begun to make their appearance at the beginning of the century. They provided models for part of the expansion of state university systems.

The expansion was motivated by the laudable notion that higher education should not be limited to the elite. It should be open to all. But many students were not interested in traditional liberal arts education. They were motivated to continue their education in order to improve their prospects for good jobs. Businessmen and industrialists also supported the expansion in expectation of getting well-trained employees.

State universities responded to these expectations by offering more and more training programs for particular types of jobs. Postbaccalaureate professional schools also grew in number and size. Even research-oriented graduate programs were increasingly geared to the needs of the market. The college was redefined largely as a program of preparation for graduate and professional schools, and the function of these was to prepare people for leadership positions in the marketplace.

There have been movements from time to time to strengthen general education requirements at universities so that students will receive some education that is not market-driven. In this way the liberal arts tradition maintains a place in higher education. Fortunately, some business leaders have found that those educated in this way have more staying power in management than those who study in more specialized ways.

There is a second source of resistance to the dominance of the market mentality on university campuses. The research-oriented disciplines control the graduate schools. The professional goal of studying in these schools is often college and university teaching. Most of the faculty in the university, even in its job- and profession-oriented branches, have studied in these graduate schools, belong to guilds for their disciplines, and have been thoroughly socialized into disciplinary thinking. They are quite willing for others to find what they teach to be useful in the market place, but their teaching is geared to introducing students to their disciplines. Research in some of these disciplines is prized as a contribution to business and industry, so that their leaders also have status with market leaders.

As more and more students in public schools look forward to higher education, public school teachers are assigned the function of preparing their graduates to succeed in academic disciplines. In this way the market orientation of the public schools is somewhat restricted. Nevertheless, the pressure to prepare students for jobs is great. For public schools as well as universities, the primary justification is now the need to educate workers for the marketplace.

V. Multiculturalism and Public Schools

The function of the public schools for a hundred and fifty years was to acculturate the children and grandchildren of immigrants into a common culture based on British Protestantism. Even the desegregation that brought black children into the school system with whites was sought by African Americans for the purpose of continuing this process more effectively with their children.

Nevertheless, developments in the African-American movement and reflection on the part of more recent immigrant groups have shifted the goal. We now recognize that it is wrong to impose one culture on all. This prevents the diverse cultures from making their proper contribution to the whole, and it disadvantages those who are forced to live by an alien culture in order to gain an education and to participate in the society.

The initial phases of the process focused on religion. Most public educators were only vaguely aware that the public schools strongly favored Protestantism. Catholics, on the other hand, already in the eighteenth century, responded at great cost and sacrifice by creating their own system of schools. Jews also developed schools of their own, or, when they took part in public schools, provided supplementary Hebrew schools for their children. Jews, Muslims, and, later, atheists protested the Christian character of the schools. They successfully argued on constitutional grounds that public moneys should not be spent to support any one religion.

In the past thirty years, the schools have been engaged, not very successfully, in an effort to be neutral among the values of the religions represented in their student bodies. As we become increasingly conscious of the wider cultural values that also need to be respected, this quest for neutrality becomes even more difficult. Such neutrality changes the nature of education drastically, since heretofore all education has been largely acculturation of one kind or another, and cultures are primarily identified by their values. If the schools do not transmit these values, acculturation will have to take place in other contexts. This requirement presses itself on us at just the point at which other value-oriented institutions, such as churches, are growing weaker.

We noted previously the extent to which schooling is now in the service of the market. This is partly the result of separating it from religious values. It seems that parents in almost all cultures today want their children to get ahead in the marketplace. This has become a common value. Each culture has other values that check this one and subordinate it to larger human goals, but these other values are religiously tinged and may prove diverse. Hence schools can avoid controversy about values by giving priority to preparing workers for the marketplace.

A second result of moving toward a value-neutral stance in the public schools is that the culture of the students is no longer greatly influenced by that of their teachers. Of course, their teachers have values, which are often quite apparent. But because the school as such does not have shared values beyond the market, the values of individual teachers have a lessened effect on students. The actual value system on the campus is, therefore, an expression of youth culture rather than a youth version of adult culture.

It could be argued that the schools are not in fact value-free, and that is correct. As the values of the religious traditions and the cultures they have informed proved divisive, they have been removed. Only the Enlightenment heritage tends to remain. Secular humanism is the quasi-religion whose values present themselves as not being specialized values at all, but simply human ones. The schools are committed to ensuring the rights of individual students and due process in administering discipline. They treat students as free and responsible persons. They place a high value on science and technology. They appeal to a more or less utilitarian ethics.

From a postmodern perspective, secular humanist values are just one set among others, to be respected as such, but not to be given hegemonic control. Their continuance, therefore, does not solve the problem posed to the schools by multiculturalism. As the modernist response, secular humanism shares responsibility for the poverty of culture in the schools.

Near the end of Section III, four possible ways of dealing with multiculturalism were identified. The first was decentralization. In Yugoslavia, General Tito successfully ruled a multicultural state. It differed from the United States in that cultural groups were somewhat separate geographically. Tito gave them considerable autonomy as long as they respected his overall control. It was the withdrawal of that autonomy from Kosovo that began the struggles that eventually drew NATO into a war with Serbia.

Because multiple cultures exist in so many localities, the United States cannot solve its political problems by giving autonomy to its several regions, but an analogous move is possible in education. We insisted on homogeneous public schools when those schools had the homogeneous purpose of acculturating students into a homogeneous society. Now we want a multicultural society. Schools have long played a central role in the transmission of cultures. Perhaps each culture that wishes to perpetuate itself within the American multicultural context should have its own schools.

Some forms of postmodernism support the idea that there can be no overarching principles or values, only culture-bound ones. In this case, a multicultural school will need to devise a distinct approach to the education of each cultural group within it. In the process it may have to polemicize against the supposed universals that the British Enlightenment bequeathed us.

Needless to say, this would pose an almost impossible task on curriculum and teachers. A more practical step to allow changes in that direction would be to institute the voucher system. Parents could then send their children to schools that teach the values and culture they want their children to learn.

If multiculturalism is primarily a matter of allowing each culture to continue and transmit itself, this is a desirable solution. If, on the other hand, multiculturalism involves members of each culture learning how to relate to members of other cultures, how to work together with them, and how to discover the meaning of being American in that process, then separation into cultural groups is not an adequate answer. At a minimum, it would need to be combined with elaborate patterns of cooperation and interaction among the schools.

The second way of dealing with multiculturalism identified previously was to allow the majority in each area to decide. This could be applied quite directly to schooling, with the majority in each school district determining the culture and values that would be taught in its schools. Because school districts would opt for different cultures, some multiculturalism would be realized, but it is obvious that many minorities would be returned to the situation of being forced to conform to the local majority culture.

The decision of the majority could be to allow different values and cultures to dominate different schools within the district. Parents would then also be allowed to send their children to other schools in the district. This would move in the same direction as a voucher system, while keeping public control over the process. Public control could prevent some of the feared consequences of private education, such as the teaching of hate in a neo-Nazi school. It might be easier to institute multicultural activities in a system under one management than among completely independent institutions.

Under this system, the majority of parents would be able to send their children to schools whose values they approved. But some would not. The problem for minorities would return, on a smaller scale, to what it was in the days of British Protestant hegemony.

The third response to multiculturalism is to decide that we have given up on shared values too easily. On a global level Hans Küng led in a project to formulate a quite elaborate set of values on which he believed that contemporary representatives of many religious traditions could agree. He has, in fact, secured many signatures. It is his conviction that peace among the religions can be furthered by a common ethic acknowledged by all, and he believes that peace among religions is prerequisite to peace among nations.[2] His document could be tested in school districts all over the country, and if there were common acceptance, it could function as a basis for renewing the role of adult values in the schools.

Another proposal of this kind with a specific focus on the United States comes from the recently institutionalized communitarian movement. In its platform it asserts: *"we ought to teach those values Americans share,* for example, that the dignity of all persons ought to be respected, that tolerance is a virtue and discrimination abhorrent, that peaceful resolution of conflicts is superior to violence, that generally truthtelling is morally superior to lying, that democratic government is morally superior to totalitarianism and authoritarianism, that one ought to give a day's work for a day's pay, that saving for one's own and one's country's future is better than squandering one's income and relying on others to attend to one's future needs."[3]

Diane Ravitch offers a third formulation of what we should be teaching all our children. "Race hatred is wrong, racial chauvinism is wrong, and racism is wrong. People are people. Cut us and we bleed. If we lose a child, we cry. The human heart is the same in all of us, regardless of skin color or language."[4]

One problem with this approach is that the values that seem to the authors to be universal to the world's cultures, or universally American, may seem to others to be particularly informed by the British Enlightenment. Ravitch, for example, while asserting that the democratic values she wants taught are found in many cultures, recognizes that in the United States "the democratic tradition was shaped by the Enlightenment."[5] Certainly her emphasis on the superficiality of cultural differences seems to have this root. Some have noted that the representatives of many religious traditions who have affirmed Küng's formulations are usually those who have been most influenced by the European Enlightenment.

Furthermore, there are problems with this approach even when there is agreement on carefully formulated sentences. Although particular statements can be interpreted in ways that are acceptable in diverse cultures, they cannot be implemented and transmitted without interpretation. Here differences reappear.

In any case, direct verbal statements alone rarely teach values. They are learned more through ritualistic practices and the stories of cultural heroes. Often they are effectively grounded in a larger view of reality. In short, the effort to communicate values apart from their cultural context is a difficult one, not likely to be very successful. Nevertheless, it may be true that more is possible in this way than postmodernists, with our emphasis on difference, have expected.

The fourth possibility, which a Whiteheadian postmodernism suggests, is to work toward a new consensus. The situation of multicultural schools is new for members of all the cultures involved. The traditions, until very recently, have not thought about how to act in a twenty-first-century multicultural situation. Traditions grow through encountering new challenges. This is a new challenge.

A first step in responding to this challenge is for all explicitly to affirm the positive value of a multicultural situation. From that it may be possible to discuss the potentials in that situation that have not yet been fully developed. There may be some overlaps in the new teachings of the several cultural traditions as they respond to this new situation. These may suggest the values that multicultural schools can inculcate. They may also suggest stories of how multiculturalism developed that can be told in a way that effectively inculcates these values.

A second step may be to have a representative of each culture describe its most cherished values. When representatives of other traditions hear about these values, they may covet them for their children as well. Instead of reducing values to what is common to the cultures as they stand, each culture may be enriched by its contact with others. This may provide a guide to what can be taught in a multicultural school, and it might create a value-laden ethos in the school as a whole that can interact with the ever-changing youth culture and replace the current hegemony of the market.

The hope would be that each culture would develop through its interaction with other cultures in a multicultural society. The goal is not a museum of static cultures but the organic growth of each in a new context. The growing cultures would come to share many values and to include one another's stories in their own. Each culture would gradually be creatively transformed. Out of this creative transformation would grow a new culture, inclusive of great diversity, and always open to further change, but still having its own strong convictions. Multicultural schools can contribute to that end.

VI. Teaching by Proposal

The preceding section dealt with issues that must be decided by society at large. But teachers with multicultural classrooms cannot wait for these decisions to be made and implemented. They must teach now in a context in which they know that they are not to indoctrinate students with the values and ideas of any one community. This has pressed them in the direction of value-free teaching.

One problem with aiming at value-free education is that it leads to a focus on skills and information alone. It leaves the impression that these are neutral, so that they can and should be incorporated into every cultural perspective. From a postmodern perspective, however, they are far from neutral. If the major skill is learning the English language and none other, that fact communicates ideas about the world into which the graduate is expected to move. The selection of information is also heavily, and inevitably, weighted. If the weighting is determined by the needs of the market, that communicates a great deal to the student about what is important.

In addition, the teaching of facts is inseparable from the communication of much more. Take the teaching of a natural science as an example.

The teacher may intend only to communicate well-established facts. But it is likely that the formulation of those facts will communicate to the student, consciously or unconsciously, that we live in a deterministic world of matter in motion. Even if the teacher does not personally share that metaphysics, it underlies most high school textbooks in science. From a postmodern perspective, the effort to stick to the facts is very likely to misinform on very important questions.

More broadly the effort to achieve value-free education communicates precisely the idea that value-free education is possible and desirable. It reinforces ideas derived from modernity that have been exposed by postmoderns as erroneous. It sets up in students' minds the dichotomy of a world of highly dubious values and one of quite certain facts. Instead of preparing graduates to live in a postmodern world, it fastens on their imagination the rigid dualisms of modernity.

Can this tendency be countered without falling into the promotion of values from one hegemonic tradition? Does postmodern thought suggest styles of teaching, which can be supported by all cultural traditions, that go beyond teaching skills and communicating factual information?

Often the choices in teaching are thought of as either providing information or eliciting knowledge. Both have roles to play. With regard to the former, there is a large place for learning facts despite the limitations noted. On the other hand, this is a type of learning to which the teacher contributes little except identifying what should be learned, pointing out where the information exists, urging study, and testing. Facts can be learned from a textbook as well or better than from a lecture or discussion. Computers can largely displace this function of the teacher.

As mentioned earlier, the term "education" itself is associated with the alternative idea of teaching as drawing forth implicit knowledge from the student. This is an art that does require a teacher. Often students are not aware that they have implicit knowledge and worthwhile understanding. Discovering and articulating this knowledge can give them new confidence and assured judgments.

It is unfortunate, however, if it is supposed that all teaching that avoids indoctrination moves between these two poles. Much that a student needs is not factual information. On the other hand, much that is needed is not already present in the student, even implicitly.

This is where Whitehead provides a fresh alternative. He redefines the notion of "propositions" so as to differentiate them from simple statements about facts. Because of the association of propositions with dull logical exercises, most people are turned off by the idea that they constitute a major focus of teaching. People speak of "mere" propositional communication or knowledge as the height of dullness. They associate propositions with what Whitehead called "inert ideas."[6] Whitehead, in contrast, described propositions as "lures for feeling."[7] A proposition is a way the world, or some entity within it, may be. It is a possibility that may or may not be actual. It is a proposal about how the world may be. If one is considering repainting a room, one entertains a variety of propositions about the best color to use.

Most propositions are never entertained by anybody. There are many possible colors a room could be painted that no one considers. But when we speak to one another we give expression to propositions in language, and hearing that language evokes attention to propositions. If communication is successful, the propositions attended to by the hearer are similar to the ones entertained by the speaker, although they are unlikely to be identical.

One important part of the art of good teaching is the ability to select propositions that have importance for the students and a chance of catching their interest. The task is then to find sentences that are likely to evoke those propositions in the students' minds. If this is done well, the students will see the world a little more clearly, with different nuances. The horizon of vision will have been enlarged.

This point can be illustrated from this book. One proposition to which the book calls attention is that the actual entities that make up the world may be events rather than objects. Now if readers have long thought that this is so, that proposition will be neither important nor interesting for them. There may also be readers for whom propositions about reality in general have no meaning, or who find this kind of discussion irrelevant to their lives. There may be other readers who are so sure that reality consists in material objects in motion that the proposal made here seems simply silly. For those readers, this proposition will be neither important nor interesting. However, for readers who have some openness to thinking about the world in general, but who have not explored the possibility of the primacy of events, the proposition could be both important and interesting. It is a proposal for thinking of the world in a different way from that into which we are normally led by our language and culture.

The author of a book cannot know who will read it and may, therefore, be excused for misjudging which propositions will prove important and interesting. But skilled teachers sense what students are ready for and open to learn. Their task is to lure students into thinking and seeing in ways that make contact with their present thinking and seeing, but go beyond them. If they select propositions that are already familiar, students will be bored. If they select propositions that do not connect with where they are, students will be frustrated or indifferent. If they select propositions that contradict deeply held convictions, students are likely to reject them out of hand.

To select wisely the propositions to be considered, the teacher needs to know the students well and also be aware of many propositions as yet unfamiliar to them. Of crucial importance are timing along with effective formulation of the sentences that will direct attention to these lures for feeling. Of course, a context in which it is safe to think in new ways is also required.

Directing attention to the right proposition at the right time is the art of persuasion. Persuasion is often understood as bringing the hearer around to one's own point of view, and it can have this character. But the type of persuasion advocated here involves giving attention to possibilities to which students were heretofore blind. What they do with these possibilities is secondary, because when students entertain new possibilities, their freedom is enlarged. They can make choices in an area in which this was not previously possible. A major goal of education is the enlargement of freedom.

For example, one may view reality as composed of material particles because one has never thought about it and has simply absorbed that view through the conventional language of the time. One may also view reality that way after one has considered an alternative, such as the idea that events are more fundamental. The belief is the same, but horizons have been extended and freedom has been enhanced.

Of course, the teacher may hope that many of the propositions elicited into student attention will commend themselves as plausible, worthy of further consideration and even acceptance. I hope that some will respond in that way to the proposals in this book. But even when the propositions are not accepted, an essential goal of teaching has been attained if they have been considered.

This style of teaching can be connected more explicitly to the multicultural context. Given the multicultural situation, some of the propositions most important for students to consider are ideas that are important in cultures other than their own. To bring out these ideas for this kind of consideration should be acceptable to representatives of all the cultures involved. Even when they are not adopted, the awareness of how others perceive and think adds to mutual understanding and appreciation.

VII. A Postmodern University

There are many postmodernists teaching in various university departments. But present-day universities as such are modern to the core. Their two main commitments—to serve the market and to advance the academic disciplines—are thoroughly modern, even if some disciplines advance by adopting postmodern methods and ideas.

One sad fact about the modern university is that it contributes little to the solution of the real issues of our time. One of these problems is the marketization of society, including the educational system. But there is no place in the university where this problem is intensively discussed. Another problem is how to educate in a multicultural context. Again the university is not organized so as to propose solutions to this urgent question.

This is not to say that individual faculty members make no contributions. Fortunately, tenured faculty have considerable freedom, and some of them direct their energies to major problems facing our society. But they can usually do so only by ignoring the basic disciplinary structure of the university.

Professional schools are organized in part to deal with the practical questions involved in the social roles for which they prepare their students. To this end, they may draw on work done elsewhere in the university. For example, professors of education draw findings about multicultural reality from many parts of the university and then relate them to educational theory and practice. The university in general, however, does not see its task as responding to the needs of society, and those within it who do undertake this task are likely not to receive the greatest rewards. These rewards go to those who operate in more narrowly disciplinary channels or who do research for the military or for large corporations.

Although the traditional liberal arts college was free both from subservience to the market and from disciplinary rigidities, it does not provide the model we now need. Its graduates may have brought more wisdom to public life than the graduates of today's specialized programs. But their courses of study did not prepare them for the kinds of problems now facing society. What we need is a new form of higher education, not a return to any past form.

The use of the word "discipline" to describe the fields within which academics now work can be misleading. It suggests that disciplined thought will conform to these disciplines, and many in the university actually think so. When one suggests nondisciplinary research, it is assumed that one means undisciplined work.

Of course, this is not the case. Disciplined thinking characterized Plato's academy and the Medieval University of Paris, without benefit of academic "disciplines." To call for a different organization of knowledge is not to ask for less disciplined study. It is to ask that disciplined study be directed to solving urgent human problems.

We are living in a world that faces very serious problems indeed. The global economy is transforming political and social as well as economic institutions all over the world. It is also heating up the atmosphere of the planet and, more generally, escalating pressures on the environment, which is already badly stressed. One might expect that those institutions that have the greatest resources for research and for making proposals for change would take this critical situation as an occasion to organize themselves to help guide humanity through its crisis. But nothing of the sort has occurred. The university continues to prepare people to serve the economy that threatens us all. There are departments that do study some aspect of global warming or social change, but only in fragmentary ways.

The postmodern proposal is that universities reorganize a considerable portion of their resources around major issues faced by society. Groups of scholars from a variety of backgrounds working together for years to find solutions to public problems might well influence the course of history. Students could get their education by participating in such efforts. They would benefit from courses studying the problem as such, not simply the aspects of the problem that fit established disciplinary approaches. Graduates of such programs would be prepared to bring real wisdom to the leadership of society.

Chapter Four

Gender and Sexuality

I. Introduction

Our society is divided by religion and culture. The preceding chapters have considered whether a constructive postmodern approach can cast light on these divisions and point a way to transform them into mutually enriching differences. Other areas of difference that are currently disturbing the public order are gender and sexuality.

Culturally and intellectually, the most important movement of the twentieth century may prove to have been feminism. Culturally it has challenged patterns of social life that have been entrenched for thousands of years. Intellectually it has provided a fresh and different perspective on an extremely wide range of issues.

Through their passionate writings, feminist women have profoundly changed the nature of the discussion of gender and sexuality. They have shown that the writings of male authors are often permeated by gender and sexuality even, or especially, when they are not aware of this, as when they discuss such topics as God, justice, and equality. This chapter is heavily dependent on their influence. In part, it simply surveys a small part of their work. Much of this work is already postmodern, and some of the postmodern feminist work is constructive in the sense meant in this series. Ecofeminism in particular has this character. Much of the work of ecofeminists is satisfying and convincing, and I have nothing to add. Section II provides my perspective on a very limited segment of what feminism has taught us and on some of its present divisions.

If there is a contribution still to be made by a Whiteheadian postmodernist on these topics, it will require introducing ontological categories into the discussion. The feminist discussion has done very well, to be sure, with minimal use of such categories, but there are a few tensions within postmodernist feminist writings in relation to which more explicitly ontological reflection may help. This author, in any case, has no other contribution to make to these profoundly important, but sometimes baffling, questions.

Two questions are selected. First, in what sense is it wise or helpful to identify with our bodies? Second, does "unselfishness" work against the development of the desired form of selfhood? The proposed clarifications, accordingly, are about the ontological nature of soul, body, and self. Section III treats the relation of body and soul, and Section IV proposes a way of thinking about the self.

The issues of gender flow into those of sexuality. Our sexual nature is a special instance of how our body and soul are related. Section V discusses the implications for an understanding of sexuality of the ideas developed in the two preceding sections.

The sexual issue that is now generating most intense policy discussion and political action has to do with homosexuality. Section VI brings the conclusions of Section V to bear on the evaluation of homosexuality. The result has consequences with respect to the heatedly debated issue of homosexual unions.

II. Feminism

The history of civilization is, for the most part, also the history of patriarchal societies. Whereas the term "civilization" is often used as a positive value,[1] it is, at best, highly ambiguous. Civilization is the culture of cities, and it is in cities that slavery, warfare, and authoritarian rule achieved their highest levels.

There has been much speculation about the existence of prepatriarchal societies and about how patriarchy came to dominance.[2] Based on research on ancient Mesopotamian sites, a plausible scenario can be proposed. In their earliest stages, some cities may have been fairly peaceful places of worship and trade, with emerging artisans and professionals playing a valued role in support of predominantly agricultural communities. In some of these cities women may have had leadership roles, and the cities may be described as prepatriarchal.

However, in due course these cities were threatened by other cities or by nomadic warriors. To survive they became centers of military defense and aggression. They dominated the peasants instead of serving them. These civilized societies became highly hierarchical, organized on the basis of slavery and the domination of females by males.

In detail, there have been great differences among civilizations in class structure and in the status of women in the several classes, but patriarchy prevailed everywhere. Until recently, in most civilized societies, women have been the property of men. Whereas men have had considerable freedom to have sex with women other than their wives, respectable women have been limited to their husbands. This restriction ensured that their children belonged to these husbands.

Although male dominance became universal, the actual freedom and power of women varied greatly. When they played important economic roles, as farmers, for example, the family's dependence on them gave them status and power. Many families operated joint enterprises in which women had a large part. It would be a mistake, accordingly, to view the lot of women in patriarchy as uniformly degraded. On the other hand, the sustained abuse experienced by many women throughout patriarchal history and in our own time can hardly be exaggerated.

In the imagination of men, women are typically viewed as closer to nature, participating more fully in natural processes. The fact that women bear children has been experienced in agricultural societies as relating them to the fertility of the land and of the animals. Where nature is revered as Mother Earth, supplier of all human needs, this connection can have positive implications for the view of women, but where nature is viewed with suspicion and the human task is to subdue it and make it conform to human purposes, the connection with nature is negative. Male hostility expressed itself in extreme form in the witchcraft trials of the early modern period.

Opposing the witchcraft hysteria by denying the possibility of demonic events was one argument given in favor of the mechanistic worldview. Nevertheless, this modern model in some respects worsened the situation for women.[3] The dualism of mind and matter placed nature entirely on the side of matter. Instead of nature being viewed as the creative force on which all depend, it was seen as an object to be investigated and manipulated by men. Women, viewed as part of nature, suffered in consequence.

In the nineteenth century, after the industrial revolution, the household ceased to be an economic producer. Men went off to work. Many poor women did so also. But the wives of the wealthy were kept at home and provided with servants to do the housework. Their role was to be "angels of the household," supporting community life and transmitting cultural values to the children. Above all, they were to provide comfort and support to their husbands. They were viewed as more moral and spiritual than men. Instead of being identified with natural sexuality as in the past, they were supposed to be above such things. Men looked to other women to satisfy their grosser sexual desires. Men also maintained exclusive control of public life.

During this period, the notion of rights continued to play a large role. The right to vote, for example, was extended to more and more of the male citizens. Women of the upper classes asked why they were excluded. Much of the feminist movement from the late nineteenth century until the present has focused on securing for women all the rights to which men were entitled. It has, on the whole, been remarkably successful.

In addition to equal rights, feminists have sought equality in other ways. The equality sought has applied to participation in the public world, in business, and in the professions. It has also included equal pay for equal work and equal opportunity for advancement. It has entailed freedom from sexual harassment. Although much remains to be done, there has been a great deal of progress, and there is a large public, or at least official, consensus that women should have equality in these ways.

The success of the feminist movement in gaining these rights has been due to the continuing power of modern ideals. Despite the negative elements in the impact of modernity on women, the logic of the individualistic humanism that undergirded both modern economics and modern political theory worked in their favor. Each human being, male or female, is an individual, and each individual has rights. In the United States, it took generations to include men without property, blacks, and women, within the purview of the right to vote, but those who sought to restrict such rights to a few were put on the defensive by the basic modernist teaching.

Some in the feminist movement have been content with attaining an equal place in the public world created by modernity. But for others, this goal is insufficient. They want also an end to patriarchal society generally.

In the view of these more radical feminists, a male-dominated society is socializing women to adopt patriarchal values and to participate

in structures shaped by those values. These feminists want to depatri-
archalize the thinking of the culture and thereby its institutions. Especially since the 1980s they have worked to expose and assess the inter-
relations among gender, sex, class, race, ethnicity, and even species, as
bases for oppression. It is these postmodernist feminists who have contributed so extensively to the intellectual life of our time.

For these feminists, one problem is language. The language into
which one is socialized forms very basic habits of thought and feeling.
Our language is patriarchal. In it the male gender consistently represents
the whole of humanity in such a way that females become invisible.

The religious traditions that inform our society are also patriarchal.
Deity is depicted as male. In Christian imagery, all three persons of the
Trinity are male. Women constitute the majority of worshippers, but
their priests and ministers have been overwhelmingly male. According
to some religious teachings, there are theological reasons that this must
be so!

These male priests and ministers teach women to worship a male
deity. They also teach them to understand that their savior is a male.
The subordination of females to males and their dependence on them
are thereby undergirded and reinforced.

With respect to God, the problem is not only that "He" is depicted as
a male but also that to "Him" are attributed stereotypically male characteristics in an absolute way. The power attributed to God is that of
total control. "He" is wholly self-contained, needing nothing but "Himself" in order to exist in a blessed state. "He" acts on others but is not
"Himself" acted upon.

Postmodernist feminists want to share power, but they oppose the
patriarchal understanding and use of power as unilateral and controlling. They expose structures of such power that exclude them. They affirm that real power is that which frees and liberates those in relation to
whom it is exercised. In place of hierarchical structures they propose
participatory ones.

Because so much of the resistance to their views and proposals is
based on the supposed givenness of social patterns and ways of thinking, they devote much attention to showing how these patterns of social structure and thought have in fact been constructed by particular
societies. These patterns are not objective, natural entities, but expressions of the interests of those who have controlling power. Other
modes of life and society are equally possible. Even gender is a social
construct in the sense that how maleness and femaleness are under-

stood and the consequences that follow vary from society to society. When it is recognized that the understanding that dominates is not accidental, but expresses the interests of the most powerful, those who suffer from it can propose alternatives. That is what postmodernist feminists are doing.

In addition to the division between modernist and postmodernist feminists, there is a division among the latter. All postmodernist feminists affirm the social critique previously sketched. But some concern themselves also with the natural world, while others do not. The common cultural association of women with nature influences both, but they respond in opposite ways.

One response is to reject this association. It can be seen as a male projection on women who, in fact, are no more connected to the natural world than men. The important issues, for women who respond in this way, lie in challenging the dominant social construction of women's lives, including their supposed connection to nature. Attention should be directed to unmasking patriarchal power patterns and undercutting them.

The other response is that of ecofeminism. This response affirms the connection to nature as one that all people should have. The problem is that patriarchal society, especially in the West, has alienated males from nature and encouraged its ruthless exploitation. This alienation begins with men's objectification of their own bodies, an alienation from which their sexual partners are made to suffer. If women, for whatever reason, have a healthier relation to their bodies and to the rest of the natural world, they should not give that up! On the contrary, there is no respect in which society is in more need of change than in its understanding of the relation of humanity to nature, including the human body, and the consequent treatment of the natural world. For ecofeminists, women can and should be a voice for nature.

At the theoretical level, ecofeminists reject the mechanistic view of nature and the many dualisms that have resulted from it. They oppose in particular the subject/object dualism so foundational to modernity. This opposition leads to rejection of the objectification of what is studied, an objectification that characterizes most modern research in all the academic disciplines of the university. Ecofeminists point out its illusory character and how it excludes the perspective of women from the sciences.

The constructive postmodernism affirmed in this book agrees with postmodernist feminism. The term "agree" is misleading, however, if it is taken to imply that it has independently come to the same conclusions. This is far from true. Feminists have pointed out much to which male constructive postmodernists were blind. But once these matters are pointed out, male constructive postmodernists can only accept them.

This is especially true with regard to ecofeminism. Constructive postmodernism differs from other forms in much the way that ecofeminism differs from other forms of feminist postmodernism. These other forms seem to continue much of the dualism of modernity, neglecting human immersion in the natural world and the intrinsic value of that world. Ecofeminist experience and sensibility undergird new dimensions of the theoretical and practical meaning of the continuity of human life with all life.

III. Body and Soul

One place in which an ontological version of postmodernism may help is with respect to the understanding of body and soul. On this point feminists speak in remarkably conflicting ways. Some minimize the importance of the body; others accent it.[4]

Many postmodernist feminists regard any identification of women with the female body as leading to "essentialism." For them, "essentialism" is the doctrine that there is a distinctive essence of women—biological, or also psychospiritual—that limits the social construction of gender. This implies either that women have some special contribution to make to society as women or that they are cast into inescapable roles. Both conclusions are widely rejected.

Some ecofeminists, on the other hand, in their reaction against mind-body dualism and the denigration of the body, say that they *are* their bodies. Since bodies are so clearly either male or female, this could lead to an extreme form of the essentialism so opposed by other feminists. Usually these are not the consequences desired or intended. The intention is to celebrate embodiment, not to accent the differences between male and female embodiment, let alone to reduce women's destiny to anatomy.

Since constructive postmodernism shares with ecofeminists the judgment of the importance of human embodiment, it faces with ecofeminists the question of how this can be affirmed without the negative consequences that follow from sheer identification with the body. No one wants to be treated simply as a physical object, and feminist women certainly do not want to be viewed by men simply as female bodies. Can one affirm the bodiliness of personal existence without the kind of identification that would lead to such negative results?

The affirmation that one *is* one's body usually results from the supposition that to affirm that one is one's soul would involve detaching oneself from one's body and objectifying it. That has indeed been true, given the dominant Western doctrines of the soul. This detachment follows from the ways in which both Plato and Descartes distinguished body and soul. The body is, in their views, an object for the soul.

Traditional Christian theology, preoccupied with the salvation of the soul, warned against yielding to the body's impulses. St. Augustine taught that original sin was transmitted through the sexual act. The resulting tendency has been to view the body as evil. The church encouraged spiritual practices that detached the soul from the body's influence.

In all these philosophical and theological instances, it was supposed that the soul was metaphysically different from the body, and that it had a separate origin. The soul belonged to a realm far superior to that of the body. The identification of oneself with the soul, therefore, inherently involved detachment from the body.

Given this still effective history, to affirm oneself as soul carries a great deal of baggage from which an ecofeminist rightly wishes to free herself. She wants to affirm herself as a fully embodied being and to celebrate this bodiliness. One way of doing this is to identify herself as an ensouled body. Nevertheless, this identification with the body, if taken straightforwardly, returns us to the evaluation of women in terms of their bodily characteristics, and thereby to the dualism of male and female, from which modern humanism has helped to free us.

Whitehead offers a quite different view of soul (psyche) that does not count against its embodiment. It allows us to identify ourselves with soul, now embodied soul, without the denigration of the body and the physical world previously associated with this self-understanding. It provides a way of continuing the gains derived from the doctrine of soul without its negative consequences.

Soul consists of occasions of experience, each of which arises largely out of bodily occasions. Each psychic occasion prehends the bodily occasions; by virtue of these prehensions it includes the body. It feels the feelings of the body and is largely constituted thereby. To a significant extent, it *is* these feelings.

Nevertheless, it is something more. Each psychic occasion prehends earlier occasions of soul. Of course, these occasions of experience were also largely constituted by their inclusion of bodily occasions; so this fact marks no sharp break. Nevertheless, each of the occasions also makes a decision as to just how to constitute itself, and what is thereby constituted has a unity that is not simply given to it by body. The decision of one occasion of psychic life affects the way it is felt in the next. Over time, the accumulation of these decisions gives to the soul a considerable range of content that it does not derive from bodily occasions. It "transcends" body in the sense of including elements not provided by bodily occasions, without ceasing to include body.

There is a difference in this regard between an adult and a baby. The baby's experience transcends body very little. When there is pain in the body of a very young baby, the baby's experience is dominated by that pain. It does not remember when it was free of that pain or anticipate its end. It simply is what body causes it to be. If the pain ends abruptly, it is for the baby almost as if that pain had never existed.

With an adult the situation is very different. How one responds to pain is influenced both by memories of similar pains and their relief and by anticipation of what can be expected. Even when the body's contribution to experience is dominated by pain, memory and anticipation cause the experience as a whole to transcend the pain in the sense of including other elements that affect the meaning of the pain. It is not the case that one simply *is* one's body. One *is* one's soul, and in being soul one includes one's body.

This "transcendence" of body by the soul is very important. Because of it, one's worth as a person is not contingent on one's bodily condition. One's body may seriously deteriorate without loss of many of the qualities that give particular value to personal existence. One rightfully expects to be treated in terms of what one is as a unified center of experience and not in terms of the deteriorating body.

The transcendence, however, is only partial. Bodily changes bring about psychic ones. One may lose an arm and a leg without great change in soul, but an injury to the brain may lead to significant changes in one's experience and personality. Soul is never independent of body.

This model is relevant also to the question of the importance of gender in constituting who one is. Some feminists have belittled the influence of biology in constituting a woman or a man. The anti-essentialists, especially, stress that gender itself is a social construct. Other feminists emphasize embodiment, and even if they do not accent the differences between males and females, identification with the body cannot but be with either a biologically male or a biologically female body. The differences are real.

The ontological analysis offered here proposes a mediating position. To the extent that bodies are constitutive of the life of soul, gender is inherent in our total being. Independently of social construction, one *is* male or female. The experience derived from the body differs accordingly—partly, of course, because of the social construction of gender.

To the extent that soul contains more than the body, it is not gendered. That is, the genes that determine maleness or femaleness directly affect the body. Those genes affect soul only indirectly through its inclusion of the body.

The gender of soul is affected not only by the body but also by life experience. Most people accept the gender of their bodies and identify themselves accordingly. A few, however, consider their bodily gender irrelevant to who they really are. In extreme cases, persons who have male bodies identify themselves as female. Some of these have had sex-change operations to bring their bodies more in line with their self-identification. This variety is possible because of the element of transcendence over body that characterizes soul.

This model is relevant also to the evaluation of talk of the social construction of gender. The correct point of such talk is that the role of gender in society is not determined by biology. A great variety of gender roles are possible. Also, the self-understanding of people as male and female is deeply affected by culture. Beyond that, social organization, by shaping childcare practices, can lead to differences in the ways boys and girls develop their identities.

Sometimes, however, the rhetoric is overblown. There are many bodily functions that continue much the same regardless of how society interprets them. These bodily functions deeply inform psychic life. They establish limits to the interpretations society can give. And the differences between male and female bodies are among those that play this role. They cannot be deconstructed away, although it remains true that there is no gender difference that is not also affected by social construction.

IV. The Self

Once one understands oneself as embodied soul, more refined questions arise. Is the self simply identical with this embodied soul? If so, it would be difficult to understand much of the feminist concern about the development of the self and the ways in which patriarchal society has hindered this development in women. Patriarchy has not prevented women's existence as embodied souls.

It seems, then, that the self is not simply soul but an organizing principle within it, one that develops in the course of the soul's life and that may take more than one form. Perhaps a further ontological analysis can help to clarify the nature of selfhood, the desired form of that selfhood, and how it is attained. Perhaps this clarification can throw light on practical questions that are puzzling in feminist literature.

In discussing how patriarchy has hindered women from coming to desirable selfhood, some feminists have highlighted the inculcation of ideals of unselfish service and self-sacrifice into women. They regard these ideals as a major obstacle to attainment of a healthy selfhood. The implication is that women should become aware of their own needs and deal with them instead of giving themselves to caring for others.

Some of the same feminists, however, point out the great value of relationality and the particular contribution of women with respect to nurturing. Few of them really want a society in which individuals care only for themselves. Can an ontological analysis clarify the real problem and reorient the discussion accordingly?

The problem here is not the logical one of a strict contradiction. One may, at least theoretically, be highly relational and may nurture others simply as self-expression or self-realization without any intention to serve their needs except as this serves one's own needs. But there is, still, a tension and a puzzle to be resolved.

According to the view I am proposing, soul is a flow of experience from one occasion to the next. Each occasion is a coming together, through prehensions, of past occasions. Of these the most important is usually the prehension of the immediately preceding occasion of psychic life and, chiefly through that contiguous occasion, of earlier ones. In many adults, the prehension of this past series of occasions is the primary determinant of the decision as to just how to constitute the new occasion.

But the prehension of the personal past must compete with other prehensions for dominance in the process of making decisions. Another person may impose himself or herself on one in such a way that it is the prehension of that person, rather than of one's own past, that largely determines the decision. The prehension of one's own past is then subordinated to that of another. The self in that moment is less a continuation of one's past than an alien presence. In early childhood this is often inevitable, since the adult figure is a more powerful presence in the child's experience than the child's personal past.

If some one person repeatedly plays the determinative role, one will not develop a self that is clearly distinguished from that person. If different people play that dominating role, the situation may be even worse. One may simply not know who one is. There will not be a strong enduring self, centering the life of soul. A patriarchal culture sometimes teaches women that they should, in this way, not have a real self of their own. First the father and then the husband are supposed to be internalized as the dominant factor in decision making.

Nancy Chodorow has shown how deeply the psychological differences between men and women are shaped by the common practice of women being the primary caregivers of both girls and boys.[5] Her depiction of these differences and how they come about can be formulated in the ontological categories employed here. Of course, her account is drawn primarily from modern Western life and cannot be universalized.

Ontologically speaking, mothers are not simply external actors upon children. Children's prehensions of their mothers participate in important ways in constituting who they are. In short, mothers are internal to the self-constitution of children. Often the child's prehension of the mother is more determinative of the child's decision than is the prehension of the child's own past experiences. When this continues beyond early childhood, the child's identity is confused with that of the mother.

Society does not see a problem with this confusion so far as girls are concerned. The girl is expected to internalize her mother. But the boy must model himself on the father. Because the father usually does not have the same intimate presence, this modeling is more by imitation than by internalization. The decisions to imitate are thus made in continuity with the boy's own past experiences rather than by the current prehension of the father. The boy's personal identity is more likely to be intact.

On the other hand, to achieve this characteristically male identity, the boy must end the intimacy with the mother whereby the prehensions of the mother are often decisive determinants of decision. The distancing of the mother is a painful experience. The boy is likely to fear any renewal of this kind of intimacy, especially with women, as a further threat to his selfhood. He feels the presence of others in constituting his experience from moment to moment as a danger to be avoided. He experiences his selfhood as requiring separateness while also feeling the pain and isolation of that separateness. In short, boys learn, in a relational universe, to minimize intimate relations.

The girl's problem is the reverse. She is likely to have a confused identity, especially in relation to her mother. If she fails to develop a clear separate identity, she is open to having her decisions in later life, as well, made more by her prehension of others than by her prehension of the antecedent occasions of her soul's life. This opens her, in patriarchal societies, to control by men.

With this in mind, let us return to the question of the damage done by the ideals of unselfishness and sacrifice. These ideals are taught in many ways, and they can certainly be used as weapons against the weak. But in themselves they are not the problem for women.

The problem is not the content of the decision so much as what makes it. If the decision is made by a self that is constituted by its inheritance from its past and its anticipation of its future, it may be selfish or unselfish. Either decision will continue the ongoing process of building the self. If the prehending of another—that is, the internalization of another person—is determinative of the decision, it will, whether it be selfish or unselfish, work against the construction of the self. In this respect, selfishness and unselfishness are neutral.

In other respects, however, they are not. A well-identified self that makes decisions that take the well-being of others fully into account contributes far more to the relational matrix than one that considers only personal advantage. It actually contributes more to the personal future as well, because the strengthening of the relational matrix provides a better context for the future of that self.

It is a mistake, then, to attack the teaching of unselfishness as such as a threat to the emergence of a healthy selfhood. Any use of the teaching to make a woman feel guilty for striving to make her own decisions, is, of course, rightly condemned. Making one's own decisions is not selfishness!

The ideal that is here being affirmed is a well-developed personal self that is open to intimacy with others. This intimacy differs from that of the young child with the mother to whatever extent the latter allows the prehension of the mother to become the determinative element in the process of decision. If this ideal of maturity is realized, the personal self will decide. But a strong self will allow that decision to be influenced by the vivid presence of others in the formation of the soul moment by moment. It will be able to experience profound mutual internality with another without threat to its own identity.

The more fully the soul internalizes others, the more the well-identified self will move beyond the simple dichotomy of selfishness and unselfishness. The self will become a social self inherently concerned for the others that participate in its constitution. It will genuinely care about the effects of its decisions on the wider, rather than the narrower, society, human and nonhuman. Selfishness in the strict sense will not be an option. The call to unselfishness will then mean the call to act for a future even wider than the one that is spontaneously envisaged and cared about. But the self that decides will still be constituted primarily by its continuity with its personal past and its anticipation of its personal future.

V. Sexuality

Our bodies are profoundly sexual. Just how they are sexual depends on gender and its social construction and on much else besides. The body does not derive its sexuality from soul; it is the source of the soul's sexuality. But soul's sexuality is deeply influenced by its social context, and by successive decisions it makes, in this context, about how to relate its prehensions of the body and its prehensions of others. The soul also affects the sexuality of the body.

Sexuality is an extremely important part of psychic life. It may be one of the parts of that life in which it is least transcendent of body or in which its transcendence of body is least influential on bodily occasions. This has long been noted and has been important for reflection about sexuality through the ages. Most of this reflection has been by males and expresses the male experience.

There can be bodily arousal when soul does not wish this to happen or lack of arousal when soul desires it. Sexual desire can claim the attention of soul when it attempts to think of other things. The objects to which sexual desires are directed are not always the ones soul prefers. In short, one's sexual nature is "unruly." But bodily autonomy in these respects can also be exaggerated and reinforced by cultural stereotypes.

Sexual desires can institute powerful conflicts in soul. Even a well-developed personal self, constituted of prehensions of its past occasions and thus transcending body, can at times have the power to decide taken from it by the prehension of the sexual body. Those with weakly developed selves are easily seduced.

This situation of relative weakness of soul in its transcendence of the sexual body is the main reason that religious traditions have given so much attention to sex in their teachings. Most of the major world religions have thought of salvation in ways that omit the body and its sexuality. They offer practices for the cultivation of soul in its transcendence of body. These typically include disciplining body. The body's sexuality offers the greatest resistance to this discipline.

At this point, all too often, and especially in Christianity, a vicious circle has set in. Because sexuality resists psychic directives, it is regarded as evil. One is taught to denigrate it and to repress it. Efforts at repression fail, although they may cause sexuality to take distorted forms. They clothe its expressions and the desires themselves with guilt. Often the guilt is projected on the partner toward whom the desire, now considered evil, has been directed. Religious teaching and practice exacerbate male anger and violence toward women, engendered by the pain of separation from the mother. Preoccupation with sex increases.

Clearly this situation is intolerable. Slowly and painfully the West—including the church, where anti-sexual teaching was once most effective—has gone through a revolution in attitudes toward sex. Sexual desire and the satisfaction of that desire are now recognized as inherently good. Whereas previously the burden of proof was placed on those who wished to justify sexual activity, now it is placed on those who wish to restrict it.

But there are still many reasons for restriction. Feminists recognized that the phase of the sexual revolution that encouraged free sex was in fact patriarchal. The freedom was of males who persuaded females that their hesitations were unwarranted. Sexual activity became a casual recreation for men, free of the mutuality and commitment that is often important to women. Even in terms of patriarchal values, furthermore, males easily become possessive of particular females and unwilling to share them. The ideal of sexual freedom runs into opposition from deep-seated feelings.

In somewhat different ways, men and women both have deep needs for more than casual partners. The sexual experience itself tends to bond the partners to each other. The physical intimacy tends to generate psychological intimacy. Many find sexual relations more satisfying when that psychological intimacy is present. The sexual partners find one another playing special roles in the constitution of the occasions of their lives. The psychological intimacy prefers exclusiveness. Each feels violated if the other seeks out other partners.

Bonding can occur independently of sexual relations, and sexual intercourse can occur without bonding. But it seems that the most satisfactory sex in the long run takes place in the context of mutual commitment and that mutual commitment is strengthened and deepened by sexual intercourse. This mutual commitment is inherently exclusive.

The needs of the wider community also call for sexual intercourse to be restricted. It can be disruptive of the workplace and of many of the community's other institutions. There are special problems when it is required in exchange for employment advantages or increased power. Even outside these institutions, its free expression is likely to lead to animosity and conflict. Social order is enhanced by pair bonding.

Pair bonding is also the best context for bringing children into the world. Society depends on adults taking responsibility for children. There is a natural tendency to do so when the children are one's own. Pair bonding ensures the father's confidence that this is the case. It enhances the likelihood that the child will receive the personal attention and love needed to develop into a positive contributor to society as a whole.

None of this requires sexual repression in the sense of denial of sexual desires that fall outside the accepted pattern. But it does require discipline in the expression of those desires. There remains a tension between what well-socialized souls desire of body and continuing bodily desires. The issue of dominance and control cannot be wished away.

The point of these brief comments is to say that the problems that arose in the context of dualistic spirituality do not go away entirely when attention shifts toward social relations. Individuals are still required to discipline or control their bodies. Sexual activity needs to subserve purposes beyond itself. Recognizing such requirements does not ensure that desires for inappropriate relations will cease.

There is a danger, therefore, when the argument moves too easily from the importance of sexuality and its goodness to the ideal of sexual fulfillment as the supreme goal. This move, promoted in barely disguised fashion by many Hollywood romances, tends to reject the notion that some sexual desires should not be acted upon. The idea that some should be denied can appear to be a continuation of the old hostility to sex.

Many people in our society suppose that personal fulfillment is the goal of life and that this consists primarily in sexual fulfillment. They believe a marriage that does not provide that adequately should be ended. Social expectations that restrict the quest for sexual fulfillment are rejected. The loss of sexual potency or of the context for its expression is felt as dehumanizing.

The implication of the position developed in this chapter is somewhat different. One desideratum in the organization of society is the sexual fulfillment of its members. But this consideration must be balanced with others and subordinated to the overarching goal of the fulfillment of persons in community. The fulfillment of persons requires that they be strong selves with open and intimate relationships and the ability to give of themselves generously to others. Sexual fulfillment can contribute richly to personal fulfillment, but it does not define it. There are fulfilled people who lack sexual partners. The fulfillment of persons in community requires that the life of the community as a whole be vital and healthy. Sexual fulfillment has a large role to play, but not at the expense of the well-being of the community as a whole.

V. Homosexuality as a Test Case

Homosexuality raises questions that may be addressed in terms of what has been said. Does it arise from bodily occasions, or is it introduced through psychic ones? If the former, to what extent can the self's decisions counter bodily preferences? If it is introduced through soul, can it be changed through psychological methods? These issues are considered first, then the question is raised whether any such change is desirable.

Given the understanding of body and soul explained in this chapter, the likelihood is that sexual orientation arises in a variety of ways, that some of it can be changed, but that much of it cannot. Much about human beings is genetically determined, and there is no reason to doubt that this applies to much about bodily sexual orientation. On the other hand, much happens to us as we are formed in our early relationships to parents and other caregivers. These events, no doubt, also affect sexual orientation.

Since many people have *some* attraction to both sexes, the self's decisions can influence the direction of sexual activity. If one acts on one's heterosexual attractions, they may be somewhat strengthened. If one denies one's homosexual attractions, these may be somewhat reduced. There are those for whom sexual orientation has a significant voluntary aspect.

On the whole, however, the evidence is that this is true only of borderline cases, so that, for most people, efforts at voluntary change do not work well. Whether a person's sexual orientation is determined by heredity or by environment, it is usually fixed quite early. Conscious decisions affect it surprisingly little. Many who would like to be what society calls "normal" find this to be a place where the refusal of body to conform to the desires of soul is marked and stubborn. In a society that associates personal fulfillment so closely with sexual fulfillment and ridicules and condemns gays, this leads, too often, to the suicide of adolescent boys.

For those who are clearly homosexually oriented, the question of genetic or environmental causation seems largely irrelevant. It could become relevant if the genetic causes were established and "gene therapy" could be used. It would also become relevant if parents could be told how to avoid inducing homosexual orientation in their children. Thus the issue of genetic vs. environmental causation is worthy of continuing study, but for practical purposes it is at present irrelevant.

This whole discussion has presupposed that homosexual desires are undesirable and should be eradicated if possible. Certainly, as long as society favors heterosexual expression so strongly and makes life so difficult for homosexuals, few would choose the homosexual orientation for their children. Also, one who wants to change from a homosexual orientation to a heterosexual deserves any help and support society can give.

But it may be that instead of trying to change individuals who do not conform to current social norms, it is society and its norms that should be changed. Perhaps humanity as a whole is richer because of this diversity as well as others. Postmodernists prize diversity, so that ordering society so as to allow for it, rather than suppressing or eradicating it, is itself a positive goal. On the other hand, no one favors every form of diversity. We will not multiply diseases or injuries for diversity's sake. Is there reason to think of homosexuality in such negative terms?

If homosexuality inherently involved a personality disorder that limited the capacity of gays and lesbians to function well or enjoy life, then sexual orientation might be an area in which diversity should not be encouraged. But the evidence is that this is not the case. If homosexuals on average have more problems than heterosexuals, this is because of their treatment by their families and by society. This is a reason to change social practice, not the individuals who are its victims.

Is there a threat to society and its family values involved in full acceptance of homosexuals? What might that threat be that would warrant society's cruel methods of self-defense? Would this acceptance, for example, harm heterosexual marriages? On examination this threat seems quite minor, if real at all. It may be that if society gives homosexual bonding equal status with heterosexual bonding, some people who now participate in heterosexual unions only because of social pressure will choose homosexual ones instead. But heterosexual marriages of those who prefer partners of the same sex do not constitute the unions that are to be enthusiastically supported and affirmed. Driving people into loveless marriages cannot be the community's goal. Meanwhile the great majority of persons in heterosexual marriages have orientations that are primarily, if not exclusively, heterosexual. Other heterosexuals are a far greater threat to their marriages than is the acceptance of homosexuals.

Some suppose that if society ceased to reject homosexuality, some young people who now suppress their homosexual desires would feel free to act on them. Many parents seem afraid that their children might do so if influenced by homosexual adults. In some borderline cases, this may happen. But by adolescence, sexual preferences are generally well established. Apparently, society wants to push adolescents into heterosexual bonding even if that is not their nature. But since most of them are heterosexually inclined, allowing them the choice is no threat to the social predominance of heterosexual marriages.

In past generations, the encouragement of procreation was assumed to be the major reason for insisting on heterosexual unions. When society has an urgent need for increased population, it may regard sanctioning other types of unions as a threat. But this is irrelevant today. Many heterosexual couples choose childlessness. Some homosexual couples choose to adopt or to have children through artificial insemination. In any case, the world's problem is too many babies, not too few.

In short, there is no significant threat. Yet society has exacted a high price from homosexuals in order to ward it off! The sexuality of homosexually inclined people has simply been excluded from the positive expectations of the community. It is assigned no social role. Homosexuals have had to find their own way in this difficult area without the community's help or blessing.

Indeed, the community has posed serious obstacles to the attainment of responsible sexuality by homosexuals. If they engage in recreational sex among themselves, this activity can be secret or ignored. But if they seek to establish lasting partnerships, these are likely to become public and to evoke condemnation. The blanket moral condemnation of homosexual acts by society implies that sexual relations in the context of faithful mutual commitments are on the same level as impersonal and exploitative relationships. Indeed, in practice the social price for those who bond is higher, since their relations are more likely to be publicly visible! Homosexuals are fully accepted only if they maintain lifelong celibacy, and for this most of them have no vocation. In short, society promotes irresponsible promiscuity among homosexuals and then condemns them collectively for this practice.

The task, then, is to rethink social practice and teaching in this area. From the discussion of sexuality in Section IV, two conclusions are relevant to forming new policies. First, the sheer fact that some sexual desires are directed toward persons of the same sex does not determine that they should be acted on. Second, society should order itself so as to support sexual fulfillment along with other goods.

The first point is that the needs of the community and inclusive human fulfillment take precedence over sexual satisfaction as such. The second point is that we should find ways in which meeting the needs of the community also supports inclusive human fulfillment and provides the context for sexual enjoyment.

Our reflections suggest that for the sake of both individuals and the community as a whole, the best contexts for the expression of sexuality are those in which mutual responsibility and love are secured by long-term equal bonding. This principle applies in the same way to heterosexuals and to homosexuals. Enduring, loving, responsible bonding is ideal for both. Celibacy should be respected as a choice made by some heterosexuals and some homosexuals, but it should not be regarded as a superior choice for either.

The proper role of the community is to offer norms and ideals, and to support actions that move toward their realization. It is not, however, to prescribe restrictive rules of behavior. What falls short of these ideals should not be condemned as immoral or made illegal, except when it endangers or damages others. Few are able to attain the highest ideals. Most people, in most areas of life, fall short and settle for something less than ideal. This is true for heterosexuals and homosexuals alike.

To affirm faithful, loving, lasting bonding between two people as the ideal context for sexual expression, therefore, does not mean this will ever be available to all. Indeed, one can imagine many circumstances in which other patterns of sexual expression are the best that are possible.

Our shared concern should be to affirm all who try to express their sexuality with concern for the welfare of the whole community, especially their partners, as well as their own enjoyment and personal growth. Society should support all efforts to act responsibly.

But this needed openness to varied expressions of sexuality does not reduce the desirability, and even urgency, of encouraging stable unions of people who love one another and are prepared to care for each other. Today the most urgently needed step in the process of ending discrimination against gays and lesbians is the legal sanctioning and the ecclesiastical celebration of homosexual unions.

Although this discussion of homosexuality has been separated from that of patriarchy, in reality patriarchal habits of mind play the predominant role in the continuing persecution of homosexuals. The postmodern feminist critique of patriarchy shows the many forms of oppressions in which it expresses itself. Its demand for universal heterosexuality is one of the most obvious.

Chapter Five

Nature, Community, and the Human Economy

I. Introduction

Up to this point, this book has been primarily about culture. The culture it has advocated is one that recognizes its immersion in, and kinship with, nature. Indeed, in an important sense, culture should understand itself as continuous with nature—as, in a sense, natural. In this respect the postmodern view reaffirms that of primal peoples. It would be foolish, however, to deny that civilized human beings have created an order that transcends nature and even works against it.

Human beings have always had an economy. That is, part of their lives has always been devoted to taking from their environment the food and other goods they needed and wanted. Having an economy did not in itself distance them from other species whose behavior we regard as natural. But with time their activities as a whole, and their economy in particular, took on characteristics that did distinguish their behavior and creations drastically from those of other species. In the contemporary world, the economy is imposed on the natural world in a particularly jarring fashion. It is far from natural!

The detachment from the natural world has been accompanied by breaking down natural relations among human beings as well. Human beings come to be in communities. In a profound sense the human communities in which they live create them. The economy of the modern world has broken down traditional communities. In its current global reach, this breakdown is being effected almost everywhere.

The justification given for this disruption of relations among human beings and between them and the natural world has been the need for economic growth. Economic theory describes how such growth is to be achieved, and economic practice, following that theory, has been remarkably successful in bringing growth, thus understood, about. But there is a real question whether this growth, bought at the price of destroyed communities and a degraded environment, has accomplished much of real value. Continuing present policies threatens the habitability of the planet, with little likelihood of accomplishing what their supporters have promised. The rich, it is true, grow richer, but the masses of human beings do not gain even in narrowly economic terms.

The theory underlying these policies derives from modern thought, whose assumptions are individualism and dualism. Postmodernism rejects both of these assumptions. It proposes to develop a different economic theory based on the understanding of persons-in-community both with one another and with the wider world. This theory leads to policy proposals in marked contrast to those now being globally implemented.

Section II, accordingly, discusses the relation between humanity and the natural world. At what point does distinctive human activity become transcendent of nature and even "unnatural"? Section III traces the history of the human relation to nature, showing how the alienation that had been present for millennia became extreme during the modern period. It shows also how individualism replaced community in the thinking of the time. Section IV locates modern economic theory in this context and considers the consequences of its individualistic and dualistic assumptions. Section V evaluates the claim that acting on modern economic theory will solve many of our basic social problems. Section VI describes the beginnings of a postmodern economic theory.

II. Transcendence in Nature and of Nature

In every unit event, or occasion of experience, the primary content is the inclusion of features of past events. But every occasion of experience also involves an act of deciding just how this inclusion is accomplished. For this reason, no event is simply the predetermined outcome of its past, but this transcendence of the past is entirely "natural."

The model of the machine, so prevalent in modern thought, abstracts from this element in all things. Despite the many features of nature that can be understood mechanistically, as a whole, and in each of its indivisible units, it is characterized by spontaneity. The transcendence of the past in every unit event is the point at which novelty enters the world. It is the germ of mentality and life.

Nature is better understood as composed of organisms than of matter in motion. Matter is passive, whereas organisms not only adjust to their environment, but also modify it to their own needs. This interaction is also entirely "natural."

In modifying their environments to make them more habitable, human beings are continuing to behave "naturally." Hence the making of artificial things is a natural activity, whether it is the building of nests by birds or of huts by people. The fact that humans in varied settings build quite different types of shelter shows a role for "culture" among humans that is less apparent among birds, but there is no sharp line between human beings and other animals in this respect. Even birds are not rigidly limited by instinct. They are capable of adapting varied materials to their needs. They can learn new habits from other members of their species and in this sense develop different cultures. This diversity of cultures goes much further among apes. To develop a culture is quite "natural."

Human culture has, nevertheless, transcended nature and come into profound tension with it. The economic order now dominating the world is not natural. It is transforming the world into a primarily artificial place expressive of human purposes rather than its own. What can statements of this sort mean in terms of the postmodern understanding of nature affirmed in this book?

The meaning can be explained in terms of the relation of body and soul discussed in the preceding chapter. The distinction of the natural and the artificial is emphatically not that of the body and the soul. Soul is just as much a part of nature as is body. Bodies with central nervous systems generate unified experiences that are not those of their individual cells but derive largely from them. This is true for birds as well as for human beings. These unified occasions of experience in their succession through time constitute the bird soul or the human one. As Aristotle saw long ago, it is the presence of souls that enables animals to move around to escape danger and to find food. Souls are entirely natural.

The distinction between the natural and the artificial comes with respect to the purposes that are acted on by soul. Soul comes into existence in the service of body. It is the needs of the body that determine its primary functions. These needs are oriented primarily to survival and reproduction, but they also involve enjoyment. It is natural for animals to seek bodily pleasure. These pleasures are experienced also by the animal soul. One aim of soul is the intensification of its own enjoyment. This aim of the soul at its own enjoyment is entirely natural.

Much of human behavior is natural in this sense. An infant's actions and behavior are in the service of the body and aimed at enjoyment, and this relationship is repeated at times throughout our lives. But among human beings soul develops purposes that are not continuous with those of body. They require disciplining the body to behave in ways that are not natural to it. Soul is then no longer in the service of body. It forces the body to conform to purposes imposed on it.

Behavior of this kind can be found among primal people. They, especially males, may submit their bodies to great pain to demonstrate control over them. But their cultures as a whole remain natural in the sense of being organized around the needs for survival, reproduction, and an enjoyment that is continuous with, or at least not in opposition to, bodily enjoyment.

Humans imposed unnatural behavior on animals before they imposed it extensively on themselves. The domestic animal is required to behave in ways contrary to its own nature. A horse, for example, must be "broken" so as to conform to the purposes of its human master rather its own nature.

In primal societies, children are rarely "broken" in an analogous way. Their natural propensities to please and imitate adults and to internalize their environments are employed to socialize them, quite naturally, into the life of the tribe. But as cultures develop into civilizations in which people play specialized roles, many of which demand unnatural bodily behavior, children must be "disciplined" as well as socialized. They are required to behave in unnatural ways, and their resistance to doing so must be overcome.

This unnatural behavior may in part be simply imposed on people throughout their lives in much the way it is imposed on domesticated animals. Much slavery has this character. But this is rarely the whole story. In general, soul develops its own purposes, which lead to its independent control of body. For example, it is because of their own hopes and ambitions that runners impose pain on their bodies in order to improve their speed and endurance. It is because of my own hopes and ambitions that I sit for hours at my computer writing this book.

The previous chapter described what is natural in sexuality as following the lead of the body. For a society to prescribe heterosexual relations for all is for it to demand unnatural behavior of those who are sexually attracted primarily to persons of the same sex. There are limits to the ability of human beings to behave unnaturally even when they desire to conform.

So much of human activity in civilized societies is unnatural that some social critics regard virtually everything in society as socially constructed. This book has argued that the human body places limits on such construction. Nature cannot be ignored in the process of understanding society. Nevertheless, the extreme importance in civilized life of this human capacity to transcend nature must be recognized.

This capacity for transcendence is the source of all the distinctively human problems that beset us. Paul Shepard traces the deepening role of transcendence through human history.[1] He chooses "madness" to describe the results of the progressive alienation from nature. This alienation has introduced harmful tensions into the human psyche as well as physical destruction of the natural world. Shepard views it as unalleviated evil. Most other people prize many of the results of human transcendence, but the extent and depth of the problems cannot be denied.

The postmodernism advocated in this book calls for the use of transcendence to recover a positive relation to the natural. In the final section of the preceding chapter, an example of such a use of transcendence was given: people should be free to relate sexually to members of the gender to which they are naturally inclined. But there are many other ways in which a recovery of attention to the body's needs and desires is possible and urgent. Instead of viewing the body as evil, because of its resistance to the soul's demands, we can appreciate its goodness and its wisdom, adapting our actions far more to bodily preferences. The body can become a partner with civilization in shaping the role of soul.

The implementation of such a vision has been expressed in some proposals for infant care. The West has emphasized the "disciplining" of the child, even the infant. For some time "experts" instructed parents to impose a regular feeding schedule on babies and to ignore the crying that resulted. We are learning now that it is far better to adapt adult behavior to the infant's needs. A similar point is made with respect to toilet training, the separation of the child from its mother, and so forth. Instead of forcing the young child to conform to socially determined patterns, society can conform to the child's nature. Many cultures have done this far better than the modern West.

III. Alienation from Nature in the Modern World

Alienation from nature did not begin with the modern world. It began with the domestication of animals. Domestication was a move from interacting with nature as it was to intentionally changing what we might call "the nature of nature." It altered the relation to nature, since the domesticated animals, no longer following their own natural patterns, had to be directed by human beings. They also had to be cared for and protected.

Selective breeding for the sake of improving the use of the domestic animals for human beings rendered them even less able to care for themselves. The relation of human beings to domesticated animals was no longer the natural one of predator to prey, but one of domination and responsibility. Humans were no longer simply one species among others. They were a species that intentionally altered the behavior and even the nature of other species.

Domestication of plants had analogous consequences. Gathering plants in their natural habitat left the responsibility for their reproduction and growth to natural processes. People found them and used them much as other animals did. But when they were domesticated, it was necessary to care for them. The required human actions were not always ones that came naturally to human beings. Sometimes they had to be forced to engage in the required labor. The domestication of plants required the domestication of human beings as well.

Alienation from nature went much further when cities were built and human dependence on natural processes became less evident to their inhabitants. Attention was redirected from plants, animals, rain, sunshine, and the fertility of the soil to interactions among human beings and the structure of society. The interactions and structures were less and less natural and more and more shaped by the imposition of distinctively human desires on natural behavior patterns. This process was greatly furthered by slavery, which was common to urban civilizations.

The self-understanding of people in these ancient civilizations, nevertheless, did not separate them altogether from nature. They understood themselves as parts of a grand scheme of things that included both nature and superhuman realities that were, in turn, related both to nature and to civilization. The meaning of their collective lives came from this location, which determined the proper forms of behavior and social organization.

A further step in the alienation from nature came with the rise of the great universalist religious traditions in the first millennium B.C.E. These traditions arose in the context of cosmic visions, but they focused their attention on human beings. They saw human beings as in trouble of one sort or another and sought ways of overcoming that problem. They appealed to people in terms of their personal capacities to act in the ways that were needed to this end. They thereby replaced the idea of a fundamentally given cosmos with attention to the capabilities of human beings to change themselves and/or their societies. The relation to the natural world played, in most of them, a secondary role.

These new teachings made people more aware of themselves as beings with an inner life that had intrinsic importance. Instead of simply accepting either the inner or the outer world as given, they experienced responsibility for how they constituted themselves and acted. The meaning of life became a conscious object of attention. They recognized that reflection of this kind was unique to human beings. Their sense of difference from, and superiority to, the natural world increased. In some instances, they understood themselves to belong properly to a spiritual world and experienced the natural world in their bodies and beyond as providing temptations to be overcome. The dominant forms of Greek thought established a radical dualism between the human soul and the body, and thus also between human beings and other animals.

For the biblical writers, the fundamental dualism was between God, the creator, and all the creatures. The human soul, insofar as it was distinguished from the body, was equally part of the creation. Hence the body-soul dualism did not develop far. Also a strict dualism separating human beings from other creatures was not possible. Nevertheless, the focus was on humanity and its relation to God, not on its relation to other creatures. This latter relation was dealt with only tangentially. Humans were to play a role in the world analogous to what they thought God played—a role of "dominion." Dominion could be interpreted either as domination or as responsible service, and elements of both can be found in the writings. When Christianity moved into the Greek world, it modified Greek dualism somewhat. But the sense of radical difference from other creatures was adopted along with a strong judgment of the superiority of the soul over the body.

Greek and biblical worldviews remained cosmic in scope despite their concentration on the human. Human beings continued to understand themselves in the wider context. Nature did not disappear from the horizons of their thought. Whether it was celebrated as God's creation or dreaded as a temptation, nature remained important.

The belief that nature was God's creation led some to observe it appreciatively in aesthetic detail. It led others to inquire into the order expressed in the natural world, as that which God had given it. The latter response proved the more influential result of the doctrine. Because God had created nature, and because God was a perfect Mind, it could be assumed that nature embodied an ideal order despite the superficial appearance of infinite variation. Christians began to seek the uniform laws that underlay natural diversity.

Alongside these pious Christian reasons for beginning the scientific enterprise, there were other, more anthropocentric motives. There was the desire to improve life. Western Europe, through the influence of the Benedictines, emphasized the development of technology as a suitable way of serving God.[2] Francis Bacon saw that if men wrested nature's secrets from her, they could compel her to serve them better.

For reasons of this sort, nature regained importance for Westerners. But it did so, not as the context of human life, but as the object of human investigation and control. The dualism of soul and body was transformed into the dualism of subject and object. The subject was understood as the human mind. The object was all that the human mind investigates. Because nature as object was conceived as passive, it could be exhaustively understood as matter.

Matter appears to human perception in variegated forms, but it was the purpose of distinctively modern science to display all these as results of processes that were themselves lacking in these qualities. Although the appearance may be aesthetically pleasing, the characteristics that make it so belong only to our subjectivity. The sensuously experienced beauty does not belong to the reality of things. Any beauty to be found in nature itself is a beauty that appeals only to the mind, the beauty of mathematical elegance. Nature itself is to be seen as matter, basically understood as mass, in motion. With such a world, the subject/mind has no kinship whatsoever.

A great deal of Western science and thought continues to reflect this early modern vision. Much of the university is based on it. Its adoption appears to be hardheaded or tough-minded. Nevertheless, its problematic character, which could never be completely hidden, has become increasingly apparent with the passage of time.

From the first, one problem with dualism was the relation of the human mind to the human body. People experience mind and body as remarkably coordinated. According to the theory, however, they cannot naturally have anything to do with each other. The most "tough-minded" approach is to deny that mind exists at all, except, perhaps, as an epiphenomenon of brain activity. Everything, including human experience, is to be explained by matter in motion. But even the announcement of this solution leaves us with the subjects who are announcing a relation among objects of their thought. For practical purposes the dualism of mind and matter, subject and object, remains.

The other problem soon raised by philosophers is that there appears to be no way that the subjects can have access to the matter of which they speak. The content of human experience, in the dominant model, is exhausted by the variegated patterns of sense data that the motion of this matter is said to cause in us. How can we posit the objective reality of that of which we have no experience at all? How can we describe its characteristics as modern physical science claims to do?

While much of science went on its way with the early modern paradigm, the philosophical tradition went in another direction. In its dominant form it was shaped by philosophers such as Berkeley, Hume, Kant, and Hegel, who gave up the notion of matter altogether. Thereby the natural world lost all independent existence. It was nothing more than the sensory content of human experience.

In its unvarnished form, this is probably a doctrine no one really believes, but especially through its formulation by Kant it has had a profound effect. Kant began with the well-established dualism of modern thought. Everything must belong either to objects or to the subject. Insisting that we can perceive only through the senses, while recognizing that sense experience gives us nothing but qualities, he saw that we had no access to an object. He also saw that these sense qualities are always ordered in terms of categories such as time and space. If time and space are not features of an objective reality that imposes itself on the subject, then they must be contributed by the subject. Kant reasoned, in this way, that what we know as the natural world is almost entirely constructed by the human mind.

Kant's interpretation of this constructive work of mind was that it was timeless, characterizing human mind as such at all times and places. But Hegel historicized it. Mind has created the world in changing ways, which the thinker can trace. The deepest level of history is the developing ways in which mind constructs reality.

Today few accept the details of Kant's or Hegel's theories. But the idea of the constructive activity of the human mind has played a large role in subsequent history. Currently it takes the form of unmasking the social construction of social reality that is so often misunderstood as an objectively given, and therefore unchangeable, situation. It has contributed significantly to the development of postmodernism.

With respect to nature, however, this tradition tends to carry alienation to its furthest point. Nature not only has no character of its own, according to this type of postmodernism, it performs no function. It is what it is known to be, and how it is known is a function of how humans construct it. It is one social construction among others, to be studied as such.

Striking, from the perspective of the twentieth century, is the lack of interest among early modern thinkers in relations among minds. They were preoccupied with the scientific knowledge of nature and how such knowledge was possible. They did not discuss the social character of the development of science or how one mind acted on, or in, another. They seemed to assume that they, like the units of the material world, existed atomistically.

Even when they turned their attention to society, the early modern thinkers retained this atomistic view. They reacted against the organic models of the Middle Ages and chose individualistic ones instead. Just as subjects and objects were external to one another, so also were objects to other objects and subjects to other subjects. There was no idea of communal relations.

In detail, the picture of mental subjects and material objects, whether actual or constructed, has taken many forms. Philosophers endlessly debate it. It has deeply influenced the course of modern theology. But its most important role in shaping our situation today has been through economic and political theory. The next two sections of this chapter will sketch the assumptions of contemporary economic theory as they were shaped in the modern context and critique its claims. Chapter Six will then treat its effect on political thought and develop the missing idea of community more fully.

IV. Modern Economic Thought

In early modern thought the bits of matter that move about are unrelated to one another except in changing relative location. They may bump into one another and affect patterns of motion. But what they are in themselves is in no way affected. With respect to minds, this is not as explicit, but individual minds, as well, are presented as fully external to one another. Whatever effects minds have on one another, they cannot change the underlying subject, self, or "I."

The understanding of human beings for economic purposes derives from the atomic character of the units of reality as conceived by modernity. This time the "atoms" are the agents of economic activity. Although these units are sometimes recognized to be households, they are more commonly treated as individuals. The difference plays little role in the theoretical development. Hence the focus here can be on "economic man" (the male of the species, indeed, being largely in view), often called *Homo economicus*.

Economic man is abstracted from all relationships to other people or to the natural world. He is like a material atom in that he is unaffected by his environment. Movement from one environment to another does not change him inwardly. As such, therefore, this movement involves neither gain nor loss.

Economic man desires to possess as much as possible and to work as little as possible. Accordingly, he sells his labor and his goods for as much as possible and purchases goods and services as cheaply as possible. This behavior is both natural and rational for him. If he is a producer, he produces those goods that bring the highest profit. If it is his labor that he sells, he acquires those skills that command the highest wages, if the cost of doing so does not exceed the gain. Accordingly, his behavior is sensitive to market demand.

Economists show that when individuals behave in these "rational" ways, workers become more productive. Producers organize their workers so that they can produce more per hour of work. They purchase machinery that also improves the productivity of labor. This increased production per hour of work reduces costs per item. Since other producers are in competition to sell, all are pressed to economize and reduce prices. Workers are able to buy more goods. Profits to manufacturers are invested in new productive enterprises. Goods and services available per person increase. In short, the standard of living rises.

There are two corollaries of these principles. The first corollary is that governmental interference in the market inhibits this growth by distorting investment. This fact does not mean that the government has no function at all in relation to markets. It should supply those elements of needed infrastructure that are not profitable for private enterprise to build. This infrastructure usually includes a system of highways, for example. The government should also ensure public order by providing a police force and a court system to adjudicate disputes. It should prevent deception in sales and keep dangerous poisons off the market. It should provide some limits to the danger and unhealthfulness of the workplace and to the involvement of children. It should restrict the pollution of the environment caused by business activities. It should educate the future workforce. It should make some provision for those unable to participate in the market. And it should prevent monopoly control of the production of needed goods.

The second corollary of these principles is that the larger the size of the market the better the process can work. The larger market allows greater specialization, which contributes to efficiency. Raw materials and labor can be obtained more cheaply. Political boundaries, accordingly, should restrict the movement of capital and goods as little as possible. The ideal is a single global market.

There is some tension between these two corollaries. Whereas the first conceives of a national market supported and checked by a national government, the second corollary points to the advantages of a global market. In a national market, the government not only serves the market but also controls it for purposes that are its own. In a global market, the government may support economic activity, but it loses control. If it imposes on a producer conditions that add to the cost of production, the producer cannot compete with those who produce in countries that do not have these rules. Producers of carpets in a country that forbids child labor, for example, have higher costs than those who are allowed to employ children at very low wages. In a global market, a government that imposes restrictions drives its producers away.

Viewing individuals as examples of *Homo economicus* does not involve the claim that people are nothing more than that. Certainly the early economists were quite aware of the abstraction involved in attending only to economic behavior. But if, in fact, people are more than what is captured in this image, then two further questions arise. First, does this *more* affect economic behavior? Second, does recognition of this more affect judgments as to the place of economic activity within the whole of society?

The answer to the first question is Yes. Real people do have other motives in their economic activities. Many give money generously to causes in which they believe. Many choose jobs that are interesting and rewarding, where morale is high, and where there are good relations among employees, over those that pay better. Many decide where to work according to family considerations, such as where they want their children to grow up. Some purchases are made in order to support particular producers. Some boycotts are for the purpose of encouraging unionization.

In the first decades after World War II, those engaged in promoting development complained of the cultural difficulties they faced in persuading Third World people to subordinate their communal life and their traditional values to earning money on an individualistic basis. There was much talk of the need for modernization or rationalization of these societies so that people would behave more like *Homo economicus*.

Nevertheless, more impressive than these exceptions is the success of many predictions based on the model. Overall the model proves useful, especially in countries that have long been influenced by the Enlightenment and modern thought. Over the years, our behavior has become very like that expected of *Homo economicus*. This is now increasingly true in the Third World as well, as modern development breaks down the communities in which traditional values were nurtured.

The second question has to do with the relation of economic theory and prediction to public policy. Few deny that human beings are *Homo politicus, Homo ludens,* and even *Homo religiosus,* as well as *Homo economicus*. Public policy should, presumably, take the multidimensionality of people fully into account. It should seek the good of the whole person, and the common good of all.

Prior to World War II, it can be argued, *Homo politicus* was primary. Education in the United States defined itself primarily in terms of the cultivation of citizens and of social leaders. Nationalism was the primary force in shaping personal loyalties and commitments. Adam Smith presupposed the power of nationalism when he spoke in the title of his book of "the wealth of nations." In the nineteenth century it was assumed that the economic order should subserve, and be regulated by, the political order. Governments were expected to regulate international trade for the benefit of their nations. Much of government activity was for the sake of the national economy, but this activity was guided by the conviction that a strong economy is good for the nation.

Since World War II, the situation has changed. The primary function of the local political order is now to serve the global economy. The arrival of the global market is the triumph of the second of the two corollaries previously identified. The welfare state is under pressure because it is in tension with "competitiveness" in the global economy.

Since economic man is understood to be independent of community, it is not surprising that economic theory supports policies that are directly destructive of community. In the United States, the effects of these policies can be readily illustrated by two phenomena. Rural America, with its thousands of small towns, was once the backbone of the nation. But the application of industrial principles to agriculture, combined with the enlargement of markets, has led to the depopulation of the countryside and the destruction of most of the small towns.

The closing or moving of factories whenever it is profitable is systematically affirmed as good in dominant economic thinking. It is viewed as irrational to maintain a factory when the capital invested could be more profitably used elsewhere. According to the theory, the more profitable use is better for society as a whole. Society as a whole is understood to be the sum total of individuals making it up, and their good is measured by their purchasing power. The theory is that workers will move to locations where more profitable investments provide new jobs. Given the standard model of *Homo economicus*, there is no problem in this, since individuals are unaffected inwardly by their context.

The destruction of established community in developing countries is more dramatic and devastating. Modernizing agricultural production entails displacing millions from their small plots and driving them into urban areas poorly equipped to receive them. Their per capita income may benefit from the move, but usually their quality of life does not. Much that previously gave meaning to their lives is certainly lost.

Another quality contributing to community is the ability to make the decisions most important to one's life. The enlargement of markets normally reduces this possibility at the local level. The globalization of the market means that persons in distant places, who have no interest in the consequences for local communities, make many of the most important decisions.

A second feature of the modern economic model is equally reflective of modern thought. The natural world is viewed simply as matter, that is, as object for human use. The value of any part of this world is the price that some human being will pay for it. Human enjoyment is intrinsically valuable, and the whole system is set up to support and increase that enjoyment. Everything else is only of instrumental value to that end.

There is a powerful tendency here to encourage the transformation of natural resources into artificial goods. Of course, economists know that people also value scenery and the availability of game for hunting.

Hence they can put some kind of price on these things. But the assumptions written into modern economics preclude the assignment of intrinsic value to other species or to biosystems.

Nature entered economic thought only in the form of "land." In the beginning of modern economic theory, land was taken somewhat seriously because it was recognized as the basis of agriculture. It was identified, along with labor and capital, as a factor of production. As time passed, however, land became simply one form of capital, or a commodity to be bought and sold like any other. Little attention has been paid to the distinctive characteristics of nature in relation to artificial capital.

Economists are not much concerned about shortages of natural resources. Since such resources are mere matter, they substitute readily for one another. The particular form in which they are found is of little importance. If one resource grows scarce, its price rises. Either users find a cheaper substitute or they develop technology that enables them to use lower grades of the resource. Economists can point to many occasions on which shortages have been solved by technology. Since shortages are solved in this way by normal market processes, no special attention is given to them.

Students of the physical world in its variety and complexity point out that shortages pose problems of a sort that economists continue to ignore. One of these is the shortage of arable land. Current economic practices are in fact eroding and exhausting large tracts of land without protest from economists, who assume that the investment of capital will provide the basis for producing the requisite products. But these generalizations ignore the problems of desertification, salinization, erosion, the exhaustion of aquifers, and loss of land to expanding cities. Economists are likely to point to the Green Revolution to celebrate the gains that can be made by the application of technology to agriculture. But in doing so they often ignore its downside: the increased dependence on oil, the loss of genetic diversity, the increasing need for chemical fertilizers and insecticides, the deteriorating food value of the products, and growing vulnerability to pests.

Economists similarly assume that the availability of seafoods can be increased by the investment of capital. Thus far these investments have been disastrous. More intensive fishing on a larger scale has exhausted fisheries, some of which may never recover. Replacing mango groves with shrimp farms threatens the breeding grounds of fish. The short-term increases in production encouraged by modern economic thinking threaten the future of the oceans as a source of food for human beings. In the real world, the notion of sustainable use is important. The idea is absent from modern economic theory.

With regard to pollution, economists are more open in principle. They have come to recognize that market transactions beneficial to both seller and buyer may impose costs on society. For example, the fumes from the use of gasoline cause pollution. Ideally, they say, the buyer should pay to society in taxes the social cost of such pollution. This cost will encourage more efficient use of gasoline and provide funds for responding to problems of pollution.

Unfortunately, this excellent proposal follows from peripheral aspects of economic theory that have thus far generated little energy from economists. The commitment to increasing market activity is far more central than the commitment to dealing with pollution. When the U.S. government appointed a commission under the chairmanship of a leading economist to consider responses to global warming, the report asserted that we should not allow the prospects of such warming to deter us from our growth-oriented policies. With sufficient capital, generated by these policies, we can respond to problems as they arise. In the words of Jerry Taylor, director of natural resource studies at the Cato Institute: "The best 'insurance policy' we can buy is one that increases the amount of wealth at society's disposal to handle whatever problems might occur in the decades to come."[3]

The understanding of human beings according to the individualist model and of nature as matter for human use has had enormous consequences. Since community has no value in economic thinking, it is not surprising that traditional communities everywhere have been undercut and that the life of new communities is fragile and temporary. Because the natural world has no value in itself and exists only to be exploited by human beings, it is not surprising that natural systems are being degraded everywhere and that efforts to respond to glaring environmental problems are subordinated to growth-oriented programs.

The understanding of economic man as universally normative has increasingly reshaped humanity in its image. Cultural diversity depended on traditional communities that have been everywhere replaced by modern cities replete with slums. Tourists travel around the world, staying in hotels that are indistinguishable from one another. Similar factories offer similar conditions of work in every country that is "fortunate" enough to be able to attract them. The same franchises are found in the cities on every continent and the same architecture is employed in their commercial buildings. Cultural diversity is replaced by modernist homogeneity.[4]

Much the same is true of the natural world. As the global economy expands, standard types of agribusiness replace the great variety of traditional agricultures. Family farming gives way to monocultural plantations. The insatiable desire for lumber destroys the forests that were once home to millions of species of living things. Despite all efforts, biodiversity diminishes rapidly.

V. Promise and Failure of Growth-Oriented Policies

The loss of cultural and biological diversity along with the loss of community and the richness of the natural environment are widely recognized, but these and other costs are accepted on the grounds that the primary concern must be economic growth.[5] It is widely assumed that such growth benefits people greatly and that, in a world in which there are still so many urgent economic needs, the goal of growth must be pursued. This section examines the claims for the value of economic growth that have been used to justify current policies.

Thinking people have recognized that the world faces multiple crises. One reason that so many have accepted the goal of growth as primary is that its supporters have argued that growth can solve a wide range of otherwise intractable problems. Here we will consider six.

First, it was argued that economic growth would solve the problem of excessive population growth. This expectation was based on the European experience in which, when industrialization reached a certain level, population leveled off. It was assumed that economic growth in Third World countries would have the same effect.

This argument is still heard occasionally, but it is not convincing to many. Even after fifty years of growth, the level of per capita income thought to be required for the population transition to occur is not being approached in most "developing" countries. Even where overall economic growth is considerable, it is usually concentrated in the hands of a few. Their wealth has no effect on the reproductive habits of the vast majority.

It is now widely recognized that one major obstacle to increasing per capita income is the population growth that has accompanied development. It is far easier to increase per capita income in a nation whose population growth has been slowed by other means! Instead of touting economic growth as the solution of the population problem, population programs are now being instituted partly to make economic improvement possible.

Second, a similar argument was made with regard to environmental problems. Sufficient economic growth, it was claimed, would solve environmental problems. This claim was also based on the behavior of affluent people, who give more attention to solving environmental problems than do the poor. When their immediate basic needs are met, people are more able to consider goods that are important for the longer term.

The problem with this argument is twofold. First, as above, the fruits of development are concentrated in relatively few hands. The masses of the people are struggling as hard or harder than ever to survive. There is, therefore, little if any improvement in the behavior of the majority toward the environment.

The other reason economic growth does not help the environment is that the policies directed primarily by the desire to increase production are typically *destructive* of the environment. Hence, instead of solving environmental problems, working for growth greatly increases them. Many now realize that attention must be given to the environment directly, that we cannot wait for economic growth to solve such problems as the eradication of species, soil erosion, the loss of forest cover, global warming, the exhaustion of nonrenewable resources, and pollution. Indeed, the deterioration of the environment is making growth more difficult.

The third claim made for the gains that would follow from economic growth was that it brings political harmony, human rights, and democracy. This argument has two parts. First, it is thought that the experience of freedom in economic activity leads people to demand freedom also in the political arena. It is argued, second, that rising prosperity brings satisfaction to all, so that class struggle diminishes.

History has borne out these claims only to a very limited degree. It is true that many countries with market economies have adopted the institutional forms of democracy and have publicly committed themselves to observe human rights. There may be some real gain here. But many of these same countries, such as Mexico today, have also waged low-intensity warfare against their own poor. This use of force against their own people reveals the growing desperation of the poor after fifty years of national economic growth and entails horrendous violations of human rights.

Furthermore, democratic governments in most countries today have little power over the issues of greatest concern to their citizens. They must conform to the dictates of the Bretton Woods institutions and act as the international financial markets require. Generally, as Marx noted, the economic elite within each country dominates it politically. Hence most developing countries are in fact more oligarchic than truly democratic.

That all benefit from economic growth is still further from the truth. It is now acknowledged that economic growth increases disparities of income both between nations and within nations. Some still argue that even though they benefit much less, the poor as a whole still benefit. Others argue that in absolute as well as relative terms, the condition of the poor has been worsened by global development. In either case, the growing disparity between rich and poor and the growing despair of the poor are a far cry from the claim that growth enables people to accept class differences.

A fourth expectation encouraged by the supporters of the priority of economic growth was that, when there is more wealth, people become freer to achieve goals other than wealth. Health, education, and culture can all improve. Hence, it is better to give priority to growth by emphasizing investment in productive facilities rather than spending much money now on health, education, or culture.

This proposal has, however, proven unwise. The effective pursuit of economic growth requires a healthy, educated populace. For reasons similar to those given previously, the vast majority of the people of Third World countries have still no prospect of attaining the level of income that would allow them independently to gain the health, education, and culture they might desire. Meanwhile, for the sake of supporting growth-oriented policies public spending in these areas has been cut.

The fifth claim for economic growth is that it is the only way to give employment to the currently unemployed and underemployed. The theory is that a growing economy requires more workers in order to produce the needed goods. Since unemployment worldwide is massive, a great deal of growth is needed.

The fact, however, is that in many countries development has led to increased unemployment. A central feature of modern development policy is to use labor more productively, that is, to produce more goods with fewer workers. For example, development usually replaces subsistence farming with agribusiness. Millions of people must leave the land where they have eked out a living and migrate to the slums surrounding large cities. Most of them are unemployed or underemployed. Similarly, huge retail stores such as a Wal-Mart can put hundreds of small retailers out of business while employing only a fraction of that number as clerks. The theory is that these changes will generate or attract new capital that will employ more people. But the fact is that new jobs lag behind the losses.

The sixth argument for giving priority to growth typically focuses on the need for growth to overcome the vast poverty that still afflicts the world. This is the argument most often heard today. It points to the issue that, to a considerable degree, underlies the first four claims for growth previously criticized. The reason that the population transition is not occurring, that the majority continue to give priority to immediate issues of survival rather than to long-term environmental considerations, that there are revolts of indigenous peoples and peasants against their governments, and that vast numbers of people are not able to use their own resources to take care of their health and education, is, in part, that they have not benefited from the vaunted economic growth of the past half century.

If policies directed toward growth would, in fact, overcome poverty, then it might be that they would contribute to the other goals as well. But since they have done little in this regard over a fifty-year period, it seems unlikely that a continuation of these policies will have this result. Thus far growth-oriented policies have concentrated wealth in the hands of the few and have increased the gap between rich and poor both in individual nations and among nations.

This is not an accident. The market, when left to itself, tends to concentrate wealth. This is not hard to understand. The strength of players in the market is not measured by their numbers but by their wealth. Those with much to invest will gain at least proportionately to that investment. Even if there were no distorting factors further favoring the rich, and if all gained proportionately, the absolute gap between rich and poor would grow. One who begins with $1000 and doubles these assets will have $2000. One who begins with one billion dollars and doubles them will have two billion.

But the problem with the market is much worse. Governments have long recognized that great concentrations of wealth work against the market's proper functioning. They enable their possessors to buy out or bankrupt their competitors and to move toward practical monopolies. Most countries have had laws to counteract this advantage of the rich in the market, but the growth-oriented climate has weakened their enforcement. Indeed, the growing power of corporations enables them to shape laws for their own interests rather than for the good functioning of the market.[6]

Wealth gives many additional advantages in the market. The rich can hire lawyers to win cases in the courts. They can influence public opinion through their control of the media. They can exercise disproportionate influence on governmental actions. The global evidence is overwhelming that both through standard market practices and governmental support, wealth is being concentrated in fewer and fewer hands. That this is one reason the poor do not benefit from growth goes without saying.

To solve the problem of too rapid population growth, we need programs geared to just that problem. To solve the problem of the environment, we need regulations that are directed to that end. To bring about better respect for human rights and more participation in government on the part of all, we need to work specifically for those goals. And to improve health, education, and culture, we need to devote ourselves directly to those purposes. To provide useful employment for all who want work requires that we give focused attention to that issue in our policies. To improve the lot of the poor requires the development of an economic system that has just that effect. Policies geared to economic growth do not help.

VI. A Postmodern Economic Theory

The economic assumptions that guide global activity today are rooted in the dominant model of modernity. Of greatest importance are the individualistic view of human beings and the dualism of humanity and nature, with its resultant anthropocentrism. The modern economic model abstracts radically from human community and the interconnectedness of human life with other creatures.

Postmodernism sees matters quite differently. People are constituted by their internal relations to their bodies, to the wider world of nature, and especially to other people. Apart from these relations, they do not exist at all. They are formed and informed in human communities. It is in and through communities that they achieve true individuality and personhood. The model that describes this best is that of persons-in-community. In attenuated form, the community in question includes the natural environment.

All models abstract from the full concreteness of actuality, but this one abstracts much less radically than the current idea of economic man as a self-contained individual. It allows us to include much of what has been learned using the individualistic model. For example, adopting the model of person-in-community in no way denies that the persons who live in community and are deeply affected thereby also function to a considerable extent, especially in their business dealings, as the competitive individuals depicted in the standard modern model. The difference is that the question of *how* individualistic and *how* communal people are becomes an empirical one to be studied in particular cases and in different cultures.

Other important questions can be asked. Is it desirable that society organize itself, as at present, so as to push people to become more individualistic? Granting that individualistic behavior may do more for the increase of goods and services, are there other values lost in this process that are more important than increased production?

The issue is not, then, whether growth as such is desirable or harmful. There can be considerable growth that is not destructive of community or the environment. The issue is whether increasing the size of the economy, in the sense of market activity, is inherently good. The postmodern answer to that question is negative. We should establish policies and programs to solve our real problems. The size of the market is not one of them.

Of these real problems the most important is the destruction of community itself. For the modern economic model, human beings are abstractable from their relationships to other people as well as to the natural environment. These relationships are external and replaceable. Nothing is lost when established communities are destroyed and nature is degraded, since communities are not distinguished from multiplicities of individuals and nature can be improved or replaced by capital.

For the postmodern model, people are constituted by their participation in relationships with others just as much as communities are constituted by the interactions of these people. Their well-being individually and communally depends on a healthy and beautiful natural context. From this perspective, the quality of individual lives is deeply affected by the quality of the community and of the natural environment in which they occur.[7] Certainly it is important that people, individually, have sufficient goods and services. Because many people now lack sufficiency, what can be learned from modernist economists about how to increase production is important. But what is learned must be used for the purpose of meeting the needs of those whose needs are not now met, not to advance growth in general. And the increase should be achieved without weakening human relationships and community or continuing the degradation of the natural environment.

Because individuals are most fundamentally persons-in-community, they gain when the condition of the community improves. This improvement benefits the relationships of which they are constituted even if it does not increase the goods and services they personally receive. Policies geared to improving the general well-being of the community, accordingly, deserve primary support.

In development policies, the difference is quite clear and simple. In India, for example, Gandhi wanted to improve village life by introducing simple technologies that could increase the earning power of the villagers without disrupting community or the relation of the people to the land. The sewing machine was the symbol of this type of development. Nehru was a Western thinker who wanted to industrialize. He brought in a large steel mill. Nehru's type of development triumphed, and village life did not improve. Postmodern theory supports Gandhian development.

From the postmodernist point of view, nature in its full diversity, remarkable capabilities, and severe limitations must be taken very seriously. If there is to be a sustainable future, the complexity and interdependence of natural processes must be considered in ways that are discouraged by the modern economic model. The human economy is a subordinate element in the natural economy rather than an autonomous system that can exploit the natural one indefinitely.[8] We must find ways of meeting the real human needs of all and attaining a satisfying life that are far less consumptive than the lifestyles of the affluent today.

Chapter Six

Governance

I. Introduction

The preceding chapters have emphasized the reality and value of diversity. They have stressed the importance of allowing diverse groups and communities to retain their identities and to respond to new situations out of those identities. The ideal for the future is a world that contains a great variety of mutually enriching religious traditions, cultures, biological species, and landscapes. It will have a place for diverse patterns of gender roles and sexual relationships.

In fact, unfortunately, the world is now moving toward greater homogeneity. The economic steamroller is flattening everything. Diversity is tolerated only when it is superficial and does not interfere with the deeper sameness. Many current affirmations of cultural distinctiveness appear to be little more than fruitless reactions to this basic homogenizing trend. Only in the area of class are differences becoming more marked, and these are not the sort of differences favored by postmodernists.

The subservience of most of our institutions, including governments, to economic actors requires explanation. Partly it is the result of the power of those actors to influence governments in corrupt ways. But it has also been the persuasiveness of the ideology that has supported this shift of power.

According to this ideology, Chapter Five pointed out, economic growth would solve a whole gamut of the major problems with which humanity is confronted, including political ones. This conviction persuaded conscientious statesmen to adopt the policies needed for such growth, including freeing transnational corporations from the control of national governments. However, this promise has not been fulfilled, and, on many points, this failure is now, at least partly, recognized. The remaining argument, that economic growth is required to solve the problems of unemployment and poverty, was also challenged in Chapter Five on the basis of the record as well as by analysis of how what is generally called "growth" works.

Economic growth has failed to fulfill the promises made by modern economists to justify the hegemony of the economic order over the political one. This judgment is informed by the postmodern appraisal of the importance of community. This appraisal is rooted in a model of the human being quite different from the ideas underlying modern economic theory. The constructive postmodern model agrees with most earlier theories in calling for ordering society to multiple values rather than exclusively to economic growth. In our new situation, it requires that the community reorganize itself so as to subordinate the economy to its shared purposes rather than simply to serve the needs of the economy. In short, it calls for the restoration of the primacy of the political over the economic.

One obstacle to getting a hearing for this proposal is the dismal record of the dominance of the political order in the past. From the middle of the seventeenth century to the middle of the twentieth, such dominance existed, and in the twentieth century the resulting nationalism led to two world wars and the Holocaust. The untamed nationalism in Eastern Europe, especially in the former Yugoslavia, shows its continuing destructive power.

The turn from the primacy of nations to joint efforts at economic improvement has brought peace between France and Germany, the two nations whose historic rivalry repeatedly plunged the world into war. International war among the major industrial nations now seems unlikely. If the call for the restoration of the primacy of the political over the economic order required a return to an extreme nationalism of the sort that has been, and continues to be, so destructive, it could not be supported.

The primacy of the political over the economic does not, however, entail this kind of nationalism. The postmodern model of persons-in-community in no way commits us to national sovereignty as that has been understood in the past. It could point forward to a world in which both local and global political bodies exercise power that is not compatible with traditional ideas of national sovereignty. To explore this possibility requires a more careful account of what is meant by "community."

Community is a notion that is widely used with more or less common meaning. There is sufficient vagueness and diversity in its use, however, that a proposal systematically to reconceive the political order in terms of community requires a careful statement of how it is here understood. Its specific meaning is informed by the postmodern ontology that underlies this book.

The affirmation of community in this book is based on the doctrine of the primacy of internal relations. Although there have been communitarian thinkers in the Enlightenment tradition, the most influential forms of modern thought have excluded, or at least ignored, this idea. Modernity has developed two major ways of understanding human beings for political purposes, both based on the understanding that relations are external. These are notions of the collective and of the individual.

If in fact people are internally related to one another and to other creatures as well, then political theory based on ignoring these relations distorts historical reality and leads to expectations that are not fulfilled. Chapter Four showed how this has happened in the area of economics. Sections II and III of this chapter do so more briefly with respect to the political order. Section IV discusses the idea of community more fully. Section V derives norms for community and considers the possibility of organizing political life on a bottom-up basis. Section VI considers the most common abuses of political life and how they may be countered in the context of this model. Section VII concludes the chapter with a discussion of how the economic order can be brought back under political control.

II. Collectivism and Community

In many traditional societies, human beings were defined chiefly by their social roles. These roles located them in classes. These classes functioned primarily collectively and were treated in that way. One member of a class was largely substitutable for another. People were expected to know and accept their place in the inevitable ordering of things.

Christian thought cut against this viewing of individuals in such collective ways. In theory, it subordinated one's social role to one's standing before God. This standing was highly individual. In Medieval society, nevertheless, the definition of individuals by their social role and collective treatment of classes remained prominent.

The Enlightenment accentuated the individualistic elements of Christianity. Although class continued to play a large role in society, the philosophies and theologies of the Enlightenment largely ignored it. They focused instead on autonomous and separate individual human beings. Chapter Five showed how that emphasis worked out in the dominant economic theory.

Karl Marx found that this individualism was in fact the ideology of the bourgeois class. He showed that it obscured the reality of the new class structure produced by the industrial revolution. Capitalists and workers, the bourgeoisie and the proletariat, now replaced lords and peasants. To understand present reality, it was necessary to see these classes as collectives in inevitable conflict. They could be defined by their relation to the means of production, and the whole history of civilization could be understood in terms of class struggle related to changing systems of production.

There can be no question of the illuminating power of Marxist class analysis. Much can be understood in these terms that is missed in traditional historical study and standard treatments of the current situation. Nevertheless, Marx's views—that class analysis is primary and that behavior of individuals can be deduced from it—proved erroneous. Members of the proletariat were more complex than this analysis in terms of collectivity allowed.

Already in 1848 Marx and Engels had asserted that "national differences and antagonisms between people, are daily more and more vanishing, owing to the development of the bourgeoisie, to freedom of commerce, to the world market, to uniformity in the mode of production and in the conditions of life corresponding thereto."[1] If this were true, then one would expect that by 1914 national loyalty would be subordinate to class loyalty. Many Marxists did think this way.

But they were proved wrong. The French proletariat fought the German proletariat under the leadership of the French bourgeoisie. In the great majority of cases, their bond as French outweighed their bond as workers.

Viewing people as persons-in-community, internally related to one another, provides a better way of understanding what actually happened. French workers were strongly affected by their internal relations with other workers and appreciated their shared interests. These relations participated in making them what they were, but they were relations primarily with other workers with whom they were acquainted. Community with workers whom they did not know, workers in other countries, was highly attenuated.

Furthermore, these same persons were internally related to other French citizens many of whom were not workers. Here, too, they appreciated their shared interests. They were likely to be participants in other communities as well, such as a family, a village, and a church.

Finally, French citizens were heirs to French history. They, like all of us, were constituted by their history. Our internal relations are, technically, entirely to the past. Some of this past is the immediate past, but partly through that, and partly directly, we have internal relations to the more distant past as well. The past of the workers was much the same as that of other Frenchmen. The community to which they belonged extended through time.

When called upon to act for the sake of one or another of these communities, the inclination was to do so. Their own being was bound up with all the communities in which they participated. Since there were conflicts among these loyalties, there was a test of their relative strength. It turned out, not surprisingly, that the national community, continuous with family and village, was far more constitutive of their being than their shared interests with proletarians of other countries.

Marx was, obviously, not wholly ignorant of the power of nationalism. But, like all thinkers, he was deeply affected by the categories he employed. Viewing workers collectively, he could not take account of other groupings in which they participated. No doubt he was aware of them, but he could not allow them to play a role in his analysis. Believing that the relation to the means of production determines behavior, Marx thought that the proletariat could be described collectively without regard to other individual involvements. Clearly he was wrong.

The collectivist bent of Marxist analysis had disastrous effects in the Soviet Union. Perhaps the greatest error of that nation was the decision to eliminate the kulaks, the most successful peasants. As a class they constituted an obstacle to the collectivization of agriculture, an ideal more important to the Soviet leaders than the lives and skills of millions of Soviet people. If one thinks collectively of classes, then one can view people simply as members of classes. One can then evaluate the classes collectively in relation to the goals of society and eliminate those that do not, as classes, fit in. Apart from the horror of the suffering inflicted on millions of innocent people, one may judge that Soviet agriculture never recovered from the extermination of its best farmers.

In any case, collectivization rarely works well because it underestimates individuality. It subordinates the individual to the collective in such a way as to discourage personal initiative. Individuals are treated as if they were more or less substitutable for one another, with individual differences too little recognized. Functioning collectively becomes more important than achieving goals; so individuals avoid rocking the boat by proposing more effective ways of action. They are rewarded more for conformity than for creativity.

A persons-in-community model leads to a different arrangement. It emphasizes doing together what can best be done together and separately what can best be done separately. Personal ambition is supported as long as it is not at the expense of other members of the community. Diversity of roles according to diversity of abilities is affirmed. Patterns of cooperation are encouraged as these prove to be in the best interest of those involved. The community is responsible to see that all its members are cared for, but those who do the best work legitimately profit from their labors. As collectives failed and more land was given over for private cultivation, Soviet agriculture began to develop in the direction I have sketched. But the development was inhibited by the collectivist ideal.

III. Individualism and Community

In comparison with collectivism, the postmodern model proposed here is markedly individualistic. The underlying assumption is that, however much persons are formed by their internal relations to others, they make their own decisions moment by moment. These decisions are free in the sense that they are not predetermined by antecedent conditions. They are acts of self-determination. This freedom is precious. Society should structure itself so as to expand its scope.

Accordingly, individual differences, individual freedom, and individual initiative are to be emphasized and encouraged. All intrinsic value is to be found in individual experience, so that ultimately the values pursued are individual. The group must be judged finally according to how well it serves the individuals who make it up. Much about the individualistic model of the Enlightenment and the political conclusions drawn from it, therefore, should be affirmed.

Paul Tillich pointed out that individualization and participation belong together. Only a centered self can truly participate in the larger world. Only through such participation can one become a centered self. The separation of individualization and participation is a mark of estrangement.[2] This means that true individuality and true community are a polarity rather than a duality, that is, they stand in a relation of mutual support rather than in dualistic tension.

Despite the support of individuality, therefore, the model of persons-in-community developed here is quite different from the standard individualistic one, and leads to quite different results in theory and practice. The *Homo politicus* of the Enlightenment is much like *Homo economicus*. It is a self-contained individual related to others only externally. The model generates its own myth of the origin, and, thus, of the legitimacy, of the state. This myth is quite unsatisfactory.

In this myth, human beings initially exist in nuclear family units, each family seeking its own well-being at the expense of its neighbors. This situation, it was supposed, made the life of all unpleasant and insecure. Reasoning that everyone would be better off, all of them surrendered some of their freedom to a government that would ensure the security of each against all the others. They entered into a "social contract" to this effect. The primary function of the state, therefore, is to maintain law and order. As long as it does so, according to Thomas Hobbes, it rightfully demands total obedience.

However, in its most influential version, that of John Locke, the contract is understood to withhold considerable rights from the state. Since people enter it voluntarily, they are understood, in the words of the Declaration of Independence, not to give the state the right to take away, without due process, their lives, their liberty, or their right to pursue their own happiness.

Locke emphasized that the state also violates the contract if it takes the property of its citizens. Their agreement was to give it the power to protect their individual possession of that property. On this reading, a state that denies its citizens any of these basic rights has become tyrannical, thereby losing its legitimacy.

This myth fails to explain the actual sentiments, loyalties, and commitments of citizens. The behavior of people in time of war, used previously to show the inadequacy of collectivist theory, can be used here as well to indicate the failure of social contract theory to account for the facts of history. People who really understood the nation to be the result of a contract entered into for purely selfish reasons would be unlikely to volunteer to serve the nation at enormous personal sacrifice and risk.

If the only purpose for agreeing to obey is the personal security gained, then to sacrifice that security out of devotion to the nation makes no sense. Such sacrifice, however, has been a common phenomenon in our actual history. The patriotic spirit is far better understood when we recognize that we are largely constituted by our internal relations with other citizens of the nation, past and present, that much of our personal identity is bound up with our participation in this community, and that the well-being of the nation is our shared well-being.

The myth of a social contract has also contributed to misleading and destructive notions of sovereignty. According to the myth, there is a single contract among individuals granting sovereignty to a single government. If authority is given to any other level of political organization, this authority must be derived from the single sovereign. It is assumed that sovereignty resides in the national state. Thus, although legitimacy rests on the consent of the people, they grant it to a single authority. From this contract is derived national sovereignty, which in turn encourages the hypernationalism from which the world has suffered so acutely.

Although the myth of the social contract did not, by itself, create the sovereign national state, it encouraged its development. This type of political system had been only one of the actually existing patterns of political organization in the eighteenth century, and the idea of national sovereignty led to political structures more like what it described. Still, in most places, it has not fit the actuality well.

The lack of clear fit has marked the history of the United States. The myth requires that sovereignty be located at some one point. The implication was that either the individual states were sovereign or the national government was. In theory, sovereignty could not be divided between the two levels. To this day, however, both in fact claim it. The victory of the Union in the Civil War determined that the "sovereignty" of the individual states cannot extend to seceding from the Union. Nevertheless, states remain sovereign in some respects.

This state sovereignty is particularly clear with respect to the political units into which the state is divided. These subunits have only those powers that are granted them by the state, and these powers can be removed by decision of the state. The dominant myth provides no assured basis for local self-rule.

In Germany and Italy, national sovereignty came into existence only in the nineteenth century. To this day, local feelings and loyalties remain strong contestants with nationalism. Recently the nations of Europe have given considerable authority to the European Union. The question of where sovereignty "really" lies becomes increasingly meaningless.

The notion of independent individuals contracting with one another to grant sovereignty to a single government led to a kind of nationalism that proved disastrous while not explaining actual national feeling. In fact, individuals are born into communities. Indeed, members of our species become individual human beings only in and through communities. They have never existed as atomic units and could never have done so. Their very being as well as their behavior is constituted by participation in communities. The idea of complex patterns of community can do far more justice to what has actually happened in the past as well as to what is happening now.

IV. The Meaning of Community

Thus far, the meaning of community has been explained chiefly in terms of internal relations. This one idea is sufficient to show the errors of both collectivism and individualistic social contract theory. It places this postmodern approach squarely in what came to be known in the 1990s as the communitarian camp. At the same time this ontological approach, along with the deep concern for ecology and economics through which it comes to politics, differentiate it from most of the recent communitarian writers. Among them this explicitly ontological note is rare, although it is not wholly absent.

Robert Bellah notes that the dominant thinking of our culture is rooted in "ontological individualism," which he rejects in favor of the view that "individuals are realized only in and through communities, and that strong healthy morally vigorous communities are the prerequisite for strong healthy, morally vigorous individuals."[3]

In his critique of Rawls, Michael Sandel moves the debate to the ontological level. He writes: "the Rawlsian self is not only a subject of possession, but an antecedently individuated subject, standing always at a certain distance from the interests it has."[4] As a result, Sandel argues, community and its values can enter in for Rawls only as an individual's choice, not as a part, as Sandel believes, of who the individual is.

Charles Taylor deplores the lack of attention to ontological issues in the liberal-communitarian debate, noting rightly that liberals who avoid ontological issues actually think in atomistic terms. Taylor sees the alternative as "holism," and he identifies himself as a holist in his recognition that human beings are ontologically embedded in society, but he follows Humboldt in greatly prizing personal liberty and individual differences.[5] His own ontology seems to add a level of holism to that of atomistic individuality.[6]

These are exceptional instances of communitarian engagement with ontological questions. Etzioni was led to emphasize community, not through ontological reflection but when he learned that most young Americans demand their rights in the courts but are not interested in fulfilling their responsibilities.[7] For him communitarianism is the right balance of rights and responsibilities. This balance enters into the name of the communitarian platform: "The Responsive Communitarian Platform: Rights and Responsibilities." This platform begins by contrasting a situation in which each individual pursues private interests with one in which each also devotes some attention to shared projects and institutions.[8] It emphasizes that the former situation is ultimately self-defeating.

Standard forms of communitarianism seek to balance concern for the rights of individuals and the well-being of the community. They want behavior to be directed to socially constructive actions chiefly by moral suasion rather than by state coercion. State policies should strengthen the family and encourage the schools to teach morality. Only when individuals care about others will their individual freedom support community life.

Although communitarians recognize that there are many forms of community, their political interests lead them to focus on those that are geographically defined. They worry that identity politics, which is, of course, based on one type of community, will fragment the communities about which they care most. International or global concerns play a minor role in their writings. According to Etzioni, "some aspire to a world community that would encapsulate all people. Other communitarians object to such globalism and suggest that strong bonds and the moral voice, the essence of communities, mainly are found in relatively small communities in which people know one another."[9]

An important exception to this neglect of the global picture is Michael Waltzer. In *Thick and Thin* he discusses in depth and with great realism the importance of tribalism in world affairs. He recognizes that "our common humanity will never make us members of a single universal tribe. The crucial commonality of the human race is particularism: we participate, all of us, in thick cultures that are our own."[10] He favors allowing each tribe to have as much self-determination as possible, while recognizing that each situation must be dealt with in its own terms. The implications of the vision developed in this book are very similar to his conclusions.

The proposal here developed undertakes to deepen and clarify this communitarian thinking by grounding it in an understanding of the way reality is. This understanding does not follow Taylor in adding a holistic layer to the atomistic one.[11] Instead, it changes the way the individual is viewed. According to this vision, all actual entities whatsoever are internally related to other actual entities. The individual's experience already includes, indeed, is largely constituted by the presence within it of the experiences of others.

Nevertheless, these relations are not always of the sort that generates societies. Societies are constituted only when some common patterns emerge through these internal relations. Further, there are many types of social relationships, and not all of these constitute communities.

Consider as an example the society that is constituted by the flow of one's experience through time. In previous chapters this society has been called the "soul" or the "person." It has a linear order like a subatomic particle or a molecule. But it is quite different. In the particle or molecule, the identity of the society through time is constituted by the repetition of patterns inherited from the past occasions by the current one. Of course, that kind of repetition also characterizes the identity of a person through time. But in the person's case, new ideas or feelings that emerge at one moment enter into the subsequent stream of occasions. These novel elements may alter the person in other respects. One may, without ceasing to be the same person, grow and change quite markedly.

Each of the momentary occasions of a person's experience is also a member of other societies. That is the case because each occasion inherits in significant ways from other occasions of experience besides those that constitute the personal past. For example, each occasion of my experience inherits very importantly from the events in my brain and through them from events in other parts of my body. Accordingly, the entire psychophysical organism is an important society of which each occasion of human experience is a member. Through this, one is related to a wider physical context and is a member of larger societies.

Even more important for political purposes than participation in the psychophysical organism are relations with other persons. With them, too, one constitutes a wide variety of societies. Not all such societies, however, are *communities*. The task now is to specify how this term is being used here.

The preceding sections described collectives and contractual organizations. Insofar as these are actual institutions, they involve elements of community, sometimes intensively. But to whatever extent they embody the understanding that promotes them *as* collectives or purely contractual organizations, the characteristics of community are absent. This is, first of all, because they are organized around external relations and do not encourage internal ones. In the case of collectives, the subjectivity of the members is ignored; they are treated in terms of their social role. In the case of contractual organizations, personal relations among the contracting parties are ignored or minimized. In a true community, by contrast, all members affirm the inwardness or subjectivity of all the others who are involved. Each is open to the influence of the others.

The clearest instances of community are those in which all participants know one another and are personally concerned about one another. Families constitute such communities, and they are extremely important for the well-being of their members. But to restrict the use of "community" to these small units would make it unhelpful for the discussion of political theory. For this reason, the approach toward a definition in the preceding paragraph was more open. Affirming the subjectivity of others and being open to them do not require personal intimacy or even face-to-face relations with all other members of the larger community.

To be properly called a community, relations among the members of the society must be important to those members. This is, of course, a matter of degree, and what is sufficiently important to some members to constitute the society as a community may not be that important to others. There are, accordingly, no sharp lines distinguishing communities from other social patterns.

A useful measure of this importance is the role of the society in determining how persons identify themselves. If some identify themselves primarily as African Americans, then African Americans constitute an important community for them. We can test the degree of importance by considering the marks of community that have been identified. We would expect that those who identify themselves in this way would care a great deal about what happens to African Americans as a group and individually. They would give more support to African-American causes than to others. They would also care about the directions taken by the group, perhaps even participate in trying to influence decisions. They would take more responsibility for other African Americans than for members of other groups.

Those who identify themselves as African American may be quite critical of directions now taken by leaders of this community. Indeed, the most heated debates take place within strong communities. It is those who care most whose disagreements are most intense.

If only a few African Americans identified themselves in this way, then it would be hard to speak of "the African-American community." But this is not the case; so the consequences previously described do follow for many people. There are, of course, other African Americans who do not identify themselves in this way. Drawing the boundaries of the community is somewhat arbitrary.

Among those who identify themselves as African Americans, some may also identify themselves as Baptists. This identification, crossing ethnic and national lines, can also be significant for many. In principle it *could* be equally important with identification as African American, but because of the history of race in the United States, this is rare.

The identification with a specific African-American Baptist denomination is likely to be stronger. That identity involves a bond to other members of the denomination not felt with members of other churches. Those who identify themselves in this way are more concerned about false steps taken in the name of their denomination than about similar errors by others.

Identification with a large denomination has fewer practical expressions than identity with a local congregation. This latter identity is likely to be expressed by significant commitments of time and money, personal caring for other members, and openness to them. But it would not be true to suppose that the face-to-face community is the only meaningful one. If the denominational membership provides part of one's identity, then when one moves away from one's local congregation, one will seek out another local community of that denomination.

For the success of governance, it must be hoped that one important form of identity will be geographically defined. People need to find some of their identity in terms of the city, precinct, town, or suburb in which they live. Otherwise, they are unlikely to be willing to invest time and energy in participating in the political process. Or if they do, it will only be for the sake of benefiting themselves or the group with which they most strongly identify. The geographically defined local society cannot become a community unless its citizens identify with and care about its inclusive well-being. Fortunately, there is a strong tendency for people to do so.

V. The Norms of Community

All communities have power. This power is always, to some extent, exercised hierarchically. That is, it is never distributed equally among all its members. Nevertheless, to whatever extent a society is truly a community, power is exercised in a participatory fashion. All members of a community have some influence on the decisions that are made and on the direction in which the community moves. The greater the participation, the healthier is the community.

To whatever extent a society is truly a community, it will take some responsibility for its members. The kind of responsibility it takes depends on the nature of the community. A community that involves people in only quite specialized aspects of their being is unlikely to take responsibility far beyond that aspect. If a community involves individuals more holistically, it will take much broader responsibility.

To whatever extent a society is truly a community, power is exercised persuasively more than coercively, although coercion cannot be excluded altogether. No community can tolerate all forms of behavior. Some behavior strikes at the very fabric of community. For voluntary communities, the limits of coercion are the limits of what a member will endure before leaving. For other communities, coercion may go much further, including fines and imprisonment. But it must be recognized that all such coercion expresses the failure of community. Where community is healthy, persuasion will dominate.

The dominance of persuasion is required by the definition of community in terms of subjects who are recognized and affirmed as such. Members, including those in authority, respect the feelings of other members. They work to enhance the freedom of all. Freedom can be enhanced by persuasion, but it is inherently restricted by coercion.

The intention of a community to enhance the freedom of its members works against the tendency to make exclusive claims upon them. Its members are members of other societies as well, and some of these other societies are also communities. To the extent that a society is truly a community, it will be respectful of the claims of other communities upon its members.

A community's awareness of its own limits can evoke openness to relating, as a community (as well as through its individual members) to other communities. Today we speak often of "networking." A network can develop into a "community of communities,"[12] in which the inclusive community, made up of the smaller ones, relates to these smaller ones much as they relate to their members.

This general reflection about the nature of communities is designed to set a context for discussing one particular type of society: the type that is geographically defined. These are the societies that can work to recover a preeminent role in relation to the economy. However, if the reassumption of power by these societies is to be an improvement over the present dominance of economic institutions, *these geographically defined societies must function as communities and as communities of communities.*

For a geographically defined society to function as a community, it must provide for the participation of all its citizens in governance. It must relate to them persuasively. It must support their freedom in many ways, including encouraging their participation in other communities. It must take responsibility for the essential well-being of all its citizens. It must also, recognizing that it is but one geographical community among others, seek to be part of a more inclusive community of communities.

Geographically defined societies may or may not correspond to "nation-states." For present purposes, nevertheless, these are especially important. As the world is now organized, nation-states are the only available candidates to recover the power to subordinate economic institutions to the general good, as the people of a nation understand this.

As noted earlier, however, nation-states are associated with a myth of legitimation derived from a highly individualistic understanding of human beings. If, instead, we understand that individuals are constituted largely by their membership in numerous societies and that, for the well-being of the people, some of these must have the form of communities, then we may envision a quite different structure of geographically defined societies.

Few nation-states are spontaneous creations of community. Many of them have resulted from military invasions and conquests, some from colonial rule, others from agreements among smaller political units. In many instances, smaller geographical areas exist in which there are more fully communal societies with greater possibility of individual participation and shared responsibility. These can be communities in a fuller sense than can large nation-states such as the United States or China.

There are advantages in having more decisions made in these smaller units, closer to the people involved. They are better able to tailor policy to local conditions. They have more ownership of the decisions, and they are in better position to judge how they are best carried out.

The Catholic Church has long taught the principle of "subsidiarity." That is, every decision should be made at the lowest level at which it can be carried out. The family should be free to make many decisions. Those that involve other families should be made at the level of the village. And so on up. This is very different from the Enlightenment idea of the transfer of sovereignty from individuals directly to the nation-state. It fits much better the emphasis on community derived from an understanding of how people are internally related.

The principle of subsidiarity suggests a bottom-up organization of political life. Local communities should govern themselves according to the town-hall model still practiced in parts of New England. Here participation is personal and direct, and the sense of mutual responsibility is kept alive. The ideal of community is quite fully realized.

Even the town meeting, however, neglects the fact that participants are also members of other communities. It may take that into account in the content of its decisions. But a local community might also experiment with taking the identities of its citizens seriously in the process of decision making.

In some instances, if the local community is fairly small, it may correspond to a cultural group. The political unit is then likely to correspond more closely with a more intense form of community. This community may have its own ways of decision making that are participatory but do not follow the Anglo model of formal voting. This different model should be affirmed. The requirement for participation should not be formulated so that only the Anglo method of voting is recognized.

If this kind of political unit proves successful, political lines can be redrawn to make it a larger factor in the whole scene. It can be one way in which cultural groups can make more distinctive and diverse contributions to the tapestry of American life. At the same time, the homogeneity of the local community will accent the importance of its being in communal relations with other communities.

Nevertheless, American residential patterns are such that many local units will be multicultural. For example, a geographically defined community might be made up chiefly of Vietnamese, Hispanics, and Anglos. If the identity of these citizens is strongly shaped by their ethnicity, then they might caucus in separate groups and choose representatives to a committee that would negotiate disputed issues. Formal voting on an each-one-counts-one basis might be contingent on a satisfactory agreement being worked out on procedures that would allow for more real participation of all the people.

Such a procedure has its own problems. If, in addition to the main groups, there is a scattering of others, their role would be awkward. Also, while some Hispanics might be comfortable in an "Hispanic caucus," others would not. Some would acknowledge a Chicano identity, for example, but not a general Hispanic one. Others would prefer to identify themselves as part of Anglo culture. The problems would go on and on, but caucuses have played an effective role in many institutions, and there are many people who are able to participate seriously through them who are silenced in a general town meeting.

No one system of this sort could be built into the general plan. The situation in different locations varies too much for that. But the plan can specify that the requirement for participation is not that each one acts individualistically in a voting process. It is open to other participatory patterns that recognize that the identity of many citizens is derived largely from membership in nongeographical communities.

There may be other locales in which class divisions are more important than cultural ones. In some instances it might be that the more prosperous and highly educated persons would dominate a town meeting in such a way that the interests of the working poor or the unemployed were not expressed. In such cases also, caucuses along the lines of primary self-identification of the citizens may provide for more authentic participation.

In still other situations religion may provide the primary identities of which a truly participatory process should take account. Muslims, for example, may identify themselves primarily in that way, even if they come from different parts of the world. The decision-making process can adapt to their preferred styles as well.

As the teaching of subsidiarity recognizes, there are many decisions that cannot be made at this level. Hence higher levels are required. The question is how representatives are chosen to govern at these levels and how the relation of the higher levels to the lower ones is understood.

One possibility is for people to vote as individuals directly for their representatives at each of the higher levels. In this case the power of the individual is preserved and the relation of the levels left open. In most instances, the higher levels will have authority over the lower ones.

A second possibility takes community more seriously and accents bottom-up organization. In this model, the town meeting would send representatives to the next higher level. The members of the town meeting would participate knowledgably in this selection, but they would not then directly participate in the further process of selecting representatives at still higher levels. They would vote for persons they know and trust, and it would be for these persons to select representatives to the next level.

In such a model, the relation of what we now call nation-states to larger units would simply be an extension of the same pattern. This pattern would apply to the relation between the European nations and the European Community. Similar patterns could develop elsewhere. Representatives of these communities would then be sent to a reorganized United Nations (or its successor), which would be granted power to achieve goals that cannot be achieved at regional levels.

Present notions of the sovereignty of the nation-state lead to the assumption that military power is located only at that level. This is, in fact, not the actual situation. Local police power is continuous with military power. In the early history of the United States, state militia were an important expression of military power. Even today a governor can call out the National Guard. More important, international armies serving under the auspices of the United Nations or NATO have fought recent wars.

Accordingly, the idea of dispersing military power at various levels is not a total break with the past. If local and regional governments have increased ability to make decisions, they may have greater need of power to enforce them. If continent-wide organizations become important, they may require organizations somewhat like NATO would be without U.S. participation. For example, the Organization of African States may need its own army to enforce peace agreements on warring countries or parties to civil wars. Certainly the United Nations will need an army to carry out its global peacekeeping mission and to make sure that planet-wide international agreements are enforced. As more real power is transferred to the United Nations as the highest level of community of communities, those responsibilities will increase and the need for military power at the world level will grow.

This bottom-up model has implications for the current debate as to whether government should be guided only by questions of procedural justice or should also support other values. In general, communitarians argue that a nation cannot live by just procedures alone. Liberals counter that support of particular values always privileges some groups of citizens. The implication of the bottom-up model is that self-determining local governments have every reason to deal with more concrete values, whereas the farther up we ascend the less this should be the case. How far up there is sufficient consensus about the more concrete values to allow government to support them will differ greatly from one place to another. In the United States there may even be many local communities that must eschew such a role, whereas in China there are likely to be some cultural values that are common through large regions and can be supported by government without oppression.[13]

It should hardly be necessary to point out that the adoption of this model would require drastic changes at every level. The highest is an important example. If nations were organized everywhere into such organizations as the European Community or the Organization of African States, then it would be these, rather than nation-states that would be represented at the global organization. Strictly speaking, it would no longer be the United "Nations." Obviously the present separation of the General Assembly and the Security Council would disappear, and no nation or region would have veto power. Ideally the regions represented would be of roughly comparable size and each would have equal power.

VI. Antidotes to Abuses

No system is free from the possibility, even the probability, of abuse. Knowing this, political theorists need to consider how to check these abuses. Top-down approaches have led to totalitarianism and untold horrors. But local governments have also inflicted severe evils on the people within their jurisdictions. In the United States, we think especially of the way state power was long used to disenfranchise and segregate blacks and to deny them justice in the courts. How can smaller, more local, units be empowered and yet prevented from exercising their power in such destructive ways?

The larger units must be able to check abuses at the smaller levels. But the power to do so can easily become the power to disempower these units and thereby the citizens. How can the respective roles of the various levels be defined so as to reduce the extent of either of these forms of abuse?

The norms of community can help here. To participate in the community of communities, each participant can be required to embody the minimum characteristics of community. The local community cannot exclude any segment of its population from participation in the process of decision making, and it must take responsibility for the basic well-being of all its citizens. It must be concerned for the enhancement of their freedom. If these conditions are not met, then the larger unit should work to see that they are.

The exercise of this responsibility would first take the form of efforts to persuade. But coercion cannot be ruled out. The representatives of any society that egregiously failed to meet the norms of community would not be allowed to participate at the next level of governance. If this stipulation did not suffice to change the unacceptable practices, then other sanctions would be used, including force as a last resort.

Similarly, any local government that solved its problems by burdening its neighbors would have to be stopped from doing so. It is not acceptable to export pollution or appropriate an undue portion of the water from a river that flows on to other jurisdictions. Higher levels of government must have the power to deal with problems that cannot be solved at lower levels, and this power includes the capacity to impose and enforce sanctions.

This pattern of higher levels having some power over lower ones should continue to the highest levels. The United Nations must have the authority to implement its decisions on global issues even against the resistance of regional communities or nation-states. It should also have the power to impose sanctions on those nations or regions that fail to measure up to the minimum standard of community.

The opposite risk is that the power possessed at higher levels to prevent abuse at lower levels will itself be abused. The local people are then disempowered with respect to the issues over which they should exercise primary decision. They are alienated from the whole system, and the ideal of community is lost. Carefully spelling out the limits of interference allowed from above at each level and charging the legal system with responsibility to adjudicate disputes can check this danger. It can also be checked by the dispersal of military power at various levels.

In the Enlightenment theory, the main way of preventing the tyranny of the majority or of the authorities was through affirming the "rights" of individuals. As noted, this notion could be derived from the founding political myth. The idea of rights has played, on the whole, an extremely positive role in Western society and increasingly around the world. It may be the greatest contribution of the West to global politics. Yet it also has its problems, which are especially apparent to those who approach matters from the side of community.[14]

Rights were conceived as a way of protecting individuals from excessive control by either popular majorities or political power. This protection was needed and still is. Many of the specific rights affirmed in this way are given new form in the proposal that societies be required to embody the minimal norms for community.

One problem is that rights tend to be conceived absolutistically. If one has the right of free speech, one tends to exercise it, whatever the cost to others. As more and more rights are defined, one's exercise of one right often interferes with someone else's exercise of another. In the adjudication of such situations, the appeal must be to something beyond the relative strength of competing rights.

Further, the emphasis on individual rights can also work quite directly against community. This is especially true with respect to property rights, which today are in the ascendancy. Communities cannot function well without the freedom to determine land use and to protect the natural environment. When individual rights are asserted in such a way as to block needed community action, all lose.

It is preferable, therefore, to build the case for the protection of individuals around the notion of persons-in-community. The political community is healthy only as it encourages the participation and the freedom of all and takes responsibility that the basic needs of all are met. The person is well-off only as the community as a whole flourishes. Unless it is understood that the true interests of the community and the individuals who make it up lie with the synergy of both, both lose.

Limits are placed on what a community may do, on the one hand, by the participation and the freedom of all persons and the meeting of their basic needs. The community should recognize that the greater the diversity it allows within itself, the greater its total richness. The freedom of its members to seek their own well-being restricts the community in its dealings with them.

The needs of the community, on the other hand, place limits on how personal freedom may be exercised. All are free to pursue their real interests, but only as they understand that these real interests cannot be the harming of others. The real well-being of each member depends on the health of the community as a whole.

VII. Recovering Governmental Control

There remains the question of how the economy is to be brought under the control of the political government. At what level should this be done? At present, the economy has become global. Does that mean that it should be subordinated to government only at the global level?

Globalization is certainly the present trend. Currently, however, the global "government" under which the economy is to function—the World Trade Organization (WTO)—is one specially created to advance the global economy through still further restriction on what national governments are permitted to do. It is carefully shielded from political influence. For these reasons, it is just the opposite of what this chapter calls for. Its creation and empowerment were one more step in freeing the economy from any obligation to serve the general good understood in any way that is broader than global economic growth.

Among those who agree that the economy should be brought back under the control of representative government, some accept the globalization of the economy as a given. They must look to a greatly strengthened United Nations as the only existing global body that represents a broad range of human concerns. At present, the United Nations is no match for the private and public economic institutions that run the world, and it is easily co-opted to support their basic policies.

Indeed, the United States has systematically disempowered the United Nations with respect to global economic issues. It has transferred power in this regard to the Bretton Woods Institutions: the International Monetary Fund, the World Bank, and the World Trade Organization. This leads to empowering transnational corporations and weakening the ability of nations to control their own economic life. This chapter and the previous one call for quite opposite moves.

Given present structures, it is still possible to propose changes that would move in the right direction. One such proposal would be to bring the World Trade Organization under the control of the General Assembly and to have the General Assembly specify its tasks and procedures. This would make it possible to direct the WTO to serve a range of purposes wider than the freeing of transnational corporations from restrictions imposed by governments.

Those of us who see the globalization of the economy as inherently destructive of local and regional communities must begin the extremely difficult, but not impossible, task of decentralizing the economy. This fits much better with the political vision proposed here. Of course, there would still be much to be done at the global level; so the proposal offered would remain appropriate. But governments at every level would have a role to play.

At present, political power is subordinated to economic power partly because economic power is far more centralized. At the global level at which the economic actors operate, there is little political power of any kind. This absence of global political power renders the economic actors quite free to ignore any values other than economic growth. But if economic actors are required to pay attention once again to political boundaries, then governments can lay down requirements for their behavior, such as paying a living wage and avoiding pollution. Such regulations will not drive capital elsewhere if there are incentives to produce where goods are marketed.

This would require control over the importation of goods. Tariffs are the traditional means of such control. Tariffs can enable local production to pay a living wage and avoid pollution and still compete with imports from places where wages and environmental standards are lower.

The moral argument against "protecting" local industries is that this would take work from laborers in poorer countries, such as Mexico. This is a complex question, but suffice it here to say that the result of free trade for Mexican workers has been a drastic decline in their wages. On the other hand, the number of Mexican billionaires has tripled.

In other words, economic developments in the two countries have been similar. The poor have grown poorer and the rich, richer. National control over national boundaries can raise wages and working conditions for all who labor without unfairly penalizing the businesses that employ them. Competitors not subject to the same requirements will have to pay a suitable fee in order to compete in the national market.

It is not altogether fanciful to imagine a global economy in which a great deal happens at quite local levels. There are already some decentralizing forces at work. Governments may recognize the appalling harm done by freeing corporations from governmental oversight. They could then move the economy back toward political control more rapidly than is often recognized. The idea that governments at all levels could have a say about the livelihood of their people is not an impossible dream.

Chapter Seven

Race and Class

I. Introduction

In the preceding chapters, community was presented in a normative light. The fundamental role that relationships play in constituting our existence determines that our very being is social. For societies to provide individuals the context for maturing into healthy persons, some of them need to be communities. Our shared concern should be to strengthen communities.

Communities, nevertheless, are also the causes of some of our most serious problems. Inevitably they are the source of we/they valuing and thinking. If people identify themselves as Buddhist, they define others as nonBuddhist. To whatever extent this identification is important to them, they will feel more responsibility for other Buddhists and for the Buddhist movement as a whole than for nonBuddhists and non-Buddhist movements. If this is their primary self-identification, the difference will be marked. The successes and failures of the Buddhist community will be their own.

Differentiating relations to others according to such we/they lines is sometimes regarded as inherently undesirable. Individualistic/universalistic thinking formulates its ethics as transcending such differences and as treating everyone in the same way. From the postmodern point of view adopted in this book, however, that is neither possible nor desirable. An infant requires from a few people a degree of loving responsibility they cannot direct toward all. People need to belong somewhere and not simply everywhere. If everyone cared equally for everyone, a world government would have to meet the needs now met by family and friends. Community, including the resultant we/they division, is crucial.

Nevertheless, it matters a great deal how the we/they relation is understood. In principle, it can be not only beneficial to some but also harmless to others. If one identifies with the extended Smith family and takes special responsibility for its members, this will be beneficial for the Smiths. If, at the same time, one respects the members of the Brown family equally, the special responsibility taken for the Smiths is harmless. The Browns constitute another community, and one expects them to take care of many of their own needs. One does not feel the same responsibility toward the Browns as toward the Smiths. On the other hand, if disaster strikes the Browns, so that they cannot take care of themselves, the Smiths will try to help.

On matters that concern both families and others, too, they will work together. Members of several families may come together as individuals, with little regard to their family identities, or they may come together as representative of their families. In the former case those who work together will constitute a distinct community, trivial or important. In the latter case, the new community will be a community of communities.

Such communities and communities of communities can be geographical. A town can have a strong community character. Its citizens are likely to take civic pride in the town's appearance and its public facilities even if they have made no personal contribution. This involves a we/they feeling toward citizens of other towns. The victory of the town's high school football team over that of the neighboring town causes a feeling of personal success in its citizens. Citizens of one town will contribute to local causes in a way they are unlikely to contribute to those of the neighboring town.

But if a natural disaster strikes the neighboring town, so that its citizens are not able to take care of themselves, this will bring forth a different response. Further, there are many issues that concern the citizens of both towns as well as others. Individual concerned citizens sometimes organize as individuals to respond to these issues, thus creating a new community. At other times people come together as representatives of their towns, working, then, as a community of communities.

This model of a community of geographically defined communities can be carried to much larger geographical areas and ultimately to the whole planet. The preceding chapter presented it as a model for governance. It expresses a way in which the natural and inevitable we/they distinction, built into the notion of community, can function positively and harmlessly.

In real history, however, community always poses dangers, and these dangers have often been actualized. There *can* be communities of nations, but more common have been wars between nation-states. Within these states there *can* be a community of communities, defined geographically or otherwise, but more often there have been conflict, exploitation, and persecution. Communities have been far from harmless.

This chapter considers two bases for community formation capable of great harm: race and class. Section II describes the features of community formation that can cause any type of community to become destructive. Section III recognizes the primary importance of race as a divisive factor in American history. It follows the postmodern pattern of turning the question about race, usually directed to blacks, back on whites. It describes how white identity in the United States developed around destructive principles.

Section IV argues that Marxist class analysis, based on European industrial society, has had little relevance to past American experience and will have less to the future. It goes on to describe how the nation is moving into a new class structure with little awareness of its class character. Since the greatest harm done by class in American society is through the elite's control of policy formation, the question is whether the newly dispossessed can develop sufficient class-consciousness to counter the new (and continuing) elite. Section V briefly summarizes the relation of race and class in the American past and the prospective situation, then suggests some policies on which African Americans and the new dispossessed might make common cause.

II. The Distortions of Community

The most basic communities have a natural character. The family is the paradigm instance. Groups of families living and working together have intimate connections with one another that they do not have with others. They share customs and modes of communication that differ from those of strangers. Through most of history, small geographically defined communities had these natural characteristics.

But communities can be formed around almost any interest or characteristic. Some of these are also quite natural. Fisherfolk have a community among themselves that does not include farmers. Lawyers have a community that separates them from those who work in the insurance business. None of this is to be deplored as long as the self-identification of people along these lines does not become so strong as to prevent participation in other communities that cut across these lines or to inhibit participation in communities of communities.

Unfortunately, history is replete with instances in which one identity subordinates others and thus rigidifies the we/they distinction. Also, loyalty to one community often precludes loyalty to more inclusive ones. A community that claims this exclusive loyalty can enter into temporary alliances with others to gain specific ends, but it cannot become part of a community of communities. The relation among such communities can only be competitive. The well-being of one requires losses by the others.

The drawing of lines in competitive ways is rendered much worse when done by those who have the power to determine the respective roles of the several communities. The examples given are likely to be relatively harmless because fisherfolk and farmers rarely exercise determinative power over one another, and the same is true of lawyers and insurers. In contrast, the ruling class in a society may draw lines around itself that negatively determine much about the lives of others. It can then order the affairs of the state for its own narrow interests. A powerful nation, in a similar way, may oppress weaker ones.

The problems generated by community were intensified by the rise of the universal religions in the first millennium B.C.E. The problem became especially intense with the subsequent emergence of Christianity and Islam. Ironically, these religions set out to overcome the divisions and animosities among peoples by pointing to that which united all. Inevitably, however, the way of identifying the universal was always particular. This particularity brought adherents of one universal loyalty into conflict with adherents of others. The universalist claims of each intensified conflicts.

Each religion claimed universal truth, so that those who opposed it were defenders of error. Victory over the other was, therefore, an extension of truth. Moral justification was added to self-interest.

When the we/they distinction corresponds to differences in culture, there is an almost inevitable tendency to regard the collective practices of one's own group as superior to those of the others. Thus "we" are in some ways better than "they," not simply different from them. As people became "civilized," this distinction of superiority was intensified. Greeks regarded others as "barbarians," a term that carried, then as now, a note of contempt. When universalistic religious claims are combined with cultural superiority, the superiority is commonly absolutized. The "pagans'" ways of acting are not simply inferior, they are wrong.

The original teachings of the universal religions rarely supported imposing them by force. They were to spread by persuasion. But in real communities, these original teachings were not followed in pure form. The actual function of the teachings was often to intensify we/they distinctions that had other bases, such as culture and nationality, or to further economic self-interest.

The model of making universalistic claims, pioneered by the universal religious traditions, can also lead to demonic imitations. Christians understand idolatry as claiming ultimate loyalty and devotion for what is not ultimate. There are subtle elements of idolatry in most religious teaching, but there are also egregious expressions in relation to objects not usually thought of as religious. Ultimate loyalty has been claimed for nations, for example, which clearly do not have an ultimate character. In a context in which people have learned to think in terms of ultimate loyalties, community feeling can be all too responsive to such idolatrous claims.

Communities with some natural or rational basis can, thus, become destructive in relation to others. The situation is still worse when communities are created around purposes that are inherently destructive. A segment of society may generate a self-identification for the purpose of imposing its will on others. Charlatans may bring communities into being simply to increase their personal wealth or power. An important evaluative question about any community is how large a place it should play in the lives of its members. In the case of some communities, the answer is: none at all.

In sum, the we/they distinction inherent in community is in itself natural and necessary, but commonly, even universally, distorted. Minor distortions, such as excessive reaction to losing a soccer match, may be accepted. But major ones have cursed human history. This curse is not diminishing.

Through most of human history the strongest identities have been tribal, religious, and ethnic or national. The greatest havoc has been created by competition and conflict among these communities. The greatest evil internal to political units, however, has been associated with classes. The exploitation of "lower" classes by "higher" ones has been almost universal.

Sometimes classes are distinguished by tribe, religious tradition, or ethnicity, as when one people conquer and rule another. But a homogeneous people also develop a class structure. Class distinctions, accordingly, must be treated as distinct.

In some places, and especially in the American colonies and the United States, race has been constructed as the most basic identification of people. Although it is related to ethnicity or national origin, it is also quite distinct from these. Race has played a large role in shaping class structure, but it can be important even when it does not correspond with class distinctions. Despite their interconnections, therefore, race and class require separate treatment.

Among whites in the United States, class structures have been relatively fluid. Upward mobility has been possible for many. The vast majority of people have identified themselves as middle class, even when their social role and economic standing did not justify such classification. Therefore, the only class that has consciously functioned as such in the United States is the upper class.

Race, on the other hand, has been a primary determinant of community. Americans have internalized race as *a*, if not *the*, primary mode of self-identification. Race has, therefore, played an unparalleled role in American history.

Although the extreme importance of racial identification continues, its role has changed since World War II. It no longer has official status and support as a basis for discrimination and exclusion. It continues to play an enormous role, but not as blatantly as before.

Class structure, on the other hand, is growing more important. Upward mobility is declining. Although class is still not a primary basis by which most people identify themselves, the recognition that their lives are in fact determined by class status may grow. It is important to consider class issues before this happens.

III. Race

Against the view that races are biologically fixed and given, something like species, there has been a sharp and necessary reaction. There is no such biological basis for distinguishing the races. Indeed the association of "race" with biological differences was not common prior to the nineteenth century. The term was used to refer to the poor and uneducated, viewed, of course, as *naturally* inferior. It was thus purely a social construct.

Nevertheless, the opposition to treating race as biologically given can lead to overstatements if it implies that actual physical differences now play no role in distinguishing people according to race. As European colonialism and imperialism grew, those to whom "race" referred were increasingly persons of color. Between Europeans and these people there are some biological differences. And it is this meaning of race that dominates usage today.

Human beings spread around the planet and interacted rather little with those at a distance. Diverse climates and economies favored certain traits in a normal evolutionary process. People living in tropical climates became darker skinned than those living in northern forests. Diets had some physical effects. The division of people into races in the dominant contemporary sense has been influenced by the diversity of physical characteristics.

It is realistic to make some generalizations about the characteristic differences of those whose body types developed in such places as East Asia, South India, Australia, northern Europe, and southern Africa. These differences persist even when the cultural differences associated with them do not. We have a natural interest in our ancestors as a part of the way of understanding who we are. Self-identification in terms of physical features associated with where most of one's ancestors lived has a place. If "race" meant only the genetic inheritance from people inhabiting one part of the world or another, it could be a harmless idea, but the history of its use makes this difficult.

Even in this limited sense, however, it is not possible to divide people into a finite set of races. There is no one set of characteristics that presents itself for such purposes, and, given any arbitrarily chosen set, divisions could proceed without limit. The actual use of physical distinctions is far more a function of social conditions than of whatever objective differences exist.

Furthermore, self-identification in terms of physical differences of the types employed in racial distinctions has no claim to be a significant principle of community formation. Sharing certain physical features is a relatively unimportant part of who people are. In principle, it has little to do with how one should think, what role one should play in society, or how one should relate to others.

There is no necessity that the physical differences associated with where one's ancestors lived play any social role at all. It seems to have been a minor issue in ancient Egypt and even in the Roman Empire. When it has been more important, this has often been because of its close connection with culture, which *is* important for identity formation and community.

American culture has been uniquely racist, in the sense that it has determined the status of its inhabitants primarily in terms of their race. Needless to say, the status of the several races has been heavily weighted against those with darker skin. The racist lens through which all are viewed has deeply affected human relations at every level. Although racism has appeared in other countries as well, its presence always requires specific explanation. It cannot be understood as a universal characteristic of human nature. The importance of the role race has played in American society requires particular historical explanation.

Despite the connection of race with genetic inheritance, American racism has subordinated physical characteristics of those categorized as belonging to different races to questions of remote ancestry. People are held to be members of the black race even when the majority of their ancestors came from northern Europe. Physical characteristics are not required for this identification. What then constitutes race for Americans, and why is it important?

Even this question is misleading. It is not about how all Americans understand race. In particular it is not asking how African Americans understand it. The question is about how Euro-Americans, having defined themselves as "white," understand it.

In white rhetoric, race is primarily a characteristic of others. Since the Civil War, the "race problem" has been the question of the space to be given and the role to be assigned to people of other races, especially to blacks. They were supposed to disturb what could otherwise be a homogeneous American society to which they did not belong. Without them, it was thought, America could function democratically and build a great civilization. But one could not simply wish them away. In this influential white perspective, the task was to define the place of other races and to keep them there.

In recent years, among more liberal whites, the problem has been redefined. The "problem" is that blacks do not have their fair share of the goods provided by American society. The deeper problem is that even when legal obstacles are removed, the majority of them do not improve their condition. What changes are required in order that the imbalance in education and income and health be reduced?

Liberal whites know that racism is still a problem for blacks. But they are typically inclined to think it also functions as an excuse. Having removed public obstacles and even supported affirmative action, they do not know what more to do. They tend to think that the ball is in the black court. Other racial groups of immigrants, especially from Asia, rapidly move up the economic and educational ladders. Surely, liberals think, blacks should do so soon.

This attitude reflects the modern understanding. It sees competitive relations among individuals in society as normative. Because people are primarily to be understood as individuals, their treatment as individuals should be decisive. If they are given, as individuals, equal opportunity, then failure in competition with others is their own responsibility. Granted, the inferior educational and economic level of parents means that some do not have full equality of opportunity; and because society bears responsibility for this lag, special help in education and affirmative action policies may be justified temporarily. But the goal is a system of individualistic competition.

The model of persons-in-community has somewhat different implications. It opposes forcing all persons into a single competitive model. Furthermore, persons are who they are largely because of the history that has formed them. They do not abruptly become someone different because of changes in law and public institutions. They must deal with this whole history, but they cannot do so alone. This history is that of the whole society and continues deeply to inform that society even when it supposes that it has changed. Real change requires uncovering the forces that have shaped us all and dealing with them together.

In any case, the dominant white approach, even the liberal one, locates the problem of race at the wrong place. Prior to the question about how the "black race" can attain an equal place in American society is the question: What is meant by American society? For most whites, American society is white American society. Until that identification is corrected, little progress can be made. Prior to the question about the condition of the black race is the question: How was the idea of race formed in American history? It turns out that the initiating act was the invention of the "white race."

Until whites recognize how deep is their self-identification as whites, they will not understand the problems they create both for themselves and for those whom they define as not white. The racial problem in the United States must be redefined as that of the social construction of the white race. Until that is deconstructed, there is no possibility for those who have been excluded from whiteness to have equal opportunity.

As long as white identity is taken for granted by those who dominate this society, it determines the definition of other identities. In this context, blacks cannot define themselves. If they could, they might not choose to define themselves as blacks at all, or even primarily as African Americans, but, instead, by characteristics that in a healthy society would be far more important. Being black is their self-identity only because it has been imposed on them. Having been imposed, it has become a strong, largely determinative, identity.

Few Europeans came to the American colonies or later to the United States with a white identity. The immigrants were English or German, Protestant or Catholic, peasant or artisan, indentured servant or landed gentry. They became Pennsylvanians or Virginians, colonials or Tories, Quakers or Baptists. They had many identities, but white was not one of them.[1]

Thandeka traces the formation of white identity in Virginia. The history is illuminating. The earliest workers on Virginia plantations were indentured servants from Great Britain. These worked side-by-side with African slaves whose numbers grew rapidly after 1660. Even after the time of forced servitude, the indentured servants were left propertyless, powerless, and miserable. In 1676, they rebelled under the leadership of Nathaniel Bacon and burned Jamestown. African slaves took a strong role in the rebellion.

In a context in which the exploited groups constituted the majority of the population, the propertied class could maintain its privilege only by introducing some significant change. According to Edmund Morgan,[2] "The answer to the problem, obvious if unspoken and only gradually recognized, was racism, to separate dangerous free whites from dangerous slave blacks by a screen of racial contempt." The method was to enact a series of laws giving increasing rights to persons of European ancestry and degrading still further the lot of Africans and Native Americans. According to Thandeka: "A new multiclass 'white race' would emerge from the Virginia laws."[3]

The new identity as white was based not only on security from being enslaved, but also on agreement that the enslaving of others was acceptable. Hence to be nonwhite was to fail to participate in those human traits that required freedom. The definition of whiteness implied that the nonwhite were legitimately enslaved. It implied also strong opposition to marriage between the races.

Matters were not quite that simple, however. The treatment of slaves was disturbing to any sensitive conscience. It threatened to complicate the new identity of whiteness. That identity must be protected from association with unjustified actions.

Justifying the treatment of slaves required that they be portrayed as still more degraded. It had to be supposed that the slave deserved slavery and that any resistance on the slave's part deserved punishment. Only then could whites be fully justified in whatever action they took to enforce their will on the slaves.

There was, of course, no connection between the physical features of slaves and any justification for their enslavement. The justification of slavery on the basis of race, therefore, could not mean "race" in any biological or physical sense. Whites had to project on blacks just those characteristics that made them unworthy of freedom and participation in the larger society. They must be ignorant, lazy, irresponsible, deceitful, uncivilized, stupid, immoral, immature, and so forth. For these reasons, they were to be forced to serve the interests of whites who were opposite in all these respects.

With whiteness so defined, it became an extremely important mode of identification. To be white meant to be accorded some measure of respect, however meager. Even if new immigrants from southern and eastern Europe or Ireland were treated with contempt by the established leadership, their designation as "white" gave them some protection and hope for the future. To this they clung. Their own low status made it all the more important to them to insist that another group was far below. They were free to heap on it the contempt they felt from others.

Many who were acknowledged as white were very insecure in this whiteness.[4] To be fully white meant to conform to patterns that were defined largely by upper-class British Americans. There was widespread anxiety as to whether one was white enough. Feelings of shame in one's inferior whiteness intensified the need to distance oneself from the despised blacks.

The definition of whiteness had enormous sociohistorical importance. Many immigrants who were accorded the status of white rapidly improved their social and economic status. This advancement was approved and supported by white society. But no such advancement was possible for blacks. Even free blacks were in danger if they became "uppity," that is, if they acted as if they thought they were as good as whites. To be safe as a black one had to behave as if one acknowledged one's inherent and indelible inferiority.

Slaves were never safe from the master's moods and whims. But the danger for blacks increased after emancipation. Freeing the slaves did not change white self-definition. Self-respect was still based on there being a group of people who were humanly inferior. The slave, being valuable property to the owner, enjoyed some protection from other whites. But the free black had no protector and was thus vulnerable to the whims of any white. Lynchings became common practice, largely as a way of demonstrating the total power of whites in general over blacks in general. Lynchings were directed especially toward any who seemed to challenge the legitimacy of this domination.

Most white Southerners were Baptists, Methodists, or Presbyterians. Many took their faith seriously. Their participation in churches gave them a strong sense of identity and thereby also of community. This self-identification of whites in principle implied some community with blacks who were of the same denomination. More broadly, shared commitment to Christian faith implied a community that cut across racial lines. Nevertheless, in the great majority of cases, white identity was stronger than Christian identity. White identity reshaped Christian teaching much more than Christian teaching altered white identity. If religion is defined as one's primary identity, then whiteness was long the religion of most Southern whites.

This throws light on the nature of lynchings. Many of them functioned as ceremonial events with audiences of ten thousand or more. Far from being merely spontaneous upwellings of mob violence, some were carefully staged, with excursion trains scheduled to bring onlookers.[5]

Furthermore, the definition of blackness attributed to it an almost supernatural power. To have any black ancestor was to be black. Even if fifteen of one's great-great-grandparents were white, the sixteenth could determine that one was black. Blackness was a kind of ontological taint that no dilution could overcome. To be white required total absence of any tinge of blackness. Even today this understanding maintains surprising power. Whereas a child who has an Asian mother and a European father is a Eurasian, a child with black and white parents is simply black.

Given this long history of use, it is not easy to turn "black" and "white" into merely descriptive terms. Indeed, it is hard to know what they would describe. Most accurately, they would describe the community that, out of a particular history, thought of itself as white and another community that, out of that same history, was compelled to think of itself as black. But those definitions would work only if people were free to move from one community to the other. Even today such movement is difficult, because race is assumed to have a more objective status.

Thandeka emphasizes that most Euro-Americans learn to be white, often in childhood, by being shamed by their parents or other members of the white community whose respect they need.[6] When they treat blacks in the way they would treat other whites, the disapproval of those on whom they are most dependent is made evident. Many Euro-Americans can remember an early instance of playing with an African-American child and discovering that this led to withdrawal of acceptance by a parent. They felt shame for violating their parents' expectations, they denied their own feelings, and learned to act as whites. Until Euro-Americans come to terms with this shame associated with being white, they will not be effective in overcoming racism. Thandeka shows that by shifting the focus from white guilt to white shame, the shared interests of blacks and whites in overcoming a system that has victimized both can provide new energy and success.

Nevertheless, we must acknowledge the role of guilt as well. Repressed guilt played a large role in the harshly negative account of "niggers" in white culture all along. At least among liberal whites, this strategy has been abandoned, but the guilt remains and affects white identity and relationships with blacks.

The guilt most easily acknowledged is historical. The crimes of whites against blacks are too numerous and too obvious to deny, although they are often ignored. Furthermore, this is not just past history. Crimes of this sort continue today.

Black and white do not exhaust races in the United States. Yet for most Americans they are the paradigm case. There have been times and parts of the country in which other racial relations have been more important for European immigrants than those with blacks. Thandeka recognizes that the experiences that teach whiteness today may involve socially excluded people other than blacks. Historically, relations with Native Americans played a formative role. It was necessary to understand these people in such a way as to justify dispossessing them of their land and often committing genocide against them. Defining them as "savages" helped in this regard. But the consciousness of identity as civilized invaders in a land occupied by savages had less effect on white identity than did African slavery and its justification.

Few whites deny that in the past other whites have been racist, but many do deny that they are racist today. They claim to have redefined whiteness in thoroughly modern terms. The white race is simply one among others, deserving the same respect as the others and equal treatment. For that reason, a majority now thinks, affirmative action is inappropriate. According to the now dominant view, whites have as much right to act in their self-interest, as individuals and as a group, as do any others. As a society, the theory is, we should ignore race in our laws and policies.

There is some gain from this change. Whiteness is no longer defined as superior. Others are, in principle, to have equal rights. Racism, meaning overt restrictions because of race, is rejected. Although it is likely that many who proclaim their white identity in this way actually continue some of the older identity, that they disclaim contempt for others is social progress.

The practical meaning of this new whiteness, however, is repudiation of any responsibility for the continuing consequences of the earlier form of whiteness. Because these whites are not now advocating exclusion of blacks from public life, they suppose that the collective acts of whites in the past are none of their doing. Current policy, many whites think, should reflect the current situation, not the past one. The result of this new definition of whiteness is to slow, if not to stop, all further social and economic progress for blacks.

There is one respect in which this new identification of whiteness is a retreat from an earlier one. As Gunnar Myrdal[7] pointed out long ago, there was a split in the white soul. On the one hand, there was the sort of self-identity as white previously discussed, one based on domination over blacks. On the other hand, there was commitment to democracy.

Actually, the strongest forms of this second commitment were shaped by Christian teaching. Martin Luther King understood this fact well, and his effective appeal to it contributed to his success.[8] The message of justice, righteousness, and human dignity was muted and distorted in the American churches, but it could not be excised from the Bible. In the nineteenth century, this message aroused the Christian consciences of some whites to end slavery. Under the stimulus of King's campaign, the biblical message also evoked some white aid in ending legal segregation. It provided an impetus to go further in the effort to rectify past wrong and to achieve a just society. To be a white American could mean accepting some responsibility for the whole society and seeking to improve it.

Unfortunately, the new definition of whiteness makes no pretense of including this element. Whites are now defined as one group among others, and each group can be expected to seek its own interests. The fact that whites remain the dominant group gives them no special responsibility to seek the well-being of the whole.

Where do we go from here? Can whiteness be redefined again so as to function positively as a principle of identification? Or should this mode of identification be rejected altogether? David Roediger calls for "the abolition of whiteness."[9] Is this possible? Is it desirable?

Roediger's argument for its possibility stems from the current vacuity of whiteness. White society has in fact lost vision, insight, and leadership in the arts. It depends on those with some other cultural identity. Much of the needed creativity stems from African Americans. Whites may be persuaded to recognize that race is a social construction and that the history of the social construction of the white race in the United States is such that they do not want to live by it. Perhaps they will drop their white identity in favor of something more specific, something with greater content. They may become Italian Americans, Polish Americans, German Americans, and so forth. These more specific identities would not pose an obstacle to the advancement of other Americans.

One problem with this proposal is that for some Euro-Americans the melting pot has worked too well. Many cannot define themselves in more specific terms. Their only cultural identity is white American. They cannot identify themselves as German American, Italian American, Polish American, or Anglo American. They are just Euro-Americans.

The question is whether they can or should, by calling themselves Euro-American, reject their identity as white. They recognize that this identity was socially constructed for purposes most now reject. An identity that was constructed for the purpose of control and oppression of others functions for some of them now chiefly as a source of shame and guilt. If redefining themselves as Euro-American would enable them to distance themselves from the crimes of whites, they could feel a sense of release.

In the long run, it is good to look forward to a society in which diversity of ethnic background is affirmed without prejudicial consequences. In that society, more and more people will have difficulty in sorting out their own ethnicity. Personal identity will be established in other categories altogether.

The question is whether adopting this strategy now is wise or beneficial. Is there not the danger that it would lead to ignoring the legacy of racism in society? Would it not support the move to redefine whiteness as one ethnicity alongside others, ignoring its privileged position and the history of oppression?

Is there not an argument for the alternative strategy of accepting the reality of the community constituted by the social construction of whiteness and, as a member of that community, undertaking to move it to repentance? Such repentance is not a matter of feeling guilty but of changing direction.

For many Euro-Americans the question of how to understand ourselves in the current scene is a deeply personal one. My personal struggle is intensified by being a Southern white whose ancestors owned slaves and loudly offered a theological defense of slavery. Can, or should, I now, by defining myself as Euro-American instead of white, disconnect from that history? If that would free me of participation in responsibility for the evils inflicted on blacks by whites, would that contribute positively to the deracialization of American society?

The form of postmodernism advocated in this book works in a different direction. It emphasizes that I am not an individual separate from the communities that have formed me. I am what I am by the internalization of others. Many, if not most, of those others have had, and acted on, a white identity. Internalizing them has made me white. It is from that white perspective that I see others. What has been socially constructed actually plays a large role in constituting my identity.

For me the way forward is through understanding how I have come to be what I am as a privileged white male. This means acknowledging the ugly history of whiteness and repenting. It also means freeing myself from disempowering guilt and shame. It means celebrating what I can of my history, reaffirming that in it which holds promise for the future. It means identifying the role that I am now called to play in terms of the capacities that my position in American society, as an advantaged white, affords.

IV. Class

Class lacks even the very limited biological reality of race, and, like race, it includes large elements of social construction. But it is not pure social construction, for it is partly an *economic* construction. That is, it is based on virtual inevitabilities of economic and political life.

Classes are functions of the dominant forms of economic and political life. The former may be more determinative, but similar modes of production can be associated with different political systems. Marxists themselves have illustrated this fact as they employed a bureaucracy to perform the functions played by the bourgeoisie in capitalism. This change did not eliminate classes, but it substituted a bureaucratic class for an entrepreneurial one.

Division into classes is not inherently evil. Even in a utopia in which all chose the roles they played in society, some would choose roles of lesser authority than others. Some like to administer institutions, others do not. Some prefer to concentrate on making music, leaving public life to others. Some prefer the security of a modest salary. Others enjoy the risk of entrepreneurship. Some prefer manual work arranged and supervised by others. The result of such free choices would not have all the features of classes, but it would include wide differences in power and in wealth. The rudiments of class would be present.

In the real world, of course, this much freedom is not possible. The economy does not adapt to everyone's personal preferences. At best, people can make some choices among available roles. An economy that offers considerable freedom in such choices is favored by the understanding of people as persons-in-community. One hope for the future is that in a post-industrial age this kind of freedom can play a larger role.

The European societies from which a majority of immigrants came were full-fledged class societies. They were typically a mixture of two types of class system. Much of agriculture still reflected the system of landed gentry and peasants. The new industrial system consisted in the capitalist and worker classes. Alongside these classes were government officials, professionals, and trades people.

Classes constituted communities, and individuals were quite conscious of their class identities. The evil of the system was the exploitative use of power by the ruling class and the demeaning way they treated peasants and workers. One reason for leaving Europe for the new world was the restrictiveness of these identities and the frequent humiliations they involved. People sought greater opportunity and dignity.

In America, many found just that. Instead of farming for landed gentry, millions gained sufficient land for themselves to become self-supporting family farmers. Others worked in factories for capitalists, but, even in their case, there was more flexibility than was characteristic of Europe. Their children were often able to become small-scale entrepreneurs or go into professions that would have been closed to them in the old country.

As a result, class-consciousness played a much smaller role among Euro-Americans in the United States than it did in Europe. Independent farmers did not think of themselves as constituting a lower class. They were simply part of the more or less classless middle class. Factory workers who could encourage their children to find something better identified with their class much less strongly than in countries in which no such opportunities existed. The frontier provided an option for those most dissatisfied with their class role. As time went by, many families included members performing quite diverse roles in society. The families did not then develop class-consciousness. When the labor movement finally succeeded in raising wages, most industrial workers considered themselves, also, to be members of the middle class.

Modern sociologists tend to define classes without reference to the self-identification of those who inhabit them. They identify places in the socioeconomic system and those who occupy them. This classification has some uses. Much can be predicted about the prospects of children, for example, according to the class of their parents. Class in this sense exists everywhere, and is important everywhere.

However, only a few in these classes have significant class-consciousness. If the members of a class do "recognize themselves as constituting a class with its own interest then we can say that they constitute a class for themselves as well as a class in themselves."[10]

In the purely objective sense, obviously, classes have played a large role in American history. Immigrants were often intensely exploited as laborers in new industries. The capitalists were fully conscious of their class identity. The lack of countervailing class-consciousness only gave them greater freedom. Still, according to some postmodern sociologists, lack of self-identification in terms of class renders the use of the term "unacceptable."[11] At the least, for the purposes of this book, when consciousness of class is absent, class has greatly reduced significance.

For the great majority of white workers, race consciousness was more intense than class-consciousness. White racism among workers impeded the effectiveness of the labor movement. It still does. In recent years white workers have voted, against the class interests of labor, for politicians who supported their perceived interests as white. The majority of labor union members voted for Reagan and Bush. An analysis of American history in terms of class has had its value, but it also has obscured much.

Nevertheless, it is important now to reflect anew about class in America. New class distinctions are emerging and are likely to become more important in the near future. In the new global economy, these distinctions are not identical with those analyzed by Marx. Unless fresh analysis is done, class distinctions will not provide a basis for political action.

There are a number of reasons for the new rigidity of class lines. The frontier is gone. Family farming is ended and, with it, any direct access to the means of production for the vast majority of people. Deindustrializtion has wiped out that segment of the working class that was well paid and economically secure. In businesses where capital is mobile, labor unions have lost out and have little prospect of regaining the initiative.

For many people, upward mobility seems unlikely. Wages are declining along with hard-won benefits. Temporary part-time jobs are replacing long-term, full-time positions. The minimum wage has fallen further behind the cost of living. Many work in sweatshops that do not pay even the minimum wage. Meanwhile the rich are getting much richer and more numerous.

Instead of a bell curve with a few rich and a few poor and most in the middle, the future is likely to be flattened out. There may even be bulges at the two ends. It will be more difficult for many Americans to think of themselves as middle class.

In recent years, American society has developed a large underclass. These are the people who fall outside the standard economy. Some are on welfare; others are in the drug business; others live by prostitution; still others, by theft. A large and growing number are in prison.

During the past few decades, public policies have contributed to the rise of the underclass. Two are particularly direct in their effects. One of these is the War on Drugs. The decision was to criminalize drugs. When normal penalties for possession of illegal substances failed to stop their use, prison terms were made mandatory and extended. The actual violation of laws against possession is widely dispersed in society, but enforcement has been chiefly in the poorest sections. The numbers of the poor in prison for violation of drug laws has escalated.

The second policy is that of maintaining unemployment. This policy superseded efforts to achieve full employment that were in effect much of the time before 1970. Economists argued that when unemployment fell below a certain point, somewhere around 6%, labor would demand higher wages. This would lead to inflation. To avoid inflation, the approved policy is for the Federal Reserve Board to raise interest rates when the economy threatens to reduce unemployment too far.

The meaning of this policy is clear. The government aims to keep wages down, especially at the lower end of the spectrum. It has succeeded in doing so. While capital has multiplied, wages have not kept up with inflation. Further, a certain percentage of those who seek work must be denied it. This policy directly encourages the development of an underclass of people excluded from the regular economy.

Until recently, the government had another policy, namely, to provide some minimal support for those who could not find work. Now, however, this guarantee has been removed. While the government retains the policy of preventing full employment, it threatens severe deprivation to those who fail to find work.

In 1999 the Federal Reserve Board allowed unemployment to fall below the usually accepted level. The predicted inflation did not occur. Nevertheless, fear that it might occur led to higher interest rates, which in fact functioned, not to stop a nonexistent inflation but to cause some and to arouse fears of recession. By 2001 the Federal Reserve Board was lowering interest rates again, hoping to re-stimulate the economy. It is clear that, even without any evidence that low unemployment actually causes inflation, the Federal Reserve Board fears this possibility and works systematically against allowing unemployement to fall too low. With less government support for those who cannot find work, the problems of the underclass grow.

Another emerging class is that of temporary and part-time workers who would prefer regular full-time employment. They now constitute at least a tenth of the workforce and are the fastest growing segment. They have ups and downs of employment with no job security.[12] They constitute a labor pool from which business draws according to its own needs without taking any responsibility for the workers. The cost of medical care, for example, will be borne by the public rather than by the employers.

At the upper end of the class spectrum are speculators. These are not the entrepreneurs and capitalists whose positive role Marx recognized. They are those who manage money, their own and that of others, simply for the sake of making money. Profits may be made in currency or stock market transactions. The latter may help the corporations in which money is temporarily invested, but the interest is in short-term profit rather than production. The extreme expression of this is "day trading."

Speculators are closely related to corporate raiders. These raiders examine the value that the property of a corporation holds in comparison with its appraisal in the stock market. By taking control of the corporation long enough to sell off its assets, they can make large profits.

There are also real investors who have a stake in the functioning of corporations. They, too, are at the upper end of the scale. They employ executives skilled in making corporations more profitable in the short term. This skill often consists in firing many long-term, well-paid workers and drawing from the labor pool previously described. The pay of these executives has risen astronomically as they reduce the labor costs of the corporation. In the United States, the ratio between top CEO salaries and those of average workers rose from 44 to 1 in 1965 to 212 to 1 in 1997.[13]

Next to this upper class is a group of persons with unusual skills that are highly profitable to their employers. They may be tax accountants, lawyers, computer programmers, or scientists specialized in some frontier area such as genes. They can command very high salaries. There are also more and more consultants who offer specialized knowledge when needed and are well paid for doing so. They, too, are closely related to the upper class.

Others who in the recent past identified with the upper class were middle managers. Corporate downsizing, however, has decimated their numbers. Some of those who lost their jobs have landed on their feet as consultants or independent entrepreneurs. But many who once constituted an important part of the middle class have become "downwardly mobile."

An important feature of the economy has been small business people. Many of them have retail stores, restaurants, or real estate agencies. In these ways they are able to work for themselves. They feel considerable investment in the status quo. Huge retailers such as Wal-Mart and large restaurant and real estate chains render their future precarious. Most of them may be put out of business or reduced to operating franchises. If these changes occur, the middle class will be further weakened.

In other instances, such as travel agencies, the Internet is undercutting their business by encouraging travelers to make their reservations directly with the airlines. But the net opens up new entrepreneurial opportunities. The survival of a healthy middle class depends in part on how much of the economy can remain outside the control of large corporations. The net may or may not help.

There are class changes in the professions as well. Doctors, who were long among the most independent and prosperous citizens, have lost standing in the economy. They are now employees of corporations. Although they are well paid, their mentality is changing.

Lawyers are increasingly polarized in terms of class. Some are in the upper class, mainly serving corporate interests. But many are struggling to survive.

University teachers are not as divided as lawyers, but the class divisions are increasing. Universities, like corporations, are downsizing their permanent faculties and meeting their needs from pools of teachers who take part-time, short-term work. These teachers are poorly paid and have no job security or benefits. On the other hand, a few stars are in great demand and can command high salaries as well as lucrative consultantships. Most teachers are in the middle range and continue to be part of the middle class. But their security and status have diminished.

The most stable employment has been in government service. There is less downsizing there and more security. Public criticism of government expenditures may eventually hurt this segment of the labor force, but not at present.

The emerging economy has many other categories. The purpose of this survey is only to suggest that the concentrations near the two ends are likely to grow. If they do, this process will affect the political scene. On the one hand, the overwhelming American consciousness of being middle class (which means to have no class at all) will change, and the number of citizens who cease identifying with the economic status quo will grow. On the other hand, the number who profit greatly from the economy will also grow. These will be far more articulate and politically powerful, but they will not be as numerous.

The harm done by class-consciousness is usually the harm done by those in power to those beneath them. But the instances of class rebellion and their aftermath remind us that lower classes can also do harm. The nondoctrinaire and nonrevolutionary character of the dominant labor movement in the United States has been a blessing. On the whole, labor has sought a larger share in the existing system rather than to replace the power of the ruling class by taking over government.

Because the majority of the population has lacked any class-consciousness to counter that of the ruling elite, that elite has had great freedom. In general, it has been able to persuade the middle class that the policies that are in its favor are also for the common good.[14] The problem has not been too much class-consciousness, but too little. The need is for a countervailing force, a force that industrial labor can no longer supply.

The polarization of the economy that is now developing could be the occasion for the emergence of that countervailing force. But the fragmentation of those who will constitute the exploited means that the traditional labor union model cannot work. Political expression is more promising. But that will require the emergence of a shared consciousness of being the dispossessed.

V. Race and Class

The new underclass is predominantly black. The new temporary labor pool is predominantly white. They share many interests and needs. Can they work together? Or will the increasing dispossession of much of the former middle class lead to further emphasis on an unrepentant whiteness? Given past experiences of failure, the situation is not promising. But change can occur.

The need is a vision of what the future could be that simultaneously abolishes the underclass and creates new opportunities for upward mobility for the working poor. This is not impossible. But the people involved must work out the vision so that they will have ownership.

My own judgment is that attaining shared goals would require the renewal of a full employment policy and accepting the "wage inflation" so feared by our leaders. Indeed, the new policies would raise the minimum wage to a living wage. They would reestablish national borders that restrict the flow of goods so that producers paying a living wage could compete with imports. They would break up some of our corporations that have near monopolistic control. They would require corporations to be socially responsible on pain of losing their charters. They would restrict currency transactions and other ways of making money that do not contribute to the economy. They would put an end to corporate subsidies by the government, and require full payment for the use of public lands by private enterprise. They would replace the patchwork of present responses to health needs by a single-payer plan similar to Canada's. They would end the War on Drugs and greatly modify the prison system.

These policies would abolish taxes on wages and introduce taxes on the use of scarce natural resources and pollution. They would abolish the sales tax. They would raise much of the needed money through taxing land or site values, while abolishing the tax on improvements. These proposals address the needs of blacks in terms of their class interests but do not touch directly on racism. In this sense they side with those who think the most promising path forward is through alliances on economic issues. But they can be achieved and effective only as they are accompanied by the kind of deconstruction and reconstruction of whiteness discussed in Section III.

Chapter Eight

Ethics and Pluralism

I. Introduction

The preceding chapters have emphasized the reality and importance of variety and diversity. The argument has differed from some forms of postmodernism in that it has called not only for acceptance of difference but also for change through the mutual encounter of those who are other. It has not, however, proposed that otherness should be replaced by homogeneity. After each has been affected by the other, difference remains. In the instance of diverse religious traditions, one can see that each is changed through dialogue with others. Buddhists learn from Christians, and Christians, from Buddhists. For the most part, however, Buddhists remain Buddhists, and Christians, Christians. The continuing difference enriches both.

There is no all-transcending position from which a human being can view this plurality. It is always seen only from a locus within the plurality. One may construct meta-theories, but they too express what is understood from one position among others. There is, in principle, no way to overcome the conditionedness of perspective.

This is true also of the statement that the conditionedness of perspective cannot be overcome. That, too, is written from a particular point of view, and it states what appears to be true from that point of view. Although it claims universality, the claim must be recognized to be self-relativized. Postmodernists know that they are immersed in relativity.

Some theories about this relativity lead to the avoidance of universal statements. Such avoidance, however, can only be partial. The theories that lead to this avoidance are themselves universal. Some theories resolve the problem by rejecting any reference of language to a nonlinguistic world. But statements of this sort are difficult to formulate without implying such a reference.

This book adopts the opposite approach. It recognizes the impossibility of certainty but affirms the value of general theories as hypotheses with varying degrees of warrant. It regards the testing of such hypotheses as endless but fruitful. It operates on the hypothesis that the totality of the reality in which we are immersed is incomprehensibly complex. Within that complexity, it theorizes, many different patterns can be traced. The descriptions of these patterns often appear contradictory and mutually exclusive. As verbal formulations, indeed, they are likely to be just that. But more careful statement can often show that, however different the patterns are, the reality of one pattern does not necessarily deny the reality of patterns that other communities believe they have discerned.

This idea does not imply that the several compatible formulations that emerge are all true. It is unlikely that any of our verbal statements are true, strictly speaking. Language is too crude an instrument to reflect the way things are with exactitude. And our ability to transcend language in thought and to develop more accurate language, though real, is limited. Nevertheless, many of our formulations are sufficient approximations to provide good guidance to our reflections about reality.

A famous example comes from physics. The statements that composed what we know as Newtonian physics were not true. But their approximation to accuracy was sufficient to serve their users well for many generations. Einstein's formulations are more precise, but it is doubtful that they are forever beyond the need of further correction. Probably they are false, but remarkably close to the truth.

There are other statements whose distance from the truth is enormous. Most prescientific statements about the constitution of the physical world are of this sort. Our recognition that they had positive functions in their cultural contexts and expressed truths of another sort does not change the fact that, as statements about the physical world, they were usually wide of the mark and often misdirected thought.

Our acknowledgment of the relativity and limitations of all our thought should not blind us to the great differences in approximation to truth that exist. Of course, the assertion that this is so may itself be in error. I can never be certain. But for practical purposes I regard this hypothesis as well established and reliable. I will ask the reader to recognize that I know this ultimate limit of all knowing, and that all my statements, including this one, are made in that knowledge.

In the more theoretical fields, including that of religious beliefs, the hypothesis that differences are often complementary works well. But a problem arises in ethics and public policy. Attending to different features of the totality leads to divergent evaluations and normative judgments. Can these also be relativized in such a way that they are finally compatible with one another? Or must we act according to one or another judgment, thereby contravening the judgment of others? When it comes to public policy, then, must power finally be determinative?

For example, Chapter Five argued for the moral imperative of treating homosexuals on a par with heterosexuals and, therefore, encouraging homosexual unions. Most cultures, including the American one, have rejected that proposal. Does postmodern relativism compel one to regard the contrary judgments of the majority as just as valid as one's own? Should this undercut one's zeal for change?

Modernists taught that diversity in theoretical views, especially in religious ones, showed that all were to be doubted. But they often supposed that people could agree on issues of ethics and practice. This book reverses that pattern. There are ways of going beyond apparently conflicting views at the theoretical level, but differing judgments about morality and practice raise far more difficult questions.

Section II shows how a variety of approaches to ethical issues is possible. As long as none of the approaches claims to exclude the others, all of them can be viewed as complementary rather than mutually exclusive. The problem is that ethical principles, when abstracted from a comprehensive worldview, give very little guidance in dealing with practical ethical issues. This point is illustrated through a discussion of abortion in Section III.

One ethical approach that has not been wholly abstracted from its setting in a comprehensive worldview is natural law theory. Section IV considers this candidate for ethical guidance, arguing that the worldview in which it has remained embedded cannot be sustained even in the context of modernity, much less that of postmodernity. Natural law theory needs to be reformulated to reflect a postmodern understanding of nature.

Although the mutual complementarity of ethical theories may help to express the pluralism affirmed throughout this book, pluralism as such is problematic in the public arena. This is the topic of Section V. Decisions must be made, and often these decisions must reject the views of many groups in the body politic. Postmodern thinkers cannot simply support the right of all to be heard, important as that is. They must also take positions that oppose those of many they have heard.

The example of abortion shows the necessity of such position-taking. A weakness of deconstructive postmodern thinking here has been that its deconstruction of traditional supports for the sanctity of human life seems to leave that sanctity unprotected. Section VI proposes a constructive response to that danger.

Section VII returns to the problem of effective politics in a pluralistic culture. Section VIII offers some concluding reflections on this chapter and on the book as a whole.

II. Varieties of Ethics

For most people throughout history, judgments about how to act were part and parcel of an unquestioned culture. One learned how to behave as a part of one's education. There was no distinction between what we call technique, etiquette, and morality. There was only the best way to do things. Some were more successful than others in acting in that best way. To do so won praise. There were also actions that were simply not allowed—taboo. There were no arguments why such actions were taboo, although there might be narrative explanations. Much of life for many people is still lived in this way. They act as they have been socialized to act and avoid actions that are simply beyond the pale.

With the rise of universalist thought in the first millennium B.C.E., questions of better and worse, right and wrong, came to the fore. In general, such questions were still considered in the context of insights into the way things are. Ethics was not separated from cosmology and religion. In India, the religious thinkers in general accepted the mores of the time and encouraged conformity to that morality in ordinary life. They developed other rules of behavior for those who wanted to attain spiritual heights, and they described the behavioral results of such attainment.

In Israel, the prophetic movement lifted up God's demand for justice and righteousness, contrasting it with other laws and ceremonies. Ethics could not be separated from Israel's understanding of the covenant with God and God's commandments. Among these commandments, however, the ones we consider "ethical" were distinguished.

Jesus and Paul built on this distinction, but both focused on the motivation of love. To act from love is to act rightly. St. Augustine formulated this in a radical way when he said "Love God and do as you please."

Greece provides the closest approximation to what we would call ethical thinking. Plato and Aristotle both concerned themselves with the virtues. Plato's concern was with how the soul is made good. Aristotle attended to behavior of the sort that is socially admired.

These patterns all continue to the present day. Conventional morality supplemented by spiritual disciplines is one style of life. The effort to obey God is another. The concern to love and to act spontaneously out of that love is another. The effort to attain excellence of inner spirit is another. Concern for character is another.

These patterns are different, and no one can pursue all equally. But to adopt one pattern need not lead to condemnation of others. In this sense they are complementary.

In the Middle Ages, Christian thought about ethical matters elaborated a natural law theory. This theory developed out of Greek ideas, especially Stoicism, but it was influenced also by the biblical view of God as creator and giver of the law. Christians judged that, because God created the world, we can find in it an expression of God's purposes for us. These can be discerned in the purposes inherent in the world itself. We are required to live "according to nature" in *this* sense.

Because medieval science explained the natural world primarily in terms of purposes, this type of ethical thinking was very congenial. However, modern science rejected teleological thinking, so that most of the Enlightenment ethicists sought new grounds for ethical theories. Natural law thinking continued chiefly among Catholics. It still operates, however, among some jurists, and it plays an influential role in public discourse. For many people the idea that behavior is "unnatural" is a strong argument against it. Natural law theory, too, can be viewed as complementary to the others.

Modern Western ethical theories also have developed out of the influence of the Bible and Greek philosophy. Deontological ethics, stemming from the Bible, is the most distinctive form. Although many obey God in hopes of reward, the Bible also notes that such obedience is good and right even when there is no reward. Whereas the great majority of the world's thought about ethics has been broadly teleological, a note of radical or categorical obligation entered the Western tradition from the Bible, and it has found influential expression in Kant and his followers.

For some ethicists, following Kant, deontological ethics is the only true ethics. Some forms of behavior are right or obligatory without regard to the consequences that can be anticipated. According to these thinkers, acting in a certain way because one hopes for certain consequences, even the consequence of a respected character, is not truly ethical.

Even in the West, however, most ethicists continued to understand ethics teleologically. That is, they thought that the right act is the act that produces, or at least intends, the best consequences. In the extreme case, the relevant consequences might be only those to the actor. In its most influential expressions, in contrast, one was to consider consequences to all. Even the possibility of considering consequences to other animals was proposed,[1] although this proposal was not influential until quite recently.

Although these ethical systems continue to be influential, the twentieth century has been characteristically skeptical. When morality is defined, as it is by both utilitarians and Kantians, as doing that which is right regardless of personal gain, the question can be asked: Why should one be moral? From the point of view of the questioner, the only acceptable answer would be that one wants to be moral or that one will gain something one desires in that way. Hence, whereas both the utilitarians and Kant believed their views were required by reason itself, the twentieth-century doubters have been free to ask: Why should one be rational in that sense?

These skeptics leave us with an extreme relativism. If being moral is something other than self-interested behavior, then it is simply a matter of taste. One who wishes to be moral will choose to be so. If it is a means of achieving a desired goal, then the attraction to one goal or another is decisive. The idea that one act or another is truly right or good becomes meaningless.

There is some justification for this skepticism. When ethics is separated from its context in social thought, cosmology, and religion, it is not fully self-justifying. A few formal statements may survive despite the skeptical attack, but what remains is a far cry from an account of how we are to live. In separation from a wider context of beliefs, several conflicting conclusions can be drawn from such formal principles about how to act.

III. An Illustration: Abortion

This point can be illustrated in considering almost any significant ethical issue. Abortion will serve as an example. Utilitarian ethics asks us to consider all the consequences that will follow and to act so as to produce the best. In its original formulation, it proposed that the desired consequence was pleasure and the avoidance of pain, but richer interpretations of consequences can be offered.

The problem is both that predicting consequences is difficult and that evaluating the anticipated consequences is equally so. If the woman has an abortion, how will she feel bout it in months and years to come? If there are questions about her physical health, will she be better if she has the abortion? Will differences between the prospective parents over the abortion poison their relationship? If the woman's professional life is a factor in the decision, will its success bring her great satisfaction or contribute significantly to others?

If the fetus is brought to term, what kind of life will it have? What effects will the negative attitudes of the parents toward having another child have on the child? Especially if there are doubts about its health, will its physical problems prevent it from having a satisfying life? What effects will the new infant have on its siblings if there are any? Or if the child must be put up for adoption, what are its chances of having a good life?

No one knows the answers to these or the many other relevant questions. The practical merits of utilitarian ethics are largely exhausted in encouraging us to consider these matters seriously and to come to what judgment we can. This stance is quite different from looking for absolute laws to which we should conform. But our decision is still likely to be shaped by our overall sense of what is real and important, a sense informed by our cosmological or religious vision.

Kantian ethics appear to free us from the need to consider consequences at all. We are invited instead to ask ourselves one question: Can we will that everyone adopt the maxim governing the act under consideration?

In actual practice, however, we are not freed from considerations of consequences. There are maxims whose generalization we cannot will because the consequences of all acting in that way would be horrendous. Kant's effort to say that the reasons for being unable to will this generalization are independent of consequences is not convincing.

Consider now the issue at hand. Much depends on how the maxim is formulated. Kant seems to favor very broad formulations. We might then ask: Can we will that every pregnant woman, when she finds some inconvenience in a pregnancy and its anticipated consequences, terminate it? Formulated in this way, most of us would answer negatively.

But we can equally well, indeed much better, ask: Can we will that, in a situation quite similar to this one, every woman would terminate a pregnancy? That is, with similar problems about the woman's work and health, about the resources available for other children, about the financial security of the family, or about the probable health of the child, and with similar ethical views, might every woman so choose? In this case, many of us would find that it depended on just what the circumstances were.

The categorical imperative as such reminds us only that we should not make an exception in our own case from what we believe is right for people in general. It is a good reminder. But it does not take us far toward an answer about how to act. That will be decided in the context of our views of life and death and family and human well-being and the nature and status of a fetus.

Kant introduces another valuable principle. He tells us that we should always treat other people as ends and not only as means. This is again an important reminder of something that all the great religious traditions have taught, that we should respect the dignity of other people. But like the utilitarian and categorical principles, it does not carry us far toward a solution of our ethical problem. It does not tell us whether the fetus is one of those people we are to treat as an end. Also, even if it is, are we not to treat the pregnant woman and others involved in the situation also as ends? How are we to adjudicate when their interests conflict? Are there instances when some are properly treated more as means than as ends, and others more as ends than as means?

There is another problem with this principle. It expresses the humanism and the anthropocentrism of modernity. By its silence it implies that everything except human beings is to be treated only as a means. The adoption of that principle has had appalling consequences for other animals. It expresses and contributes to the objectification of nature that has endangered the carrying capacity of the Earth. That criticism does not mean that the principle as such should be abandoned. It only reminds us that the role of formal ethical principles by themselves should be recognized to be quite limited.

To operate effectively, ethical systems must be reincorporated into the types of larger vision from which they have been abstracted. Without such a wider context, the issues so important to modern philosophers are condemned to playing a minor role in most actual ethical debates. For example, the definition of a "person," with its answer to the question whether a fetus is a person, makes far more difference to the outcome of the discussion than do formal ethical principles.

A larger vision, however, can show at least some limited role for all the approaches considered. Thus multiple approaches to ethics and diverse ethical theories need not lead to skepticism. They all have their place and value. They err only when they claim to exclude others or to be independent of other aspects of belief.

IV. The Application of Natural Law Theory

Because classical and medieval ethics were embedded in larger systems of thought, they have more concrete implications. In terms of present issues, this fact is most clear with respect to natural law theory. To operate effectively in the public debate today, it must be abstracted from its full theological context in medieval theology. But the abstraction does not go very far. The theory is not abstracted from its understanding of the created order.

Natural law theory is particularly important today in relation to issues of sexuality. It holds that sexuality came into the world for a purpose, namely, for procreation. To employ sexuality to that end is good. To employ it for other conscious purposes, while remaining open to its fulfillment of its own intrinsic purpose, is also acceptable. But to be involved in sexual acts that intentionally prevent conception, or that cannot serve that end, is morally wrong. It is against nature by thwarting the intrinsic purpose of this important aspect of creation.

In the course of the centuries, the Catholic Church has modified its teaching somewhat. But the resistance to birth control and to homosexual acts remains. Particularly in the latter area, it is able to generate considerable support from those who consider homosexuality unnatural even though they know nothing of natural law theory and would not follow it on other points. It may be that the deepest obstacle to freeing homosexual acts from their taint of immorality is the association of the moral with the "natural."

Moderns sometimes side with premoderns on the association of the natural with heterosexuality. They appeal to the biological fact that sexuality and gender emerged as a strategy of nature for reproduction. Nature's requirement was heterosexual sex. This is profoundly natural. For moderns it can be emphasized that nature's strategy here as elsewhere was profligate. Just as plants have far more seeds than needed under favorable circumstances to reproduce themselves, so nature made sex pleasurable in order that there would be far more sexual activity than needed if it were carefully directed toward procreation. Thus, unlike medieval Catholic thinking, modernity declares it fully natural to engage in heterosexual activity for pleasure's sake. But because the evolutionary function of sexuality was procreation, some moderns have still drawn the conclusion that homosexual acts are contrary to nature.

Although some moderns speak in this way, they are in fact rejecting true modernity when they do so. Modern science, including evolutionary theory, denies that there is purpose in the process. In the modern evolutionary view, sexual bimorphism developed accidentally and happened to lead to a new form of reproduction. This form proved successful. Sexual reproduction has been a central part of the evolutionary process ever since. But that does not mean that there is anything unnatural about expressing sexuality in ways that are unrelated to reproduction. The notion that some things that happen in the natural world are unnatural is meaningless in the modern vision.

The postmodern vision developed in this book reaffirms the presence of purpose in the natural world. Purpose is present in each occasion. It is present moment by moment in every cell in the body and especially in each of the occasions whose succession makes up the human soul. It is wrong to deny that these creaturely purposes have played a role in the evolutionary process.

Moderns who affirm the purposelessness of the evolutionary process often deny that creaturely purposes are real chiefly because of their fear that acknowledging them will allow for the reintroduction of cosmic purpose. They are not wrong. Creaturely purposes reflect a larger purpose in the whole of things. But the relation of purpose to evolution in this vision is quite different from the one against which evolutionary theory was formulated. Chance and necessity continue to play a large role in this postmodern vision. The effort to treat them as exhaustively explanatory of all that happens fails, but any effort to interpret the entire course of events as expressing a cosmic divine purpose also fails.

In this context, what is "natural" for an individual cannot be read off the grand story. If we use the term at all, we may mean what we find given as opposed to what we choose. Sexual orientation is experienced as given, not chosen. If an individual's orientation is to members of the same sex, then for that person homosexuality is natural. If that individual enters into heterosexual relations only by an act of will, these relations are unnatural.

Some may say that because most people are heterosexual, that is more natural. Quantitatively that may be, but it has nothing to do with what is natural for the minority. For them to act according to nature, that is, their own nature, is to express physically their feelings for other members of the same sex.

This analysis shows that the abstraction of natural law theory from its full context greatly weakens its plausibility. In that context, the basic patterns of nature were believed to be directly expressive of God's purposes and intentions. Even in the context of that understanding, other conclusions would have been possible, but in that context, the one that was drawn was reasonable. Without that context, and in view of the very different understanding of nature brought about by modern and postmodern science, its weakness should be exposed.

V. Practical Problems

The theory that multiple approaches to ethics can all find their place does not resolve the issue of what to do in a concrete situation. Different conclusions will follow from different approaches in combination with the larger belief systems in which they are embedded. Although one may entertain the truth of diverse doctrines, including diverse doctrines about how to do ethics, one cannot both act and not act in a certain way. Sometimes one can devise more complex responses to a situation that satisfy persons coming from different approaches. But often there is an either/or character to the action that cannot be further nuanced. One cannot both have, and not have, an abortion.

In an instance of this kind, postmodernists will leave the decision largely to those most immediately involved. There is no need to impose homogeneity. Religious, cultural, and philosophical relativity can be respected. The problem arises at the level of public policy.

We must have laws protecting each group and each individual from serious harm by others. None of us would wish to tolerate unrestricted maiming and killing and destroying one another's property. As a community we decide that certain actions are to be prohibited and that we will punish those who commit them. Although there are many debates about the exact laws and the ways they are enforced, all religions and cultures agree in general on these matters.

Some cultures, however, have practices that appear to others to violate these rules. Genital mutilation is one that has been highlighted in recent times. Here the postmodernist concern to avoid imposing the values of one culture on another comes into conflict with the postmodernist concern for the liberation of women from male oppression and abuse.

Let us return to our own issue: abortion. There are subcultures within the United States whose religious convictions and approach to ethics forbid the practice of abortion. The postmodernist can respect these convictions. But some of these subcultures also argue that abortion should be outlawed for all, and they work vigorously to this end.

They do not understand themselves as thereby imposing their particular religious beliefs on other communities. Instead they believe that our shared conviction that murder should not be allowed entails laws against abortion. Publicly they argue for this not from their sacred texts but from their factual judgments, their formal ethical principles, and their understanding of the role of law. The basic factual judgment is that the fetus is a human being. The ethical principle is that killing an innocent human being is wrong. The role of law is to forbid actions that do serious harm to others.

A postmodernist must respect the culture that cultivates this kind of thinking. Given those views, that culture cannot simply respect others who think differently. It must do what it can to protect all fetuses from "murder." This requires that it undertake to influence legislation.

Yet a postmodernist, not agreeing that abortion is "murder," believes that within limits decisions about abortions should be left to pregnant women and the others most closely involved. No one culture should impose its views about abortion on others. There arises, therefore, direct opposition to a culture that one fully respects and recognizes to be acting consistently and morally.

This illustration makes clear that postmodernism must recognize itself as one position among others. Its affirmation of diversity and pluralism does not make it any less a particular belief system. It generates its own conclusions about public policy and engages in its own efforts to implement what it advocates. Its starting point is just as conditioned as any other. It cannot claim any exemption from the relativity it notes in others.

Does this recognition weaken its commitment to its own proposals? For some postmodernists, the answer may be Yes. They speak as if the recognition of relativity and conditionedness entails that there is no truth or approximation to truth, only diverse systems of thought that are incommensurable with one another. If this were the case, then there would be reason to withdraw energy from proposals that affect people who do not share one's system. There is no basis for declaring one's own view—that it is undesirable to impose practices on others— more trustworthy or desirable than any other view. In short, the logic of statements by some postmodernists promotes a debilitating relativism, even when those who propound the logic do not consistently follow it.

Conditionedness and relativity do not have that meaning in the kind of postmodernism advocated in this book. They make clear that there is much to be discerned that is not visible from the conditioned perspective of any individual. This stance opens one to relativize what one has seen and to learn from others. It makes evident that no one ever gets beyond a fragmentary and partly distorted understanding of reality. But it does not mean that all theories about reality are equally good or bad. Constructive postmodernists will strive to develop the best theory they can, always open to correction and supplementation, and then act vigorously on the results. One mode of action will be the defense of otherness and diversity. But where that entails struggling against an other who wants to impose one view on others, even an other whose integrity they fully respect, they will not withdraw from that struggle.

In the present instance, the struggle is at two levels. One level is simply the political struggle to defend the flexibility built into present laws against efforts to reduce it. The other level is theoretical. The logic of the opposition rests on an understanding of the person that a postmodernist does not accept. To expose the weaknesses in this understanding and to spread a different understanding as widely as possible is an important part of the struggle. Knowing that the new understanding is imperfect, that it is the way things look from a conditioned perspective, does not invalidate the judgment that it does justice to more of the evidence than do the available alternatives, including the one that underlies the intense opposition to all abortion.

The best-articulated arguments that abortion is murder come from Roman Catholics. Their argument is based on essentialist thinking. According to this thinking, an entity either is or is not an embodiment of an essence. In this case the relevant essence is human personhood.

If human personhood is an essence, then its presence must have a definite beginning. Historically, as in St. Augustine, its beginning was quickening.[2] Quickening is becoming alive, and the soul is the principle of life. The human soul, therefore, was understood to enter the body at that point. From then on, one dealt with a human person. For Augustine, to kill the quickened or ensouled fetus was murder.

Others have located the initiation of personhood at later points, such as viability, or birth, or even the learning of language. Currently the dominant Catholic response is that there is no point in the development of the fetus or the child where there is a change so abrupt and significant that one can assert it to be the point at which a new essence appears. The evidence now is that the process is more continuous. The implication is that we must assume the essence to be there from the beginning, now defined as the fertilization of the ovum. At that point the genetic code defining the particular character of this unique human being is established.[3] The rest is the outworking of the human personhood there established.

Given the assumption that there is an essence of human personhood that is either present or not, this argument has considerable force. For those who find the conclusion unacceptable, therefore, it is the assumption that should be questioned. Is not human personhood a state that is gradually achieved over time rather than an essence that is either present or not? If by human personhood is meant the properties associated with a normal adult or even a child, then the evidence points in this direction. Obviously, most of what people normally think of as a human being is not present in a newly fertilized ovum. It is only if the evidence must be interpreted through a particular metaphysic that it leads to the counterintuitive notion that the fertilized ovum already *is* a human person, so that its destruction is murder.

The reasons for clinging to essentialist thinking in this regard are clear. Such thinking makes absolutist statements about all human beings possible. All have sacred and equal worth, because all participate equally in the essence. There are many desirable consequences that follow from this view. The alternative view—that there is no essence to the human person, that people are very different, and that personality develops gradually and in diverse directions—has its dangers. The universal prohibitions and affirmations about human life, to which both the church and modernity have clung, must either be abandoned or justified in nonabsolutistic terms.

The full clarification of the consequences of such a postmodern move is an important task. Until the public can trust that these consequences do not undercut convictions about the preciousness of each individual human life, many will support the absolutes that seem to offer these safeguards, even if they lead, at the edges, to unconvincing and undesirable conclusions.

VI. A Postmodern Understanding of Persons

Deconstructive postmodernism engages in its deconstruction for the sake of the liberation of persons. The prizing of difference has been directed to allowing the authentic voice of previously silenced persons to be heard. The risk, however, is that the process of deconstruction can undercut the grounds on which in the past persons have been judged to be ends in themselves, beings of intrinsic worth, rather than simply resources to be used by those capable of controlling them.

Whitehead traced the ideas that undergirded the understanding of personal worth and rights,[4] showing their history to be closely involved with the Platonic doctrine of the human soul. It is the fact that every human being possesses, or is, such soul that calls for the respect of every other human being. Being soul gives to each person a status that transcends individual differences and social roles.

The implications of the doctrine of soul, Whitehead pointed out, were not immediately appreciated. The economy of the Roman Empire was based on slavery, and even those most interested in soul rarely objected to the institution. At best, they sought better treatment of slaves. Over the centuries, nevertheless, more and more people developed the implications of the doctrine of soul, and finally, in the nineteenth century, slavery was abolished in most of the world. Doctrines of human rights were developed and they have been extended to more and more people.

Ironically, the basis for this extension of the implications of Plato's doctrine of soul has lost its self-evidence in the intellectual community. In the eighteenth century, David Hume undercut the idea of a substantial soul. He left us with only a succession of primarily sensory experiences, along with habits of interpreting them. It would be difficult to draw from his philosophy a clear ground for treating every individual human being with unconditional respect.

The term "soul" has faded from philosophical discourse, being largely replaced by "mind" and "self." These terms have also ceased to refer to substantial entities with claims to transcend the flux of empirical realities. For many postmodernists, they mean only what particular linguistic systems or cultures use them to mean. They have no ontological reference. The apparent implication is that the choice of treating others with respect is one choice among others, no more in line with reality than contrary choices.

Thus far, few have drawn the full relativistic implications. Just as most Platonists long accepted the dominant patterns of the Greco-Roman world despite the theoretical implications of their beliefs, so now most modernists and postmodernists accept the implications of the Platonic doctrine of soul despite the contrary theoretical implications of their ideas. But the fear of these implications leads others to cling to absolutistic teachings. Whitehead considered it a matter of some urgency to develop a postmodern doctrine of soul that took full account of the problems noted by Hume and later deconstructive thinkers—one that reaffirms and grounds the conviction of human worth transcending appearance, usefulness to others, and social status.

Whitehead strongly shared the deconstructive view that soul is not a substance underlying the flow of unified human experience. It is just that flow. He had no interest in identifying an essence of human nature that sharply distinguished all human experience from the experiences of other animals. He emphasized more the variety of human experiences than any universal elements within them. A human experience is the experience of a member of the biological species *homo sapiens*. The characteristics of human experiences are to be found empirically.

None of this, however, diminishes the worth or importance of human experience in all of its variety. On the contrary, the only locus of value is experience. Every experience is a value in and for itself. This is true of the experiences of other animals as well; so it is a reason for opposing the treatment of other animals as mere means for human use and enjoyment. But the fact that respect should be accorded to others besides humans in no way diminishes the fact that respect should be accorded to every human being. This is demanded by the ontological reality of intrinsic value.

The intrinsic value of every experience is greatly enhanced by its place in the "person." For Whitehead, the person is the cumulative flow of experience. That is, each occasion of experience contributes its novelty and originality to successor occasions in the flow. Most of the richness of experience in each moment derives from the intimate presence within it of predecessor occasions. Thus the person has a value that is not exhausted by the values of its individual members, since it is the personal ordering of these members that contributes so much to the potential for value in the future.

Once again, unlike the Platonic doctrine of human soul, this doctrine is relevant to the evaluation of other animals. In many of them, the personal ordering of experience plays a role. As a consequence, one individual does not simply substitute for another. There is a loss when a dog dies that is not replaced by the birth of another dog. There is an accumulation of experience that uniquely contributes to the intrinsic value of the dog's new experiences as well as to that of the human beings who love it.

There are certainly some nonhuman animals with greater intrinsic value than some human beings. For example, some chimpanzees are capable of enjoying greater intrinsic value than some brain-damaged people. This postmodern vision rejects the absolutist lines between humans and other animals that both classical and modern philosophy have drawn. This recognition does not, however, diminish the Kantian claim of every human being to be treated as an end and never only as a means.

In most of the Platonic tradition the intrinsic value of human beings has been heightened by views of their relationship to God. They are understood to be creations of God and in the image and likeness of God. For Christians, God's special concern for human beings has been expressed in the incarnation and crucifixion of Jesus. Each human being has been viewed as a child of God for whom Jesus died.

For most postmoderns, this theistic heightening of the preciousness of each human being is not possible. Nevertheless, Whitehead, like the tradition, introduces the theistic note. In his case, this note does not discriminate markedly between human beings and other creatures: all come into being from the divine initiative and all contribute to the content of the divine life. The joy of any creature brings joy to God; its suffering, suffering. What we do to one another, we do also to God. The call to be concerned for all others as ends in themselves is heightened by the fact that through harming or benefiting them, we harm and benefit God.

The implications of this postmodern approach to such issues as abortion and physician-assisted suicide are different from the implications of the modern approach. The latter issue was discussed in Chapter One. In this chapter, the focus is on abortion as a test case.

From this postmodern perspective, the fertilized ovum has intrinsic value, for like all cells it is composed of occasions of experience. But its intrinsic value is less than that of many creatures we are accustomed to destroying rather casually. The reason that we should *not* be casual about its destruction is that, in most instances, it has the *potential*, given many additional contributions, of becoming a human being.

Destroying a potential human person, nevertheless, is a quite different matter from destroying a human person. In nature generally, most such potentials are not realized. Indeed, they *could* not be realized. Only a tiny percentage of potential oaks become oaks, for example. In human beings, only a tiny percentage of sperm fertilize ova. The idea that every potential for life, even human life, should be actualized is, of course, absurd. The decision to actualize potentials should always be made in the context of considering other potentials that may be thwarted in the process. But because of the great value of the actuality that is prevented by destroying the fertilized ovum, its destruction should never be casual.

As the embryo develops, its intrinsic value increases. Nevertheless, it remains trivial in comparison with the value of what it has the potential to become. The intrinsic value of the fetus becomes a significant concern only when the central nervous system develops to the point where there are unified experiences. Causing pain to the fetus after this time should be a matter of moral consideration. This consideration increases as the subjective life of the fetus grows. Even then, however, the intrinsic value of fetal experiences is analogous to that of animals to which we assign quite limited value on an individual basis. It is still the potential value that should dominate our moral reflections.

The view presented here is opposed to treating any one principle as an absolute. Every decision about abortion must balance a variety of considerations. The values of the pregnant woman and of the fetus are especially important. As time passes, the balance shifts toward the fetus, but never to the point that the woman's life should be sacrificed to it.

Despite the special role of the pregnant woman, a constructive postmodernist cannot absolutize her rights or interests. This must be balanced not only by the rights and interests of the fetus but also by those of other people whose lives will be affected by the decision. Ideally, the decision about an abortion should be a collective one. The interests of the wider society should also enter in.

In a general way, this view supports the Supreme Court decision in *Wade vs. Rowe*. The Court saw a transition from a time when the pregnant woman should be free to determine the fate of the fetus to a time when the point of view of the fetus becomes quite important. It assumes a process of becoming human rather than an all-or-nothing essence of humanity. Despite the moral desirability that others beside the woman have a say, it wisely avoided making legal requirements about who must be consulted.

The point of these reflections is to show that a postmodern doctrine of the soul does not open the door to sheer relativism. It undergirds the central teachings stemming from the Platonic doctrine of soul. But by removing the absolutistic character of the traditional doctrine, it allows for rethinking of some of its less convincing, and sometimes cruel, practical implications.

VII. Pluralism in Politics

The previous sections have offered some reasons why the constructive postmodernist should be active in politics. The recognition of the conditionedness and relativity of one's own perspective will not block one from holding strong convictions and acting on them. The affirmation of difference will not prevent one from seeking to prevent others from imposing their will or from attempting to change policies in a favored direction. We can believe that our judgments are grounded in the nature of things. In the process of pushing our proposals, we can use critical and rational argument.

But there is also strong resistance among many postmodernists to practical political involvement. Many are more comfortable working to change cultural patterns, trusting that those changes will in turn express themselves in legislation. Feminist work has been largely of this sort and has proved remarkably effective.

With regard to basic economic and political structures, however, postmodernists are more divided. This division is seen in the green movement, which is the most comprehensive current expression of postmodern politics. Within this movement are many who refuse to engage in the compromises required for practical politics.[5] They believe that they should act with integrity in local contexts. They hope that, in the long run, creating alternative communities will undercut the now dominant style. They are often quite hostile to the role of national government, insisting on bottom-up governance against top-down.

Other greens believe that without changes in the public sphere, there is no possibility of responding adequately to the global crises now faced. They see national government as having a positive and necessary role to play and emphasize the importance of pressuring it to play that role. To influence public policy, they are prepared to engage in those activities needed to do so. Because postmodernists are too few and too weak to be effective, they must form coalitions with others. In countries such as the United States, which are fragmented into religious, cultural, racial, and class groupings, politics is the art of finding allies for particular projects and compromising one's goal sufficiently to have a chance of winning majority support.

From the postmodernist perspective of this book, these two approaches are complementary. Local achievements are too often undercut by changes in public policy. Those who engage in them often find themselves helpless before forces they have not even engaged. By themselves, local efforts will not effect the redirection of the nation, much less the world. On the other hand, the deep changes that are required will never be attained solely through national legislation, or by international treaties. And even the more moderate changes that do have some chance will not be implemented without grass roots movements that in some measure anticipate them.

One principle of postmodern thought in general, and of the greens in particular, is to be inclusive and to give voice to diverse groups and interests. Unfortunately, it is easier to celebrate diversity than to work effectively with members of diverse groups, especially with those that have a strong consciousness of their distinct identity and interests. Still, if we are to move toward a society that gives a place to diverse groups, allowing them to develop from their own history and experience, we must work together toward a conception of what that society will be like and find ways to cooperate on programs and legislation that will move in that direction.

Jesse Jackson's rainbow coalition was the right idea. Its time had not come. There was insufficient reflection about the purpose of such a coalition. It could seem to some that Jackson was co-opting other groups for his purposes. Each group was still too intent on its own interests to draw together around common ones.

That situation still prevails and makes it quite easy for the dominant culture, especially those who control the economy, to divide and conquer. But there are signs that leaders are emerging in the many separate cultures who understand the need to work together to envision a society that allows each its place and yet has sufficient unity to function. This book intends to be a contribution to such thinking. Once a vision is in place, common action will follow, continually reshaping the vision as well.

VIII. Concluding Reflections

Postmodern thinking is still in its infancy. It is fragmented, and often fragmentary. There are constructive elements or implications in all postmodern thinkers, but there is a danger that the emphasis of so many on deconstruction obscures the constructive intention. There is a danger, also, that internecine fighting among postmodernists will weaken the impact of their shared critique of modernity and their proposal of a more humane and diversified future. Since the probable future is now being shaped on a massive scale by an ultramodern global economic order, the whole postmodern discussion is in danger of becoming an irrelevant exercise among privileged academics.

This book has called for transforming many apparently conflicting positions into complementary ones that can serve as contrasts for an enriched future. Implicitly, it has argued that this can be done among alternative postmodern approaches as well. There will always remain practical decisions by which one party or another will feel rejected, but we can continue to practice the art of listening to one another and of making space for one another.

This book is in part an appeal to postmodernists who are particularly suspicious of worldviews and ontologies to open themselves to these as well. If they will respond by detailed critique of how the use of a cosmology in this book has led to the negative consequences they have observed elsewhere, this critique will be greatly appreciated and can lead to better formulations in the future. On the other hand, wholesale *ad hominem* dismissal does not advance our work together. It also alienates some thoughtful people whose support is badly needed if we are to make a positive difference in the public world.

In one sense, the modern world is dead. But its dead hand structures our universities as well as our public life. Those who understand the negative consequences of this continuing power must find ways to work together. If this book can contribute to that project, it will have succeeded.

Notes

Preface

1. David Ray Griffin, "Introduction," in David Ray Griffin, William A. Beardslee, and Joe Holland, *Varieties of Postmodern Theology* (Albany: State University of New York Press, 1989), 3.

Introduction

1. Alfred North Whitehead, *Science and the Modern World* (New York: The Free Press, 1925).

2. David Griffin has researched the use of "postmodern" in this tradition. John Herman Randall used it already in 1944 in "The Nature of Naturalism" (in Yervant H. Krikorian, ed., *Naturalism and the Human Spirit*, Morningside Heights, NY: Columbia University Press) to refer to a changed understanding of nature (of which Whitehead's work was one expression), which is open to human values and religion. Uses more directly influenced by Whitehead can be dated to 1964. Floyd W. Watson advocated "postmodern science" in *The Broken Image: Man, Science and Society* (Garden City, NY: Doubleday & Co.). Also in 1964, I may have been the first to use the term in a title, thus making it somewhat more visible: "From Crisis Theology to the Post-Modern World," *Centennial Review 8*. I made more systematic use of the concept in *Christ in a Pluralistic Age* (Philadelphia: Westminster Press, 1975). Griffin himself began using the term in 1972, and in recent years has given it rich definition and content. He organized a Center for the Postmodern World in Santa Barbara, and in 1988 he inaugurated this series on constructive postmodern thought. In 1973 Charles Altieri wrote an essay entitled "From Symbolist Thought to Immanence" (*Boundary* 21/3), in which he argued that Whitehead's philosophy is the best support for the relation of fact and value affirmed by a group of American poets he considered postmodern: Robert Bly, Robert Creeley, Robert Duncan, Denise Levertov, Charles Olson, and Gary Snyder. Frederick Ferré published *Shaping the Future: Resources for the Postmodern World* in 1976 (San Francisco: Harper and

Row), and "Religious World Modeling and Postmodern Science" (*Journal of Religion* 62/3) in 1982. Stephen Toulmin picked up the Whiteheadian use of the term from Ferré in *The Return to Cosmology: Postmodern Science and the Theology of Nature* (Berkeley: University of California Press, 1982).

3. See Friedrich Schleiermacher, *On Religion: Speeches to its Culture Despisers* (English Translation, London: Kegan Paul, Trench, Tribue and Co., 1893) and *The Christian Faith* (English translation, Edinburgh: T&T Clark, 1928).

4. George Lindbeck and Stanley Hauerwas are important leaders here.

5. See Mark C. Taylor, *Erring: A Postmodern A/Theology* (Chicago: University of Chicago Press, 1984).

6. Alfred Loisy, 1857–1940.

7. George Tyrrell, 1861–1909.

8. Modern Churchmen's Union.

9. Shailer Mathews, *The Faith of Modernism* (New York: Macmillan, 1924).

10. See Bernard Smith, *Modernism's History* (Sydney: University of New South Wales Press, 1998).

11. See especially, Alfred North Whitehead, *Process and Reality: An Essay in Cosmology* (Corrected Edition by David Ray Griffin and Donald W. Sherburne, New York: The Free Press, 1978), Part V.

12. John B. Cobb, Jr., *Christ in a Pluralistic Age.*

Chapter One: Can Christians Contribute to the Postmodern World?

1. John Hick, *An Interpretation of Religion: Human Responses to the Transcendent* (London: The Macmillan Press, 1989), Part Four.

2. George Lindbeck, *The Nature of Doctrine* (Philadelphia: Westminster Press, 1984).

3. Alfred North Whitehead, *Adventures of Ideas* (New York: Macmillan, 1933), 214–15.

4. Ibid., 20–21.

5. "Creative transformation" is a term used equivalently with "the creative event" and explained by Henry Nelson Wieman in *The Source of Human Good* (Chicago: The University of Chicago Press, 1946), 58–66. My use is explained in *Christ in a Pluralistic Age,* Part One.

Chapter Two: Religious Pluralism and Truth

1. See, for example, Pinchas Lapide, *The Resurrection of Jesus: A Jewish Perspective,* trans. Wilhelm C. Linss (Minneapolis: Augsburg Press, 1983). Also Pinchas Lapide and Jürgen Moltmann, *Jewish Monotheism and Trinitarian Doctrine,* trans. Leonard Swidler (Philadelphia: Fortress Press, 1981).

2. Hans Küng, "Christianity and World Religions: Dialogue with Islam," in

Leonard Swidler, ed., *Toward a Universal Theology of Religion* (Maryknoll, NY: Orbis Press, 1987), 192–209.

3. Ernest Simmons, "Mystical Consciousness in Process Perspective," *Process Studies* (Spring 1984), 1–10.

4. Paul Tillich, *Biblical Religion and the Search for Ultimate Reality* (Chicago: University of Chicago Press, 1955).

5. For a detailed account of Heidegger's understanding of the implications of his thought for theology, see James M. Robinson, "The German Discussion of the Later Heidegger," in James M. Robinson and John B. Cobb, Jr., eds., *The Later Heidegger and Theology* (New York: Harper & Row, 1963), especially 34–40.

6. Alfred North Whitehead, *Process and Reality*, 21.

7. Raymond Bailey, *Thomas Merton on Mysticism* (Garden City, NY: Doubleday, 1975), 174.

8. See Gene Reeves, "The Lotus Sutra and Process Thought," *Process Studies* (Summer 1994), 108–10.

Chapter Three: Culture and Education

1. See Paul Tillich, *On the Boundary* (New York: Scribners, 1966), 68–74.

2. Hans Küng, *Global Responsibility: In Search of a New World Ethic* (New York: Crossroad, 1991).

3. "The Responsive Communitarian Platform: Rights and Responsibilities," in Amitai Etzioni, ed., *The Essential Communitarian Reader* (Lanham, MD: Rowman & Littlefield, 1998), xxix–xxx.

4. Diane Ravitch, "Pluralism vs. Particularism in American Education," in *The Essential Communitarian Reader*, 281.

5. Ibid., 280.

6. Alfred North Whitehead, *The Aims of Education and Other Essays* (New York: New American Library, 1949), 13. Originally published by Macmillan in 1929.

7. Whitehead, *Process and Reality*, 25.

Chapter Four: Gender and Sexuality

1. Whitehead used the term to identify the sum of all values. Alfred North Whitehead, *Adventures of Ideas*, Part IV.

2. I am indebted to the doctoral research of Anand Veeraraj for this overview.

3. Carolyn Merchant, *The Death of Nature: Women, Ecology and the Scientific Revolution* (New York: Harper & Row, 1980).

4. For a far more nuanced discussion of this issue in recent feminist writings see Catherine Keller, *Apocalypse Now and Then* (Boston: Beacon Press, 1998), Chapter 6. For Keller's own formulation of the role of the body, see page 178.

5. Nancy Chodorow, *The Reproduction of Mothering: Psychoanalysis and the Sociology of Gender* (Berkeley and Los Angeles: University of California Press, 1978).

Chapter Five: Nature, Community, and the Human Economy

1. Paul Shepard, *Nature and Madness* (San Francisco: Sierra Club Books, 1982).

2. For an account of how the Benedictine's altered the evaluation of technology in the West, see David F. Noble, *The Religion of Technology: The Divinity of Man and the Spirit of Invention* (New York: Alfred A. Knopf, 1997).

3. Jerry Taylor, *The Washington Times*, Dec. 5, 1997, A21. For more extensive and detailed discussion of the economist's view of how to respond to global warming, see William Nordhaus, ed., *Economics and Policy Issues of Climate Change* (Washington, DC: Resources for the Future, 1998).

4. Despite his enthusiasm for economic globalization, Thomas Friedman takes this problem seriously in *The Lexus and the Olive Tree* (New York: Farrar, Straus, Giroux, 1999).

5. See Friedman, *The Lexus and the Olive Tree*.

6. See David C. Korten, *When Corporations Rule the World* (West Hartford: Kumarian Press; San Francisco: Berrett-Koehler Publishers, 1995).

7. For rich discussions of this topic see William Vitek and Wes Jackson, eds., *Rooted in the Land: Essays on Community and Place* (New Haven: Yale University Press, 1996).

8. This point has been made repeatedly by Herman Daly. See, for example, Herman E. Daly and John B. Cobb, Jr., *For the Common Good* (Revised Edition, Boston: Beacon Press, 1994), 143–46.

Chapter Six: Governance

1. Karl Marx and Friedrich Engels, "The Communist Manifesto," in D. McLellan, ed., *Karl Marx: Selected Writings* (Oxford: Oxford University Press, 1977), 235.

2. Paul Tillich, *Systematic Theology*, Vol. II. (Chicago: University of Chicago Press, 1957), 65–66.

3. Robert N. Bellah, "Community Properly Understood: A Defense of 'Democratic Communitarianism'," in *The Essential Communitarian Reader*, 17–18.

4. Michael J. Sandel, *Liberalism and the Limits of Justice* (Cambridge: Cambridge University Press, 1982), 62.

5. Charles Taylor, *Philosophical Arguments* (Cambridge, MA: Harvard University Press, 1995), 185.

6. See his paradigmatic discussion of the move from individuals separately

attending to the weather to their coming through conversation to attending to it together. "This attending-together is not reducible to an aggregation of attendings-separately." Ibid. 189.

7. Amitai Etzioni, "Introduction," in *The Essential Communitarian Reader*, xvi.

8. "The Responsive Communitarian Platform: Rights and Responsibilities," in *The Essential Communitarian Reader*, xxv.

9. Amitai Etzioni, "Introduction," in *The Essential Communitarian Reader*, xiv.

10. Michael Waltzer, *Thick and Thin* (South Bend, IN: University of Notre Dame Press, 1994), 81.

11. In "The Politics of Recognition," Taylor comes much closer to the ontology presented in this book. He recognizes that the "crucial feature of human life is its fundamentally dialogical character." He asserts: "If some of the things I value most are accessible to me only in relation to the person I love, then she becomes part of my identity." Amy Gutman, ed. *Multiculturalism: Examining the Politics of Recognition* (Princeton: Princeton University Press, 1994), 32, 34.

12. The phrase "community of communities" appears in Etzioni's book as the heading of Part IV. In Part IV there is discussion of identity politics; so the implication is that the geographically defined community is a community of communities defined ethnically, by gender, and by sexual preference. My use of the term includes that, but extends to communities of geographically defined communities as well.

13. Charles Taylor points out differences in this regard between the United States and Canada as well as the special case of Quebec. Op. cit. 203.

14. A much fuller and more nuanced discussion of rights from a perspective very similar to that of this book is found in Douglas Sturm, *Solidarity and Suffering: Toward a Politics of Relationality* (Albany: State University of New York Press, 1998), Chapter 2.

Chapter Seven: Race and Class

1. Thandeka, *Learning to be White: Money, Race, and God in America* (New York: Continuum, 1999), Chapter 3.

2. Edmund S. Morgan, *American Slavery, American Freedom: The Ordeal of Colonial Virginia* (New York: W. W. Norton, 1975), 328.

3. Thandeka, *Learning to be White*, 47.

4. This is a major theme of Thandeka's book.

5. David R. Roediger, ed., *Black and White* (New York: Schocken Books, 1998), 15.

6. Thandeka, *Learning to be White*, Chapter 1.

7. Gunnar Myrdal, *An American Dilemma* (New York: Harper), 1944.

8. See, for example, Martin Luther King, *Where Do We Go From Here: Chaos or Community?* (New York: Harper & Row, 1967), 97.

9. David Roediger, *Towards the Abolition of Whiteness* (London: Verso, 1994), especially 12–17.

10. Richard Breen and David B. Rottman, *Class Stratification: A Comparative Perspective* (New York: Harvester Wheatsheaf, 1995), 179.

11. Alain Touraine, "Sociology and the Study of Society," in Patrick Joyce, ed., *Class* (Oxford: Oxford University Press, 1995), 88.

12. See Barbara Hilkert Andolsen, *The New Job Contract: Economic Justice in an Age of Insecurity* (Cleveland: Pilgrim Press, 1998), Chapter 3.

13. For these and other statistics showing the loss of status of workers in relation to the elite in the United States, see Patrick J. Buchanan, *The Great Betrayal* (Boston: Little Brown, 1998), 8–10.

14. See John Kenneth Galbraith, *The Culture of Contentment* (New York: Houghton Mifflin, 1992).

Chapter Eight: Ethics and Pluralism

1. See, for example, a passing reference to the feelings of other sentient beings in John Stuart Mill, *Utilitarianism*, Chapter II.

2. Augustine, *Questiones in exodum*, 80.

3. See, for example, *Documentation of the Right to Life and Abortion* (National Conference of Catholic Bishops, Washington, DC: United States Catholic Conference, 1974), 9.

4. Alfred North Whitehead, *Adventures of Ideas*, Part I.

5. Robyn Eckersley, *Environmentalism and Political Theory: Toward an Ecocentric Approach* (Albany: State University of New York Press, 1992), 181–85.

Note on Supporting Center

This series is published under the auspices of the Center for Process Studies, a research organization affiliated with the Claremont School of Theology and Claremont Graduate University. It was founded in 1973 by John B. Cobb, Jr., Founding Director, and David Ray Griffin, Executive Director; Marjorie Suchocki is now also a Co-director. It encourages research and reflection on the process philosophy of Alfred North Whitehead, Charles Hartshorne, and related thinkers, and on the application and testing of this viewpoint in all areas of thought and practice. The center sponsors conferences, welcomes visiting scholars to use its library, and publishes a scholarly journal, *Process Studies,* and a newsletter, *Process Perspectives.* Located at 1325 North College, Claremont, CA 91711, it gratefully accepts (tax-deductible) contributions to support its work.

Index

SUNY series in Constructive Postmodern Thought
David Ray Griffin, series editor

David Ray Griffin, editor, *The Reenchantment of Science: Postmodern Proposals*

David Ray Griffin, editor, *Spirituality and Society: Postmodern Visions*

David Ray Griffin, *God and Religion in the Postmodern World: Essays in Postmodern Theology*

David Ray Griffin, William A. Beardslee, and Joe Holland, *Varieties of Postmodern Theology*

David Ray Griffin and Huston Smith, *Primordial Truth and Postmodern Theology*

David Ray Griffin, editor, *Sacred Interconnections: Postmodern Spirituality, Political Economy, and Art*

Robert Inchausti, *The Ignorant Perfection of Ordinary People*

David W. Orr, *Ecological Literacy: Education and the Transition to a Postmodern World*

David Ray Griffin, John B. Cobb Jr., Marcus P. Ford, Pete A. Y. Gunter, and Peter Ochs, *Founders of Constructive Postmodern Philosophy: Peirce, James, Bergson, Whitehead, and Hartshorne*

David Ray Griffin and Richard A. Falk, editors, *Postmodern Politics for a Planet in Crisis: Policy, Process, and Presidential Vision*

Steve Odin, *The Social Self in Zen and American Pragmatism*

Frederick Ferré, *Being and Value: Toward a Constructive Postmodern Metaphysics*

Sandra B. Lubarsky and David Ray Griffin, editors, *Jewish Theology and Process Thought*